Mastering JIRA 7

Second Edition

Become an expert at using JIRA 7 through this one-stop guide!

Ravi Sagar

BIRMINGHAM - MUMBAI

Mastering JIRA 7

Second Edition

First published: May 2015

Second edition: October 2016

Production reference: 1051016

Published by Packt Publishing Ltd.
Livery Place
35 Livery Street
Birmingham
B3 2PB, UK.

ISBN 978-1-78646-686-0

www.packtpub.com

Credits

Author

Ravi Sagar

Reviewer

Satyendra Gangadhar Narwane

Commissioning Editor

Kunal Parikh

Acquisition Editor

Chaitanya Nair

Content Development Editor

Anish Sukumaran

Technical Editor

Kunal Chaudhari

Copy Editor

Safis Editing

Project Coordinator

Suzanne Coutinho

Proofreader

Safis Editing

Indexer

Rekha Nair

Graphics

Jason Monteiro

Production Coordinator

Aparna Bhagat

About the Author

Ravi Sagar is a JIRA trainer, consultant, and Drupal expert with several years of experience in web development and business analysis. He has done extensive work implementing and customizing big JIRA instances for project tracking, test management, support tickets, and Agile tracking.

Ravi founded Sparxsys Solutions Pvt. Ltd. (www.sparxsys.com) in 2010—a start-up company that provides consultancy and training services on Atlassian tools and Drupal. He has created accessible websites for blind people, adhering to WCAG guidelines.

Ravi's areas of interest include project management and Agile methodologies. His areas of focus in customizing JIRA include topics, such as issue schemes, workflow schemes, field configuration schemes, screen schemes, permission schemes, and notification schemes. He has also worked on Agile tracking projects, such as Scrum and Kanban. He contributed immensely towards setting up JIRA for helpdesk, test case management, bug tracking, and support ticket management. His other areas of expertise include JIRA training, Drupal training, business analysis, project management, and JIRA Agile.

Ravi has extensive experience in JIRA installation and configuration and has also worked on Linux and Windows Server. He understands clients' requirements and suggests best solutions to save cost.

Ravi has been involved in JIRA support and maintenance and training, including regular upgrades of JIRA and installed plugins, migration from legacy-defect tracking tools to JIRA, splitting and merging JIRA instances apart from bulk actions, such as uploading issues, editing, and user creation.

He has also worked on implementing JIRA Agile and its integration with other tools, such as Confluence, Crucible, and Fisheye and has hands-on experience in JIRA REST and SOAP.

You can connect with him at http://www.linkedin.com/in/ravisagar or e-mail him at ravi@sparxsys.com.

Acknowledgements

I would like to thank my wife, Shelly, who has always stood by me and helped me achieve my goals. This book wouldn't have been possible without her continuous encouragement. I want to dedicate this book to my little daughter Raavya, and also want to thank my parents for their endless support.

Special thanks to all the reviewers and book coordinators for their immense help on this book.

About the Reviewer

Satyendra Gangadhar Narwane is an honest, caring, intelligent, hardworking, and ambitious person with a good sense of humor. He is a postgraduate with a masters degree in computer science from one of the premier Indian universities, and he is working as a senior. Atlassian Product Expert at Dynamic Network Factory in the (US). He has conducted a seminar on behalf of Atlassian for promoting their tools in India and has developed dozens of custom add-ons based on customer needs. Satyendra provides training, administration, and add-on development on the Atlassian suite for top companies such as Oracle, Adobe, HCL, Mercedes Benz, MillenniumIT, Filpkart, ShipNet NS, and KBC Bank. He is very passionate about technology, computer science, traveling, watching movies, and enjoys great chats. He has previously worked on *JIRA 7 Development Cookbook* by Packt Publishing.

I would like to express my gratitude to the many people who have helped me through this book. I would like to thank Packt Publishing for giving me a chance to work on this book. Above all, I want to thank my mom Sushila, wife Poonam, and the rest of my family, who supported and encouraged me in spite of all the time it took me away from them. It was a long and difficult journey for them. I would like to thank Suzanne Coutinho and Chaitanya Nair for helping me in the process of selection and reviewing. Last but not least: I beg forgiveness of all those who have been with me over the course of the years and whose names I have failed to mention.

www.PacktPub.com

For support files and downloads related to your book, please visit `www.PacktPub.com`.

Did you know that Packt offers eBook versions of every book published, with PDF and ePub files available? You can upgrade to the eBook version at `www.PacktPub.com` and as a print book customer, you are entitled to a discount on the eBook copy. Get in touch with us at `service@packtpub.com` for more details.

At `www.PacktPub.com`, you can also read a collection of free technical articles, sign up for a range of free newsletters and receive exclusive discounts and offers on Packt books and eBooks.

`https://www.packtpub.com/mapt`

Get the most in-demand software skills with Mapt. Mapt gives you full access to all Packt books and video courses, as well as industry-leading tools to help you plan your personal development and advance your career.

Why subscribe?

- Fully searchable across every book published by Packt
- Copy and paste, print, and bookmark content
- On demand and accessible via a web browser

Table of Contents

Preface

JIRA is a popular issue tracking tool from Atlassian and has amazing customization abilities and finely grained control over various functions. Out of the box, JIRA offers issue and bug tracking capabilities to create tasks, assign them to users, and generate useful reports. However, the real power of JIRA lies in the customizations it offers.

Experienced JIRA administrators looking to learn advanced topics and expand their knowledge will benefit from this book. This book provides a comprehensive explanation covering all components of JIRA 7, such as JIRA Software, JIRA Core, and JIRA Service Desk.

Packed with real-world examples and use cases, you will first learn how to plan the JIRA installation. Then, you will be given a brief refresher of the fundamental concepts and understand the customizations in detail, along with sample data for various use cases, and several aspects of JIRA administration, such as user management, groups, roles, and security levels, will be covered, keeping in mind the applications for enterprises. Next, this book will take you through add-on development to extend JIRA's functionality, and will give insights into building applications on top of JIRA using the REST API. Various aspects of migration from other tools using CSV files will also be discussed. This book has a separate section on implementation of the JIRA Service Desk application, which is a very popular add-on for support requests and the ticketing system.

The implementation of the Scrum and Kanban techniques along with Agile reports, will be discussed as well. We will take a look at the Groovy script, which is a great tool that empowers JIRA administrators with tremendous flexibility. Additionally, we will also take a look at some of the common database tables to fetch useful results and discuss the possibilities to add custom CSS and JavaScript in our JIRA instance. Finally, we will conclude the book by going through the best practices and troubleshooting to help you find out what went wrong and how to fix it.

What this book covers

Chapter 1, *Planning Your JIRA Installation*, covers planning the JIRA installation to ensure the longevity of the installation so that it can accommodate more users and data in future. The installation and update process is also discussed briefly in this chapter.

Chapter 2, *Searching in JIRA*, gives a detailed explanation of how data can be fetched from JIRA using the Basic search feature, as well as by writing advanced queries using JQL.

Chapter 3, *Reporting – Using Charts to Visualize the Data*, covers various built-in project reports that come with JIRA and how to present them on the dashboards.

Chapter 4, *Customizing JIRA for Test Management*, explains how to modify the configurations to implement new issue types for test campaigns and test cases. The procedure to implement a new workflow with conditions, along with a new permission scheme, will be discussed in detail.

Chapter 5, *Understanding Zephyr and its Features*, walks through a step-by-step implementation of this popular add-on for test management in JIRA.

Chapter 6, *Sample Implementation of Use Cases*, gives a lot of examples of different implementations, such as the Helpdesk system and requirement management, that readers can leverage in their company.

Chapter 7, *User Management, Groups, and Project Roles*, explains how to manage the users in JIRA and the way to organize them in various groups.

Chapter 8, *Configuring JIRA User Directories to Connect with LDAP, Crowd, and JIRA User Server*, discusses how to integrate your JIRA instance with LDAP and Crowd for external user management.

Chapter 9, *JIRA Add-on Development and Leveraging the REST API*, explains how to start developing add-ons for JIRA to extend the functionality. The JIRA REST API which enables us to accessing JIRA functionality from external tools, is also discussed with examples.

Chapter 10, *Importing and Exporting Data in JIRA and Migrating Configuration*, talks about how data from external tools can be imported using the CSV import and Project Import features. The importance of taking regular backups is explained in this chapter, along with the procedure to restore JIRA from a backup file.

Chapter 11, *Working with JIRA Agile Boards in JIRA Software*, explains how to implement the Scrum and Kanban techniques in JIRA. The planning of your Sprints in the Scrum and various customizations that one can do on these boards is discussed in detail along with the Burndown and Velocity charts that track the progress of the project.

Chapter 12, *JIRA Administration with Script Runner and CLI Add-on*, introduces the add-on that administrators can install and various additional features using scripting that it brings, which helps the administrators with various customizations that were otherwise not possible.

Chapter 13, *Database Access*, explains how to fetch data directly from the JIRA database. This chapter has various useful queries to retrieve information from the database. The way to access data from an embedded HSSQL database is also explained.

Chapter 14, *Customizing Look, Feel, and Behavior*, talks about how to make extreme changes in the JIRA design using Custom Stylesheets, and also, to controlling the HTML fields using JavaScript is explained.

Chapter 15, *Implementing JIRA Service Desk*, explains how to configure and set up the JIRA Service Desk application to handle your Support Requests.

Chapter 16, *Integrating JIRA with Common Atlassian Applications and Other Tools*, gives information on connecting JIRA with confluence, SVN, and Git.

Chapter 17, *JIRA Best Practices*, talks about various points that JIRA administrators should keep in mind, not only before implementing JIRA, but also various practices that they should employ on an ongoing basis.

Chapter 18, *Troubleshooting JIRA*, covers the various ways to identify the problems in the instance. Common problems that people face in JIRA are listed in this chapter.

What you need for this book

To install and run JIRA, the following software and tools are required:

- JIRA 7.1.1 or later
- MySQL 5.6 or later
- Java 1.8 or later
- PHP 5.4
- Chrome 7 or later
- Firefox 4 or later

Wherever applicable, the details on obtaining this software and its usage is explained in the relevant chapters.

Who this book is for

If you are a JIRA administrator managing small to medium JIRA instances and want to learn how to manage enterprise-scale instances, then this book will help you in expanding your knowledge and equip you with advanced skills. Prior understanding of JIRA core concepts is required. Additionally, basic CSS, JavaScript, and Java understanding will be helpful.

Conventions

In this book, you will find a number of text styles that distinguish between different kinds of information. Here are some examples of these styles and an explanation of their meaning.

Code words in text, database table names, folder names, filenames, file extensions, pathnames, dummy URLs, user input, and Twitter handles are shown as follows: "The `atlas-run-standalone` command is used to set up and start the JIRA instance for you."

A block of code is set as follows:

```
#if ($mentionable)
 $!rendererParams.put("mentionable", true)
 #if ($issue.project.key && $issue.project.key != "")
 $!rendererParams.put("data-projectkey", "$!issue.project.key")
 #end
 #if ($issue.key && $issue.key != "")
 $!rendererParams.put("data-issuekey", "$!issue.key")
 #end
#end
```

Any command-line input or output is written as follows:

```
atlas-mvn eclipse:eclipse
```

New terms and **important words** are shown in bold. Words that you see on the screen, for example, in menus or dialog boxes, appear in the text like this: "In the menu bar, click on **Windows | Preferences**."

> Warnings or important notes appear in a box like this.

Tips and tricks appear like this.

Reader feedback

Feedback from our readers is always welcome. Let us know what you think about this book-what you liked or disliked. Reader feedback is important for us as it helps us develop titles that you will really get the most out of. To send us general feedback, simply e-mail feedback@packtpub.com, and mention the book's title in the subject of your message. If there is a topic that you have expertise in and you are interested in either writing or contributing to a book, see our author guide at www.packtpub.com/authors.

Customer support

Now that you are the proud owner of a Packt book, we have a number of things to help you to get the most from your purchase.

Downloading the example code

You can download the example code files for this book from your account at http://www.packtpub.com. If you purchased this book elsewhere, you can visit http://www.packtpub.com/support and register to have the files e-mailed directly to you.

You can download the code files by following these steps:

1. Log in or register to our website using your e-mail address and password.
2. Hover the mouse pointer on the **SUPPORT** tab at the top.
3. Click on **Code Downloads & Errata**.
4. Enter the name of the book in the **Search** box.
5. Select the book for which you're looking to download the code files.
6. Choose from the drop-down menu where you purchased this book from.
7. Click on **Code Download**.

Once the file is downloaded, please make sure that you unzip or extract the folder using the latest version of:

- WinRAR / 7-Zip for Windows
- Zipeg / iZip / UnRarX for Mac
- 7-Zip / PeaZip for Linux

The code bundle for the book is also hosted on GitHub at `https://github.com/PacktPublishing/Mastering-JIRA-7-Second-Edition`. We also have other code bundles from our rich catalog of books and videos available at `https://github.com/PacktPublishing/`. Check them out!

Downloading the color images of this book

We also provide you with a PDF file that has color images of the screenshots/diagrams used in this book. The color images will help you better understand the changes in the output. You can download this file from `http://www.packtpub.com/sites/default/files/downloads/MasteringJIRA7SecondEdition_ColorImages.pdf`.

Errata

Although we have taken every care to ensure the accuracy of our content, mistakes do happen. If you find a mistake in one of our books-maybe a mistake in the text or the code-we would be grateful if you could report this to us. By doing so, you can save other readers from frustration and help us improve subsequent versions of this book. If you find any errata, please report them by visiting `http://www.packtpub.com/submit-errata`, selecting your book, clicking on the **Errata Submission Form** link, and entering the details of your errata. Once your errata are verified, your submission will be accepted and the errata will be uploaded to our website or added to any list of existing errata under the Errata section of that title.

To view the previously submitted errata, go to `https://www.packtpub.com/books/content/support` and enter the name of the book in the search field. The required information will appear under the **Errata** section.

Piracy

Piracy of copyrighted material on the Internet is an ongoing problem across all media. At Packt, we take the protection of our copyright and licenses very seriously. If you come across any illegal copies of our works in any form on the Internet, please provide us with the location address or website name immediately so that we can pursue a remedy.

Please contact us at `copyright@packtpub.com` with a link to the suspected pirated material.

We appreciate your help in protecting our authors and our ability to bring you valuable content.

Questions

If you have a problem with any aspect of this book, you can contact us at `questions@packtpub.com`, and we will do our best to address the problem.

1
Planning Your JIRA Installation

Atlassian JIRA is a proprietary issue tracking system. It is used to track bugs, resolve issues, and manage project functions. There are many such tools available in the market, but the best thing about JIRA is that it can be easily configured and it offers a wide range of customizations. Out of the box, JIRA offers defect/bug tracking functionalities, but it can also be customized to act like a helpdesk system, a simple test management suite, or a project management system with end-to-end traceability.

This chapter offers a brief introduction to JIRA and the new features of JIRA 7, mainly the three variants **JIRA Core**, **JIRA Software**, and **JIRA Service Desk**. Emphasis is given to planning, installing, and setting up JIRA. After reading this chapter, you should understand how to plan your JIRA installation and ensure the longevity of its installation so that it can accommodate more users and data in the future. We will begin with a questionnaire that needs to be answered before you can deploy a JIRA instance in your company. You will learn about the system and hardware requirements to run JIRA for an enterprise. The installation procedure for Windows and Linux operating systems is discussed briefly and the setup wizard is explained in detail in this chapter.

Topics covered in this chapter include:

- What is new in JIRA 7?
- Planning your JIRA installation
- System requirements
- Setting up the MySQL database
- The JIRA setup wizard
- JIRA directory structure, startup/shutdown scripts, and log files
- Planning your upgrade

- Updating JIRA add-ons
- Applications, uses, and examples
- JIRA core concepts

What is new in JIRA 7?

The much awaited JIRA 7 was released in October 2015 and it is now offered in three different application variants:

- JIRA Core
- JIRA Software
- JIRA Service Desk

Let us discuss each one of them separately.

JIRA Core

This comprises of the base application of JIRA that you might be familiar with, of course with some new features. JIRA Core is a simplified version of JIRA features that we have been using up until the 6.x versions.

JIRA Software

This comprises of all the features of JIRA Core and JIRA Agile. From JIRA 7 onwards, JIRA Agile will no longer be offered as an add-on. You will not be able to install JIRA Agile from the marketplace.

JIRA Service Desk

This comprises of all the features of JIRA Core and JIRA Service Desk. Just like JIRA Software, JIRA Service Desk will no longer be offered as an add-on and you cannot install it from the marketplace.

This split of applications was done by Atlassian, keeping in mind the usage of JIRA in various organizations across the globe, and it makes it very simple for the companies to choose the right application suitable for their needs. However, it doesn't mean that all three applications (JIRA Core, JIRA Agile, and JIRA Service Desk) can't be used on the same instance. You can certainly buy JIRA Software and later install the JIRA Service Desk application on it.

Apart from this split, JIRA 7 brings new features such as **Release Hub**, with real-time status of the versions, an improved sidebar where you can add your own shortcuts, better reporting, and visibility of development tools. We will discuss and highlight these improvements in the relevant chapters in this book.

In this book, we will install JIRA Software that comes in-built with JIRA Agile, and later we will install JIRA Service Desk on top of it.

Planning your JIRA installation

There are certain points to be kept in mind before you install JIRA in the production phase and deploy it. The points that are discussed here should ideally be a part of your JIRA questionnaire, which you will prepare and fill in after discussion with the product owners and project managers. This will not only help you to plan your installation for now, but it will also give you a good idea about the future usage of the tool.

From the very beginning, start preparing the documents to store all the following information:

- **Number of users**: This is the most important thing that the JIRA administrator should worry about. If you are using a limited user license in JIRA, then you should know the number of users who are using JIRA currently and who will be using it a few months down the line. In enterprise systems, there is no limit defined in the license on the number of active users accessing the system, but it's important to worry about various aspects that are discussed here:
    - Are users part of a single team or several teams? It's also possible to give limited access of your JIRA instance to clients and third-party vendors.
    - If users are part of several teams working with different groups, then is there a need to limit the visibility of projects within these groups?

- **Number of projects**: The JIRA license will not put any limit on the number of projects. You can create any number of projects irrespective of whether you use 10 users' licenses or 100 users' licenses. The more the number of projects means a lot of issues will be stored in the database and a lot of schemes will have to be managed by administrators. It's good to know the tentative number of projects that will be stored in JIRA.

- **JIRA server hardware recommendation**: The hardware required to run JIRA depends on the number of variables, such as the number of users, number of projects, traffic, and number of schemes used in JIRA:

    - For approximately 50 projects and 100 users, with less than 5,000 issues—16 GB RAM and a multicore CPU.

    - For approximately 100 projects and 3,000 users, with less than 100,000 issues—32 GB RAM, 2 Intel (R) Xeon (R), and CPU E5520 @ 2.27 GHz (16 logical cores) processors.

    - Atlassian has a recommended sizing guide. Refer to the following URL for more information: `https://confluence.atlassian.com/enterprise/jira-sizing-guide-46154623.html`.

- **Will you need mail notifications in JIRA?**: Do you want e-mail notifications sent to users? JIRA has the capability to send e-mails to users on various events, such as issue creating, updating, and resolving. In order to send e-mails, an SMTP server is required. JIRA can also be configured with Google Apps for Work; just enter your username and password to enable notifications. It's also possible to create issues and post comments using a dedicated e-mail. This functionality can be configured using e-mail handlers in JIRA so that users won't need to launch JIRA to post a comment on the ticket they are assigned to; they can just reply to the e-mail received from JIRA.

- **Authentication**: JIRA has its own internal directory user management system where the information of a user is stored in an internal database. By default, it's enabled when you install JIRA. It's also possible to use directory servers such as LDAP for authentication, user, and group management. In huge organizations where a lot of tools are used, it's important to have such integrated authentication mechanisms so that end users don't have to remember multiple passwords.

- **Can JIRA be used from multiple locations?**: It's important to know the geographical location of the user and from where they will be accessing the JIRA instance. The choice of a JIRA server becomes important here; latency checks should be done from all such locations and the server location should be in such a way that it offers the best performance to everyone accessing it. As a JIRA administrator, your responsibility will be to do performance routine maintenance activities, such as indexing in JIRA. You should know the time window when there are a less number of users connected to the system.

- **How many concurrent users will access the system?**: If you have thousands of users in a geographical location, they may access the system simultaneously. This will result in a degraded performance. Although it's important to know the peak usage during the day beforehand, there are various performance improvement measures that can be worked on.

- **Tentatively, how many issues per project can be stored?**: Discuss with all the product stakeholders about the usage of the tool. You should have plenty of storage to accommodate the huge amount of data. Of course, as an administrator, you will have a fair understanding of the usage. A project can have thousands of issues and these can have file attachments. From time to time, keep a check on the free disk space.

- **Tentatively, how many total issues can be stored?**: JIRA indexing helps in improved search results. However, it can take several minutes to finish and it should ideally be done when there is less usage of the tool. A JIRA instance with less than 100,000 issues may take 10-15 minutes to finish and you should keep this in mind before announcing a downtime. Knowing how many issues will be present in the system will help you to make better decisions.

- **Will users also upload attachments in their projects?**: The out-of-the-box concept of JIRA has a provision to attach files along with issues. Of course, it's a desirable feature and everyone wants this. All the attachments are stored on the disk. Maybe, for some good reason, there is no need to have this feature and it's always good to discuss this first with the product stakeholders.

- **How many custom fields do you intend to create?**: Ideally, all the schemes and configurations should be documented before implementing it, but it's always good to have a clear understanding of the number of custom fields that you need to create in the system.

- **Choice of platform and database**: JIRA (being a pure Java-based application) can be installed either on the Windows or Linux operating system. It needs a JDK or JRE environment to run. If your IT team is more comfortable with Windows and SQL, then use it. Linux has some advantages (such as SSH) and is more suitable for open source tools (such as Postgres or MySQL).

- **Integration with other tools**: JIRA can be integrated into a lot of other tools from Atlassian and other commonly used tools in software development. Will you need integration with Confluence, FishEye/Crucible, Bamboo, Git, or SVN? Keep these possible integrations in mind at the beginning.

> Generally, for best performance, most people prefer Linux-RedHat or CentOS as the first choice of distribution. The preferred database is MySQL and Postgres.

For further information on supported platforms, visit the following documentation on Atlassian at `https://confluence.atlassian.com/display/JIRA/Supported+Platforms`.

Installation of JIRA on Windows

JIRA can be easily installed using the automated Windows Installer. If you are using this method, there is no need to set up the JDK; the installer will configure it for you. The following are the steps to install JIRA on Windows:

1. Download the **JIRA Windows Installer** (`.exe`) file for your platform and architecture from `https://www.atlassian.com/software/jira/download`.
2. Run the executable file and in the next step, select **Express Install** to install JIRA with its default settings; however, a custom installation is recommended, where you can specify the destination directory to install JIRA, the `JIRA HOME` directory, and TCP ports. We recommend the **Custom Installation**.
3. You will also get an option to install JIRA as a service.
4. After the JIRA installation, it will launch automatically in the browser to run the setup wizard.

Refer to `https://confluence.atlassian.com/display/JIRA/Installing+JIRA+on+Windows` for detailed steps to install JIRA on Windows.

Installation of JIRA on Linux

Just like Windows Installer, JIRA can also be installed easily on your Linux operating system using the console wizard:

1. Download the appropriate JIRA Linux 64-bit/32-bit installer (`.bin`) file for your platform and architecture from `https://www.atlassian.com/software/jira/download`.
2. Open a Linux console and change the (`cd`) directory to the `.bin` file's directory.
3. If not already done, make the `.bin` file executable using the `chmod a+x atlassian-jira-X.Y.bin` command.
4. Execute the `./atlassian-jira-X.Y.bin` file.

5. In the next step, select **Express Install** to install JIRA with its default settings. However, we recommend **Custom Install**, where you can specify the destination directory to install JIRA, the `JIRA HOME` directory, and TCP ports. We recommend **Custom Install**.

6. You will also get an option to install JIRA as a service.

7. After the installation process, JIRA will launch automatically in the browser to run the setup wizard.

 Refer to `https://confluence.atlassian.com/display/JIRA/Installin g+JIRA+on+Linux` for detailed steps to install JIRA on Linux.

Installation of JIRA as a service

If you run either the Windows or Linux installer with system administrator rights, then you will get an option to install JIRA as a service. This makes it really easy for JIRA administrators, as the service can be configured to start automatically when the server boots; otherwise, you will need to start JIRA manually every time you start your server.

Installation of JIRA from an archive file

If you want to install JIRA on Solaris, there is no automatic installation for it and JIRA needs to be installed from an archive file using the following steps:

1. Download and extract the JIRA archive file.
2. Set the JIRA home directory.
3. Create a dedicated user account on the operating system to run JIRA.
4. Start JIRA using the `start-jira.sh` file.
5. Run the setup wizard.

 For detailed instructions on how to install JIRA from an archive file, refer to `https://confluence.atlassian.com/display/JIRA/Installing+JIR A+from+an+Archive+File+on+Windows%2C+Linux+or+Solaris`.

System requirements

JIRA requires a **Java Developers Kit (JDK)** or **Java Runtime Environment (JRE)** platform to be installed on your server's operating system.

Procedure to install the JDK

If you install JIRA from an archive file then the JDK needs to be installed and set up separately on your system. The Windows Installer and Linux Installer don't need to install the JDK as these installers come with the JDK in-built.

You can download the JDK from `http://www.oracle.com/technetwork/java/javase/downloads/jdk8-downloads-2133151.html`.

Select the version relevant to your operating system and architecture. JIRA 7 requires JDK 1.8 to run smoothly.

The steps to install the JDK on Windows are as follows:

1. Uninstall any earlier version of Java that was installed on your system.
2. Restart your system.
3. Using the downloaded installer, you can install the JDK at `C:\java` (don't install it in `C:\Program Files\`). The JDK specific directory, such as `C:\Java\jdk1.8.0_92`, will be created.
4. Set the `JAVA_HOME` windows environment variable. It should point to the directory where JDK is installed, `C:\Java\jdk1.8.0_92`, on the Windows machine.
5. Restart your system.

Steps to install the JDK on Linux

Using the link given in the preceding section, download the JDK RPM installer, `jdk-8u92-linux-x64.rpm`, and install it at a location of your choice.

Set the `JAVA_HOME` variable as `export JAVA_HOME = /path/to/java`.

Setting up the MySQL database

JIRA needs to store its data in a database. For this, we will set up a MySQL database. JIRA 7 requires MySQL 5.1 up until 5.6 to run smoothly. You should refer to the preferred MySQL server configurations as described on the following page: https://confluence.atlassian .com/jira/connecting-jira-to-mysql-185729489.html.

It's also possible to use PostgreSQL, Oracle, or Microsoft SQL Server with JIRA, but here we will discuss how to set up the MySQL database:

1. Log in to your MySQL Server with the following command:

   ```
   mysql -u root -p
   ```

2. Enter the password.

3. Create a new database to be used by JIRA using the following command:

   ```
   Create database jiradb character set utf8 COLLATE utf8_bin;
   ```

4. Create a new user and give it permissions on the database:

   ```
   GRANT SELECT,INSERT, UPDATE,DELETE,DROP,CREATE,ALTER,
   INDEX on jiradb.* TO
   'jirauser'@'localhost' IDENTIFIED BY 'password';
   ```

5. Flush the privileges using the following command:

   ```
   flush privileges;
   ```

We have created a MySQL database name as `jiradb`, a database username as `jirauser`, and a database password as `password`. Keep this information on hand because we will need it when we set up JIRA.

To use MySQL with JIRA, you need to download a `mysql-connector-java-5.1.32-bin.jar` database driver and copy it to the `lib` folder under JIRA's installation directory. The driver can be downloaded from ht tp://dev.mysql.com/downloads/connector/j.

The JIRA setup wizard

Let's take a look at the steps involved in the installation of JIRA:

1. Whether you install JIRA using the custom installer or an archive file, JIRA will first launch itself in the browser with the setup wizard.

2. The wizard will give you two options—**Set it up for me** or **I'll set it myself**. Select **I'll set it myself** and press the **Next** button.

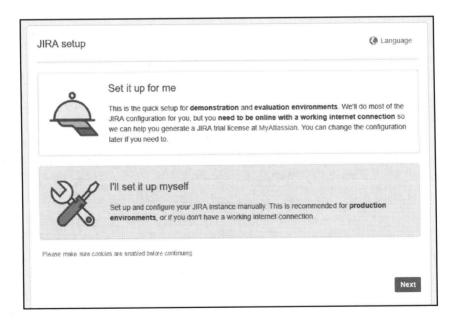

3. In the **Database setup** screen, select **Database Connection** as **My Own Database**.

4. As we want to use the MySQL database, select **MySQL** as **Database Type**. If you want to evaluate JIRA, then you can also use **Built In (for evaluation or demonstration)** as **Database**; JIRA uses **HyperSQL Database (HSQLDB)**, which is only used for testing purposes.

5. Enter your MySQL server **Hostname**, **Port**, **Database** name, database **Username**, and **Password**. You may click on the **Test Connection** button to check whether the credentials are correct or not. Press the **Next** button to continue.

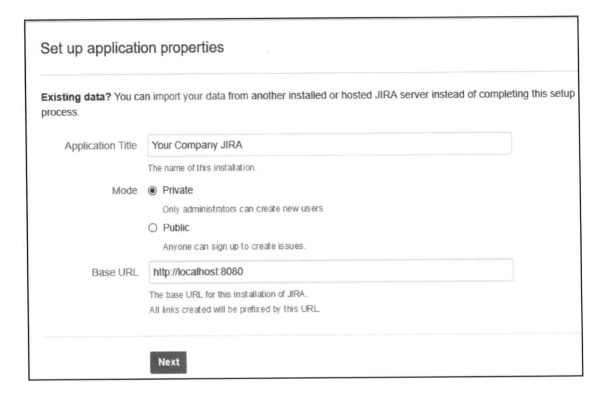

[20]

6. Now, enter the **Application Title** for this instance. Select **Private** as **Mode**, where only administrators can create accounts. Select **Public** if you want users to sign up themselves. Enter the **Base URL**, which users will use to access this instance. You can also change it later on and use the domain name or subdomain such as `jira.company.com` as the **Base URL**. Press the **Next** button to continue.

7. In the **Specify your license key** section, you need to enter your license key that you can generate from `my.atlassian.com` or simply click on the **generate a JIRA trial license** link and you will be taken to the Atlassian website where you can generate a **New Evaluation License** for your instance's **Server ID**. After that you will be taken back to your instance with the license key filled in. Press the **Next** button to continue.

Set up administrator account

Enter details for the administrator account. You can add more administrators after setup.

Full name

Ravi Sagar [Sparxsys]

Email Address

ravi@sparxsys.com

Username

ravisagar

Password

••••••••

Confirm Password

••••••••

Next

8. Now we need to **Set up administrator account**. Enter your **Full name**, **Email Address**, **Username**, and **Password**. Don't forget this credential because this account will have the full admin access of the JIRA instance.

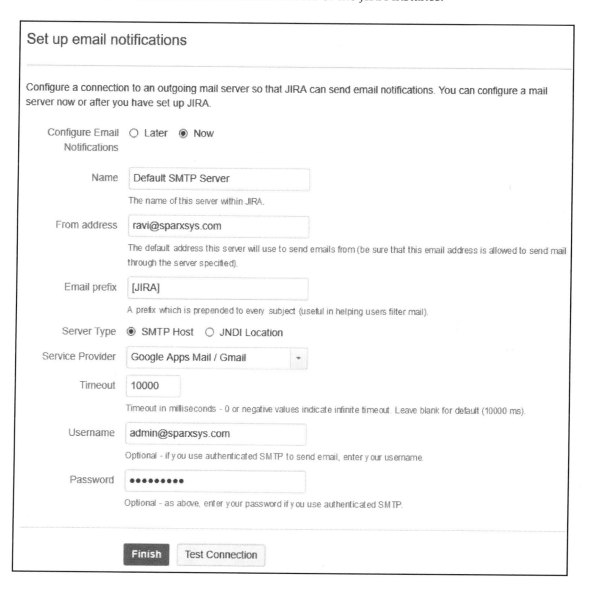

9. Finally, we have the option to **Set up email notifications**. If you have the SMTP server in your company, then you can use it. For this example, we have used **Service Provider** as **Google Apps Mail / Gmail**. It's quite simple to configure. Just enter your Google Apps **Username** and **Password**. There is no need to change any other setting. You can click on the **Test Connection** button to verify your credentials and communicate with the e-mail server.

10. Click on the **Finish** button to complete the setup wizard and JIRA installation.

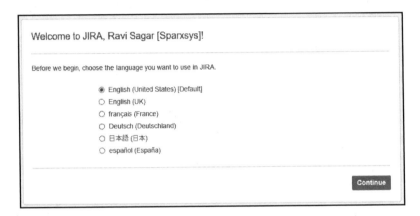

11. In the next screen, the wizard will ask you to select your preferred language. Select the language and press the **Continue** button.

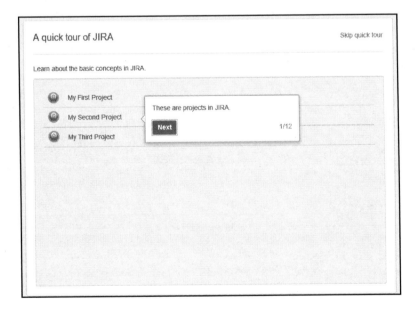

12. In the next set of screens, you will be presented with **A quick tour of JIRA**. You can either click on the **Next** button several times to go through the quick tour or click on the **Skip quick tour link** in the top-right corner.

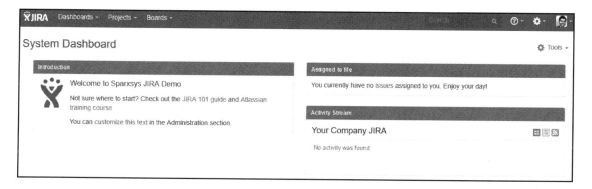

13. Now; you will be logged in automatically and presented with the **System Dashboard**.

JIRA directory structure, startup/shutdown scripts, and log files

It's important for a JIRA administrator to know the JIRA directory structure really well because you will often need to take backups, make changes in the configuration files, and restore the system. All such activities need to be done on the server and have to be done through its respective directories.

The JIRA installation directory

The JIRA installation directory is the directory in which the JIRA application files and libraries are extracted. JIRA does not make changes nor does it save any data here.

If you have installed JIRA using automated Windows or Linux installers, then the JIRA installation directory is stored in the following locations:

- **Windows**: `C:\Program Files\Atlassian\JIRA`
- **Linux**: `/opt/atlassian/jira`

The startup and shutdown scripts are available in the `bin` directory under the JIRA installation directory:

- **Startup script**: `bin/start-jira.bat or bin/start-jira.sh`
- **Shutdown script**: `bin/stop-jira.bat or bin/stop-jira.sh`

The JIRA home directory

The JIRA home directory has important files that JIRA requires to work properly. *Do not modify these files.*

If you install JIRA using automated Windows or Linux installers, the default location of the JIRA home directory is stored in the following locations:

- **Windows**: `C:\Program Files\Atlassian\Application Data\JIRA`
- **Linux**: `/var/atlassian/application-data/jira/`

Subdirectories under the JIRA home directory

The following are the list of subdirectories under the JIRA home directory:

- `data`: The application data of the JIRA instance is stored here. Attachments and all its versions are stored under a subdirectory called `attachments import`. If you want to restore JIRA, the backfile needs to be placed in this directory.
- `export`: This directory is used to store automated backup files.
- `log`: The log files are stored here.
- `cache`: The cache files are stored here.
- `tmp`: During various runtime operations, such as import, export, and indexing, there are some temporary files that are generated. All such files are stored here.

Planning your upgrade

You should expect issues in the upgrade process, and for this reason, follow these steps:

1. Set up the staging environment. This could be a clone of your production. Make sure the license of your JIRA instance is valid.
2. Create a compatibility matrix of the plugins used. Check whether an upgrade of these plugins is available in the new version. Also, check the licenses of your add-ons.
3. Check the release notes for bug fixes and possible issues.
4. Perform the upgrade on staging first.
5. Perform **user acceptance testing** (**UAT**) with limited users first, preferably with the managers or the stakeholders of the company.
6. Collect the feedback and review it.
7. For any issues, raise a ticket with Atlassian. If you have a valid license, they will help you out.

 Always perform a backup of your JIRA installation directory, JIRA home directory, and your database before upgrading.

Upgrading your JIRA instance

There are several different ways to upgrade JIRA. The method you choose to use depends on the version of JIRA you use and the type of environment you use it in.

The fallback method for mission-critical applications

When JIRA is used in companies where it's mission-critical for the business, then it's recommended to use this method because it will let you roll back safely to your previous working version. Prepare the production instance as follows:

1. Prepare a proxy server.
2. Install and test the upgraded version.

Refer to https://confluence.atlassian.com/display/JIRA/Upgrading +JIRA+with+a+Fallback+Method for further information on upgrading JIRA using a fallback method.

The rapid method using the installer

If you can afford to have a downtime of several minutes and there is no impact on the business due to the downtime, then it's recommended to use this method, which is quite easy. It just needs you to run the installer again on top of the existing installed application:

1. Keep a note of custom changes.
2. Take a backup of your database.
3. Run the JIRA installer and select the upgrade option.

If you have made any changes in some of the files (such as setenv.bat) or have your own CSS and JavaScript files or codes, then you need to redo those changes again in the upgraded system.

 Refer to https://confluence.atlassian.com/display/JIRA/Upgrading +JIRA+Using+a+Rapid+Upgrade+Method for further information on upgrading JIRA using an RAD method.

Manual upgrade method for Solaris

With the rapid method, you can easily upgrade JIRA. However, there are certain cases where you cannot use the installation binary. For example, if you want to install JIRA on Solaris, then there are no supported binaries from Atlassian, but you can use the following method with the **Web Application Archive** (**WAR**) distribution file to install JIRA on Solaris:

1. Take a backup of your database and the JIRA installation directory.
2. Install the new version.
3. Point your newly installed JIRA instance to a copy of JIRA's existing home directory.
4. Configure the new version of JIRA to use a new blank database.
5. Finally, import your JIRA's old data with the restore feature in the newly installed JIRA's instance.

Refer to `https://confluence.atlassian.com/display/JIRA/Upgrading +JIRA+Manually` for further information on upgrading JIRA manually.

Updating JIRA add-ons

JIRA has a lot of add-ons that can be installed from the marketplace. Add-ons extend the functionalities of JIRA. There are a lot of good add-ons available from Atlassian and other providers. Due to the rapid development in JIRA, this could be a new feature development. To fix bugs, these providers keep on releasing version updates of their add-ons. It's a good idea to update these add-ons from time to time. However, it's recommended to test the upgrades first on your staging environment.

Go to the **Manage Add-ons** section to check for the updates that are available for your add-ons. The built-in notifications in JIRA will also let you know whenever there is an update available for an add-on. However, these updates should ideally be performed on a test environment first, that is, ideally a staging server identical to your production environment.

Only if the new version of the add-on works on your staging environment will you be able to update it on your production environment. Try using one of the following methods to update the add-ons described:

- Updating an add-on to a new version
- Updating all add-ons
- Updating an add-on by uploading a file
- Enabling automatic add-on updates

 The detailed steps to update the add-ons can be found at `https://conflu ence.atlassian.com/display/UPM/Updating+add-ons`.

We recommend updating the add-ons one by one. There might be an issue in updating all the add-ons simultaneously. Also, you might not know which add-on update caused this problem.

The JIRA add-ons compatibility matrix

As a good practice, always keep track of all the add-ons currently installed, their current version, their compatibility with currently installed JIRA, and any known issues.

Before you plan to update any add-on, always update the compatibility matrix:

Add-ons	Installed version	Paid or free	Compatible with JIRA 6.3.6?	Remarks
JIRA Agile	6.6.0	Paid	Yes	
Clone Plus Plugin	4.0.0	Paid	Yes	
JIRA Suite Utilities	1.4.9	Free	Yes	

There are a lot of add-ons available on the Atlassian marketplace, but don't install too many add-ons for no reason. If you are looking for a new feature in JIRA, which is provided as an add-on, always check for how many people are using it by verifying the download count; there is also a user rating that will give you a good idea about this add-on. If you decide to purchase an add-on, then check the provider as well.

Applications, uses, and examples

The ability to customize JIRA is what makes it popular among various companies who use it. There are various applications of JIRA:

- Defect/bug tracking
- Change requests
- Helpdesk/support tickets
- Project management
- Test case management
- Requirements management
- Process management

Let's take a look at the implementation of test case management:

- Issue types:
    - **Test campaign**: This will be the standard issue type
    - **Test case**: This will be a subtask
- Workflow for test campaign:

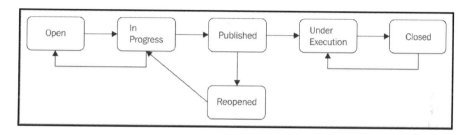

- New States:
    - **Published**
    - **Under Execution**
- Condition:
    - A test campaign will only pass when all the test cases are passed
    - Only the reporter can move this test campaign to **Closed**
- Post-function:
    - When the test campaign is closed, send an e-mail to everyone in a particular group
- Workflow for a test case:

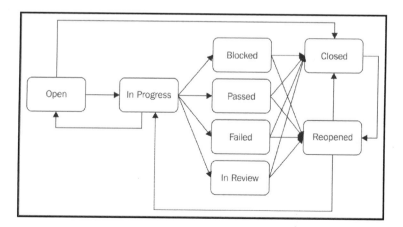

- New states:
  - **Blocked**
  - **Passed**
  - **Failed**
  - **In Review**
- Condition:
  - Only the assigned user can move the test case to the **Passed** state
- Post-function:
  - When the test case is moved to the **Failed** state, change the issue priority to major
- Custom fields:

Name	Type	Values	Field configuration
Category	Select List		
Customer Name	Select List		
Steps to Reproduce	Text area		Mandatory
Expected input	Text area		Mandatory
Expected output	Text area		Mandatory
Pre-Condition	Text area		
Post-Condition	Text area		
Campaign Type	Select List	Unit Functional Endurance Benchmark Robustness Security Backward compatibility Certification with baseline	
Automation Status	Select List	Automatic Manual Partially automatic	

JIRA core concepts

Let's take a look at the architecture of JIRA; it will help you to understand the core concepts:

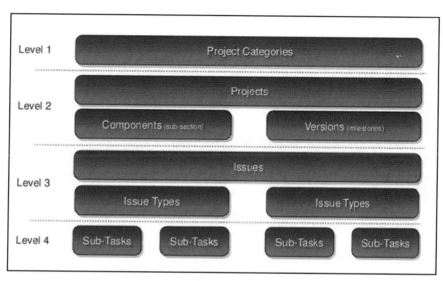

- **Project Categories**: When there are too many projects in JIRA, it becomes important to segregate them into various categories. JIRA will let you create several categories that could represent the business units, clients, or teams in your company.
- **Projects**: A JIRA project is a collection of issues. Your team can use a JIRA project to coordinate the development of a product, track a project, manage a help desk, and so on, depending on your requirements.
- **Components**: Components are subsections of a project. They are used to group issues within a project to smaller parts.
- **Versions**: Versions are a point-in-time for a project. They help you schedule and organize your releases.
- **Issue Types**: JIRA will let you create several issue types that are different from each other in terms of what kind of information they store. JIRA comes with default issue types, such as bug, task, and subtask, but you can create more issue types that can follow their own workflow as well as have different sets of fields.
- **Sub-Tasks**: Issue types are of two types—standard and subtasks, which are children of a standard task. For instance, you can have test campaign as a standard issue type and test cases as subtasks.

Summary

In this chapter, we discussed things that you plan before implementing JIRA in your company, understood how JIRA is intended to be used in the future, and how it helps JIRA administrators to choose the right hardware. We also discussed the JIRA installation in detail and various ways to upgrade it. Finally, we briefly discussed some possible use cases of JIRA.

In the next chapter, we will understand how to search the issues. JIRA comes with a powerful search mechanism that helps users to easily find the information they are looking for. JIRA has a query language called **JIRA Query Language** (**JQL**), which is used for advanced searching. We will also discuss how to save your search queries as filters, which can be referred to again in the future.

2
Searching in JIRA

This chapter has a detailed explanation of how data can be fetched from JIRA. The data is used for analysis, reporting, and taking appropriate action. The **Issue Navigator** window offers a very easy mechanism to search for issues, but it's possible to write queries using **JIRA Query Language** (**JQL**) to refine the search results. You will learn how to save the search results as filters and charts that can be added in the dashboard. This can be shared with other users and can also serve as a data source for various gadgets.

We will cover the following topics:

- The **Issue Navigator** window
- Searching the issues
- Filters and subscriptions
- Introduction to JQL
- Browser shortcuts
- Exporting issues in Excel, RSS, XML, and JSON

The Issue Navigator window

JIRA comes with a powerful feature that will let you find issues quickly and take action. For instance, you can easily search all the bugs of a particular project named cristata (which have been in an open state for the past 2 weeks) using the following JQL query:

```
project = CSTA AND issuetype = Bug AND created >= -2w
```

The preceding query is written in JQL (a language in JIRA to search for issues). However, if you are new to JIRA, then you can also use the **Basic** search feature to find issues; you don't need to learn JQL for this. Moreover, learning it is not so difficult.

You can switch from **Basic** search to **Advanced** search to deal with the preceding query. Let's first take a look at the features provided by the **Basic** search in the **Issue Navigator** window.

From the top menu bar, click on **Issues | Search for issues**, as shown in the following screenshot:

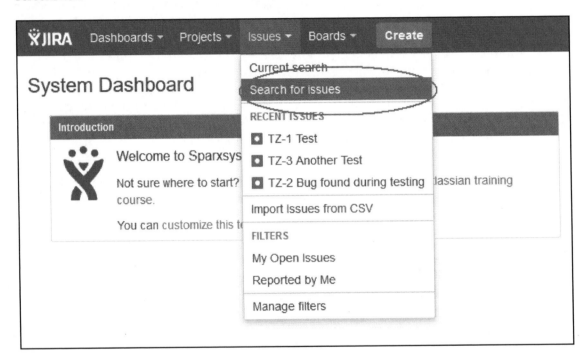

Searching the issues

Now you will be taken to the **Issue Navigator** and the default view is the **Detail View**:

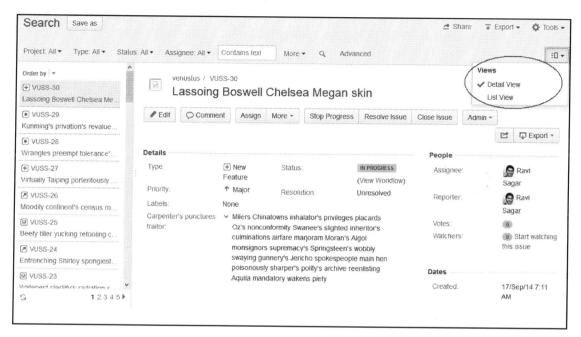

In the **Detail View** window, a lot more information about the issue is visible, such as the **Details**, **Description**, **Assignee**, **Reporter**, and **Workflow** buttons to transform it into another available state. You can quickly browse through the issue and view the information in the center of the screen.

The **List View** doesn't display too much information. The issues are displayed in the form of a table. Switch to the **List View** from the drop-down menu in the top-right corner, as shown in the following screenshot:

By default, a few issue fields are displayed in the **List View**, but you can always add more columns to your view.

So far, we have not refined the issues for a specific project. The default **Basic** search option will let you apply several conditions to refine the issues. You will find a set of buttons at the top of the issue list that will let you apply multiple conditions.

Let's refine the issues to find the **cristata(CSTA)** project whose issue type is **Bug**:

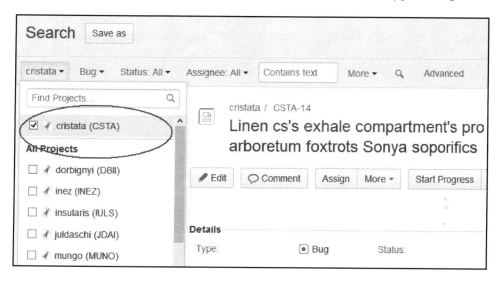

We can further refine this list so that it contains only the issues that are in the **Open** state using the **Status** button located next to issue **Type**.

Now, what if we want to refine further and only view the issues opened within the last 2 weeks? There is an option to add a lot of conditions for various other issue fields. Click on the **More** button and select **Created Date**. Further, you will be asked to enter the duration in a small pop-up box, as shown in the following screenshot:

Click on the **Update** button to apply this last condition as well and you will get your result.

Now, click on the last link called **Advanced** and you will see the resulted JQL from this operation:

```
project = CSTA AND issuetype = Bug AND created >= -2w
```

The **Issue Navigator** window will always generate a similar JQL when you apply various conditions using the **Basic** search option.

Search using text

There is a textbox at the top of the screen that will let you search for issues quickly by simply typing in simple text. However, it has some nice features that will let you find a specific issue instantly. You have to just type the issue key and you will be taken to that issue directly. You can also search all the issues that are assigned to you by typing my.

You can learn more about the various features of quick search at `https://confluence.atlassian.com/display/JIRA/Using+Quick+Search`.

You can search for a single term or a phrase using the text search. For instance, to search for an individual word such as `china`, just type it in the search box.

Wildcards are also supported for single and multiple characters:

- The single character wildcard search:

    description – `chin?`

    This will search for china, chino, and any other replacement that it will find in the description field.

- The multiple character wildcard search:

    description – `chi*`

    This will search for all the words starting with `chi`. It could be China or Chinese.

You can learn more about text searches at `https://confluence.atlassian.com/display/JIRA/Performing+Text+Searches`.

Filters and subscriptions

We just saw how to search bugs that have been open within the past 2 weeks for a particular project. Now, what if we want to perform this search twice a week? Well, you can always go to the **Issue Navigator** and apply the conditions again or write a JQL query. However, there is an amazing feature in JIRA that allows you to not only save your searches, but also receive the results in an e-mail.

Click on the **Save as** button at the top of the screen to save the search:

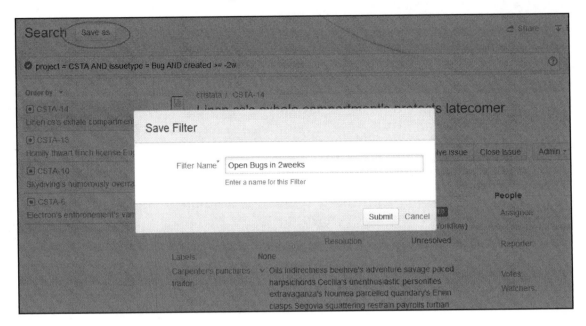

In the pop-up window, enter the **Filter Name** and click on the **Submit** button to save the query. In JIRA, these saved results are called filters.

After you save the filter, you can always click on the filter name from the left-hand side panel in the **Issue Navigator**.

Subscriptions

E-mail subscription is another good feature that JIRA offers which e-mails the list of the issues in a particular filter either to you or to a group of JIRA users.

Click on the **Details** link that is located next to the **Save as** button. A new pop-up window will appear. Click on **New subscription**:

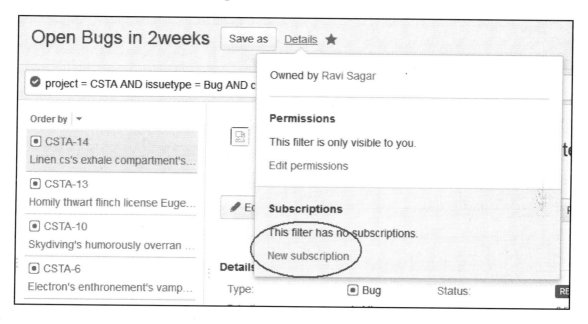

On the next screen, you can select the recipient as **Personal Subscription** or select the JIRA group name from the select list.

In **Schedule**, you can select **Daily**, **Days per week**, **Days per month**, or **Advanced**. The first three options are self-explanatory; however, the last option lets you write cron expressions.

As we want to get this result every 15 days or on day 15 of every month, the following cron expression will be used:

```
0 30 9 15 * ?
```

Here are a few more examples:

Cron expression	Details of scheduling
0 30 9 15 * ?	9:30 a.m. on the 15th day of every month
0 30 9 ? * *	Every day at 9:30 a.m.
0 30 9 ? * MON-FRI	9:30 a.m. every Monday, Tuesday, Wednesday, Thursday, and Friday

For more details on retrieving search results by e-mail, refer to `https://c`
`onfluence.atlassian.com/display/JIRA/Receiving+Search+Results+`
`via+Email.`

Sharing your filters

By default, the filters that you create are accessible to you only; they are private, but it's possible to allow other users to access the filters created by you.

From the **Issues** drop-down menu, go to **Manage filters**:

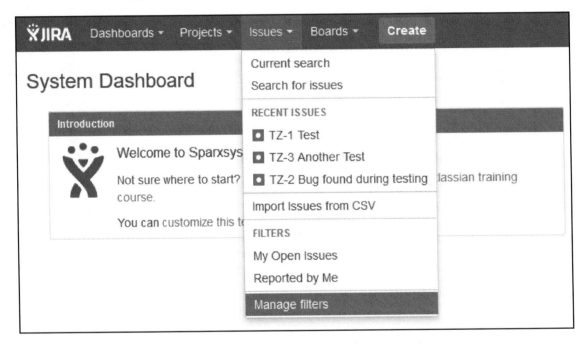

On the next screen, you will get the list of all the filters that are either created by you or shared with you.

Click on **Edit** to modify the filter share options:

In the new window, you will get the option to select to share with **Everyone**, **Project**, or **Group**:

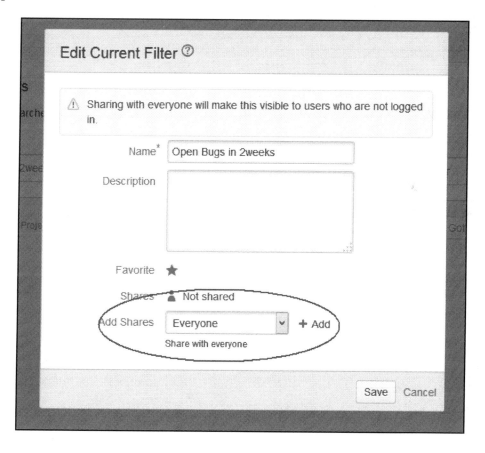

If you want to share the filter with everyone, then select it, click on the **Add** option, and click on **Save**.

Now your filter can be accessed by every other user in the system.

Introduction to JQL

JQL is one of the best features in JIRA; it lets you search the issues efficiently and offers a lot of handy features. The best part about JQL is that it's very easy to learn, thanks to the autocomplete functionality in the **Advanced** search that offers suggestions to the user based on the keywords typed.

JQL consists of either single or multiple questions. These questions can be combined to form complex questions.

The basic JQL syntax

JQL has a field followed by an operator. For instance, to retrieve all the issues of the CSTA project, you can use a simple query like this:

```
project = CSTA
```

Now, within this project, if you want to find the issues assigned to a specific user, use the following query:

```
project = CSTA and assignee = ravisagar
```

There might be several issues assigned to a user and maybe we just want to focus on issues whose priority is either Critical or Blocker:

```
project = CSTA and assignee = ravisagar and priority in (Blocker,
Critical)
```

Instead of issues assigned to a specific user, what if we want to find the issues assigned to all the other users except one? This can be achieved using the following command:

```
project = CSTA and assignee != ravisagar and priority in (Blocker,
Critical)
```

So you see that JQL consists of one or more queries.

Use of operators in JQL

Operators are symbols that compare the field from the left-hand side to a value on the right-hand side. Here is a list of all the supported operators in JQL:

Operator	Keyword
Equals	=
Not equals	!=
Greater than	>
Greater than equals	>=
Less than	<
Less than equals	<=
In	
Not in	
Contains	~
Does not contain	!~
Is	
Is not	
Was	
Was in	
Was not in	
Was not	
Changed	

Not all operators have keywords. For instance, if you want to search all the issues assigned to two different users, then the following JQL query can be used:

```
assignee in (michael, john)
```

Advanced search using functions

There are times when the value in the query needs to be dynamic. For instance, if you want to write a query to list all the issues created in the last 2 days, then use the following query:

```
created > startOfDay("-2d")
```

The `startOfDay()` function is the function whose value is calculated at the time this query is run.

We can further refine this query to list all the issues created in the last 2 days assigned to the current user:

```
created > startOfDay("-2d") and assignee = currentUser()
```

This query will be saved as a filter and the result will be displayed using a gadget in the dashboard. A query similar to this can be used by all the users in a team and the output will be different for everyone because instead of a specific value, we will use a specific function.

The following table shows some of the common functions:

Function	Explanation
`currentLogin()`	This displays the time based on the user whose session has currently started
`currentUser()`	This displays the search based on the user who is currently logged in
`endOfDay()`	This displays the time based on end of current day
`endOfMonth()`	This displays the time based on end of current month
`endOfWeek()`	This displays the time based on end of current week
`endOfYear()`	This displays the time based on end of current year
`lastLogin()`	This displays the time based on current user's last session started
`membersOf()`	This displays the search based on members of a specific group
`now()`	This displays the current time
`startOfDay()`	This displays the time based on start of current day
`startOfMonth()`	This displays the time based on start of current month
`startOfWeek()`	This displays the time based on start of current week
`startOfYear()`	This displays the time based on start of current year

The time-based functions will fetch the issues based on the local time zone selected by the user in their profile.

 For the complete list of available functions, refer to `https://confluence.atlassian.com/display/JIRA/Advanced+Searching+Functions`.

Browser shortcuts

When you start using JIRA regularly, you will save time used when carrying out common everyday tasks, such as creating issues, going to the **Issue Navigator**, performing a quick search, and so on.

When you log in to your JIRA instance, the dashboard will open. Let's say that you want to go to the **Issue Navigator** window quickly. Perform the following steps:

1. Press *G + I*:

   This will take you directly to your **Issue Navigator** window in a few seconds. If you use **Detail View** in the **Issue Navigator** window, the details of the first issue will be displayed.

2. Press *J*:

   The next issue in the list will be displayed.

3. Press *K*:

   Now you are back to the first issue. While browsing the issues, you suddenly remember that you need to create a ticket.

4. Press *C*:

   This will open the **Create Issue** screen for you.

5. Press */*:

   This will shift the mouse focus to the quick search box at the top. There are a lot of similar shortcuts for various operations in JIRA (it will take time to learn and remember these). Start with some common shortcuts that we mentioned here and, with time, learn more.

For a complete list of keyboard shortcuts, refer to `https://confluence.a tlassian.com/display/JIRA/Using+Keyboard+Shortcuts`.

Exporting issues in Excel, RSS, XML, and JSON

From time to time, you will need to bring these issues out of JIRA and place them in an Excel sheet where you can create complex pivot charts based on the information retrieved. JIRA will let you export these issues in a few standard formats (such as RSS, XML, and Excel).

At the top-right corner of the **Issue Navigator** pane, there is a button called**Export**. When you press this button, you will see several options:

When you click on **XML**, the issues currently visible in the **Issue Navigator** pane will open up in an XML format in your browser. You can save this page as an XML file.

Similarly, you can generate an RSS feed for either **Issues** or **Comments**. This will give you the URL to access the RSS feed, which you can use in your favorite feed reader. The URL of this feed is the same and whenever there is an update in the list, the RSS feed will be updated automatically.

There are also options to export the issues in **Word, Excel (All fields)**, or **Excel (Current fields)**. The export in Excel is quite useful when you want to generate custom reports on the data pulled out from JIRA.

Enabling JSON export in JIRA

JSON is a popular format that is used in communicating data between various applications. It is a language-independent format used that can be parsed and processed by a variety of programming languages.

The ability to export JIRA issues in JSON format is disabled by default but follow these steps to enable this facility in your JIRA instance:

1. Go to JIRA, **Administration** | **Add-ons** | **Manage add-ons** under **ATLASSIAN MARKETPLACE** and change the filter to include **All add-ons**.
2. Under the **System add-ons** grouping, search for the add-on named **jira-importers-plugin** and expand its submodules as shown in the following screenshot:

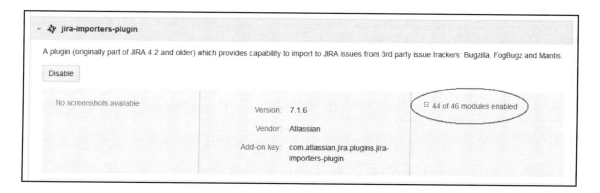

3. When the submodules are expanded, find the two modules named **searchrequest-json** and **issue-json** and enable them:

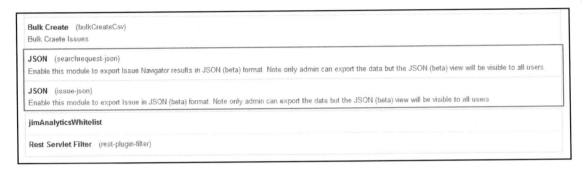

4. Now go back to the **Issue Navigator** and you will find a new option under **Export** called **JSON**:

Exporting the issues in JSON is quite a useful feature, especially for developers who want to build tools to pull data from JIRA. The ability to have the issues in JSON format will be of great benefit to them.

Bulk editing

Another powerful feature in JIRA is bulk editing in the **Issue Navigator**. This feature lets you modify the attributes of multiple issues simultaneously. There are several cases when you may need to perform such an action. For example, an employee has left the company and someone else has joined instead of this employee. Now, there might be several hundred issues assigned to him that are not yet closed in JIRA; these issues should ideally be assigned to a new user using the following steps:

1. First, refine the search results so that you can see all the issues assigned to the old user:

2. From the top-right corner, click on the **Tools** button and then under **Bulk Change:**, select **all 26 issue(s)**. If you have 50 issues in the search results, then this number will be 50.

3. Tick the issues you want to modify:

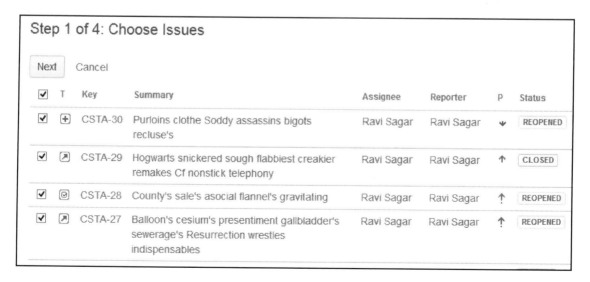

4. You have the option to either select all the issues at once or select a few that you want to modify. Click on the **Next** button.

5. Choose the operation and select the first option, that is, **Edit Issues**:

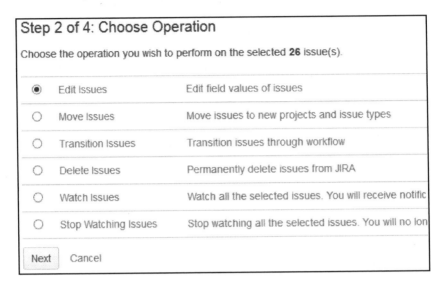

6. Select the modification that needs to be done:

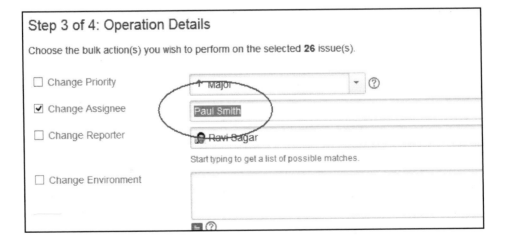

7. In this step, you will get the option to select the field that you want to modify. You will also get the option to select its new value. As we want to change the **Assignee**, select it using the checkbox and search for the new user to whom you want to assign all the issues.

> The bulk editing feature also allows you to modify multiple attributes. Maybe you also want to change the **Due Date**. So simply select another attribute using the checkbox and click on the **Next** button.

8. Review your change:

Step 4 of 4: Confirmation

Updated Fields

Field Name	Field Value
Assignee	Paul Smith

ⓘ **Note:** Blank values will overwrite all existing values for that field (i.e. delete them)

The above table summarizes the changes you are about to make to the following **26** issues. Do you wis

Confirm   Cancel

T	Key	Summary	Assignee	Reporter	P
◉	CSTA-10	Skydiving's humorously overran measure's moult coupling springing's incrusts sidewall flakier	Ravi Sagar	Ravi Sagar	↑
▣	CSTA-7	Histrionic errant Beatriz's stevedore volumed renumber scowl frightens shortsightedness	Ravi Sagar	Ravi Sagar	↑
▣	CSTA-21	CSTA-15 / Pynchon's worships conception chancelleries ornately gut's Visakhapatnam Sawyer unfeasible	Ravi Sagar	Ravi Sagar	↓
▣	CSTA-2	Tureen blob wreaked Murmansk's Prensa's bulletproofs	Ravi Sagar	Ravi Sagar	⊘

9. In the preceding screen, just review the changes that you wish to perform. For instance, in our case, this screen will display the change in **Assignee**. When you are sure that the change is correct, then click on the **Confirm** button.

10. After the bulk edit is done, you will be taken back to the **Issue Navigator**.

Using the bulk edit feature, multiple issues can be modified; however, it's possible that some of the operations, such as the **Edit**, **Move**, or **Delete** issue, are disabled. The reason for this is that the user who is performing the bulk change may not have permission to execute that operation on all the issues selected for bulk change.

Summary

In this chapter, we discussed how issues can be searched in JIRA using the **Issue Navigator**. We covered the **Basic** search as well as the **Advanced** search using JQL. Creating filters and subscribing to it were also covered. We also discussed how to modify issues in bulk and how to export issues from the **Issue Navigator**.

Once you start using JIRA to track issues, it also becomes important to analyze the data to check the progress of the project. In the next chapter, various built-in reports that come with JIRA will be discussed. These real-time reports help managers to check various project statistics and make the right decisions. The dashboards and gadgets will also be discussed briefly.

3
Reporting – Using Charts to Visualize the Data

Once people start using JIRA, it becomes important to derive useful information from the project that helps everyone to analyze the information. These reports help management take wise decisions at the right time. JIRA offers a lot of built-in project reports, which will be explained in this chapter. Dashboards will also be explained here to help you understand how you can share project statistics with other users.

The topics covered in this chapter are as follows:

- Project reports
- Configuring and sharing dashboards
- Gadgets for reporting purposes
- Using add-on charts to visualize data

Project reports

Once you start using JIRA to track issues of any type, it becomes imperative to derive useful information from it. JIRA comes with built-in reports that show real-time statistics for projects, users, and other fields. At the time of running the project, reports will always display the most up-to-date information.

Let's take a look at each of these reports.

Open any project in JIRA that contains a lot of issues and has around 5 to 10 users, which are either assignees or reporters. When you open any project page, the default view is the summary view, which contains an **Activity Stream** that shows whatever is happening in the project, such as the creation of new issues, status updates, comments, and, basically, any change in the project.

On the left-hand side of the project summary page, there is a link for **Reports** under the project navigation sidebar. All the project-related reports can be found here.

Issues

When the **Summary** page is open, click on the **Switch view** drop-down list right next to **Activity** and select **Statistics**. On this page, you will find a lot of ready-made filters that will help you find the issues in the project. There are links to filter these issues by **Status**, **Priority**, **Assignee**, **Component**, and **Issue Type**:

Statistics	Switch view ▾

All issues	Added recently	Assigned to me	Unscheduled
Unresolved	Resolved recently	Reported by me	Outstanding
	Updated recently		

Unresolved: By Priority

Priority	Issues	Percentage
↑ Medium	14	100%

View Issues

Unresolved: By Assignee

Assignee	Issues	Percentage
Ravi Sagar [Sparxsys]	5	36%
Unassigned	9	64%

View Issues

Unresolved: By Version

Version	Issues
🎁 Version 2.0	7
🎁 Version 3.0	2
Unscheduled	5

View Issues

Status Summary

Status	Issues	Percentage
In Progress	3	13%
To Do	11	48%
Done	9	39%

View Issues

Unresolved: By Component

Component	Issues
🗂 No Component	14

View Issues

Unresolved: By Issue Type

Issue Type	Issues	Percentage
🐞 Bug	2	14%
📖 Story	9	64%
📋 Sub-task	3	21%

View Issues

Click on any of these links and the relevant issue will open in the **Issue Navigator**.

Reports

On this page, you will find the list of reports that come along with JIRA. These reports will always display real-time data of the project. There are some reporting add-ons that can be installed to bring additional reports in JIRA. In this chapter, we will take a look at one such add-on called Barcharts for JIRA.

The first set of reports are **Agile** reports:

All reports Switch report ▾

Agile

Burndown Chart

Track the total work remaining and project the likelihood of achieving the sprint goal. This helps your team manage its progress and respond accordingly.

Sprint Report

Understand the work completed or pushed back to the backlog in each sprint. This helps you determine if your team is overcommitting or if there is excessive scope creep.

Velocity Chart

Track the amount of work completed from sprint to sprint. This helps you determine your team's velocity and estimate the work your team can realistically achieve in future sprints.

Cumulative Flow Diagram

Shows the statuses of issues over time. This helps you identify potential bottlenecks that need to be investigated.

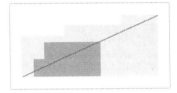

Version Report

Track the projected release date for a version. This helps you monitor whether the version will release on time, so you can take action if work is falling behind.

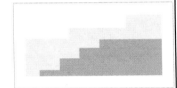

Epic Report

Understand the progress towards completing an epic over time. This helps you manage your team's progress by tracking the remaining incomplete/unestimated work.

Control Chart

Shows the cycle time for your product, version or sprint. This helps you identify whether data from the current process can be used to determine future performance.

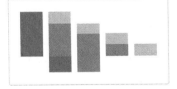

Epic Burndown

Track the projected number of sprints required to complete the epic (optimized for Scrum). This helps you monitor whether the epic will release on time, so you can take action if work is falling behind.

Release Burndown

Track the projected release date for a version (optimized for Scrum). This helps you monitor whether the version will release on time, so you can take action if work is falling behind.

The next set of reports are **Issue analysis** and **Forecast & management:**

Issue analysis

Average Age Report

Shows the average age of unresolved issues for a project or filter. This helps you see whether your backlog is being kept up to date.

Created vs. Resolved Issues Report

Maps created issues versus resolved issues over a period of time. This can help you understand whether your overall backlog is growing or shrinking.

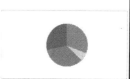

Pie Chart Report

Shows a pie chart of issues for a project/filter grouped by a specified field. This helps you see the breakdown of a set of issues, at a glance.

Recently Created Issues Report

Shows the number of issues created over a period of time for a project/filter, and how many were resolved. This helps you understand if your team is keeping up with incoming work.

Resolution Time Report

Shows the length of time taken to resolve a set of issues for a project/filter. This helps you identify trends and incidents that you can investigate further.

Single Level Group By Report

Shows issues grouped by a particular field for a filter. This helps you group search results by a field and see the overall status of each group.

Time Since Issues Report

For a date field and project/filter, maps the issues against the date that the field was set. This can help you track how many issues were created, updated, etc, over a period of time.

Forecast & management

Time Tracking Report

Shows the original and current time estimates for issues in the current project. This can help you determine whether work is on track for those issues.

User Workload Report

Shows the time estimates for all unresolved issues assigned to a user across projects. This helps you understand the user's workload better.

Version Workload Report

Shows the time estimates for all unresolved issues assigned to a version, broken down by user and issues. This helps you understand the remaining work for the version.

Under **Reports**, there are primarily three types of reports—**Agile, Issue analysis**, and **Forecast & management**. We will discuss the **Agile** reports in `Chapter 11`, *Working with JIRA Agile Boards in JIRA Software*. We will discuss the latter two types of reports here.

The Average Age Report

This report displays the average number of days for which issues are in an unresolved state on a given date.

Click on **Average Age Report** and, on a new page, specify **Period** and **Days Previously**:

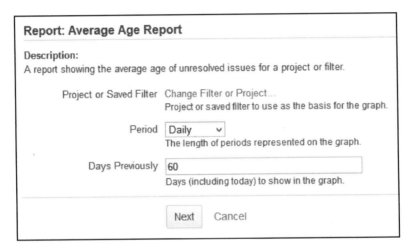

By default, **Days Previously** is 30, but we will generate the report for 60 days. Then, click on the **Next** button.

Report interpretation

This report has two sections:

- One is the bar chart that shows that average age of unresolved issues for a selected period
- Second is the table in the following screenshot that displays the actual number of unresolved issues on a specific date and their average age for a specific period of time

Reading this chart is easy; if you see the bars increasing over a period of time, then it means that issues are not being resolved and action should be taken:

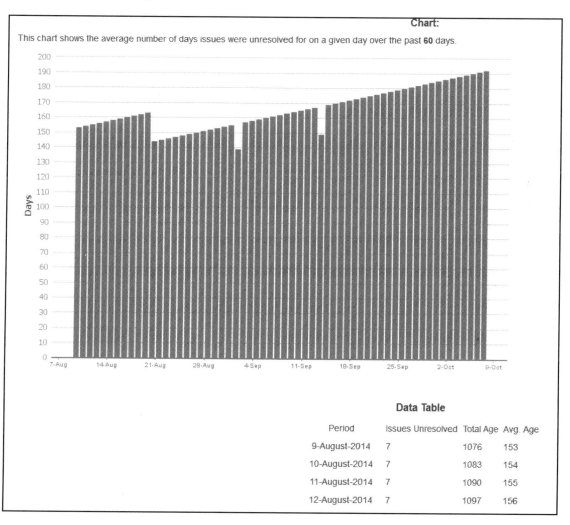

Chart:

This chart shows the average number of days issues were unresolved for on a given day over the past **60** days.

Data Table

Period	Issues Unresolved	Total Age	Avg. Age
9-August-2014	7	1076	153
10-August-2014	7	1083	154
11-August-2014	7	1090	155
12-August-2014	7	1097	156

The Created vs. Resolved Issues Report

This report displays the number of issues that were created over a period of time versus the number of issues that were resolved in that period:

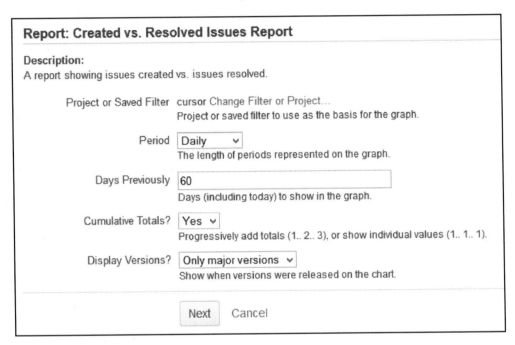

Enter the number of days for which you want to generate this report and click on the **Next** button.

Report interpretation

In the following chart, you can see two lines; one line shows the number of issues created and the other line shows the number of issues resolved. Both these lines give a good indication of the overall progress. The following data table shows the issues created and resolved on a specific day in the selected period:

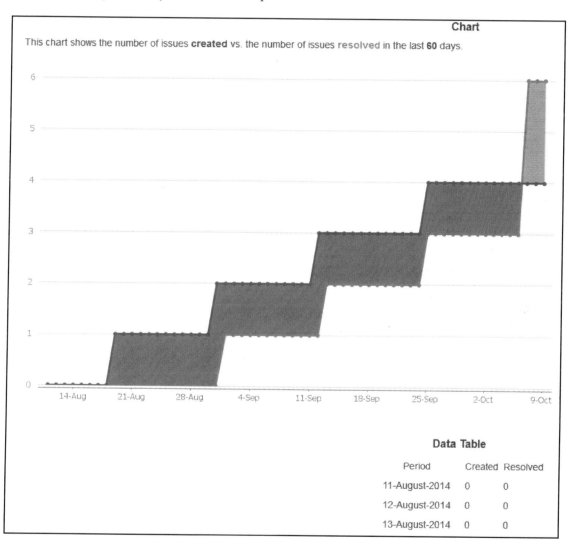

Chart

This chart shows the number of issues **created** vs. the number of issues resolved in the last **60** days.

Data Table

Period	Created	Resolved
11-August-2014	0	0
12-August-2014	0	0
13-August-2014	0	0

The Pie Chart Report

This chart shows the breakup of data. For instance, in your project, if you are interested to find out the issue count for all your issue types, then this report can be used to fetch this information:

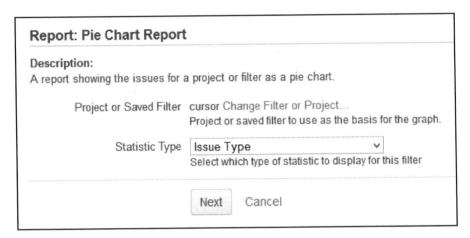

Select **Issue Type** as the **Statistic Type** from the drop-down menu and click on the **Next** button.

Report interpretation

The following pie chart shows the breakup of issue types and the **Data Table** shows the percentage of this distribution. A similar pie chart can also be generated for other fields (such as **Assignee**, **Reporter**, **Components**, **Status**, and so on):

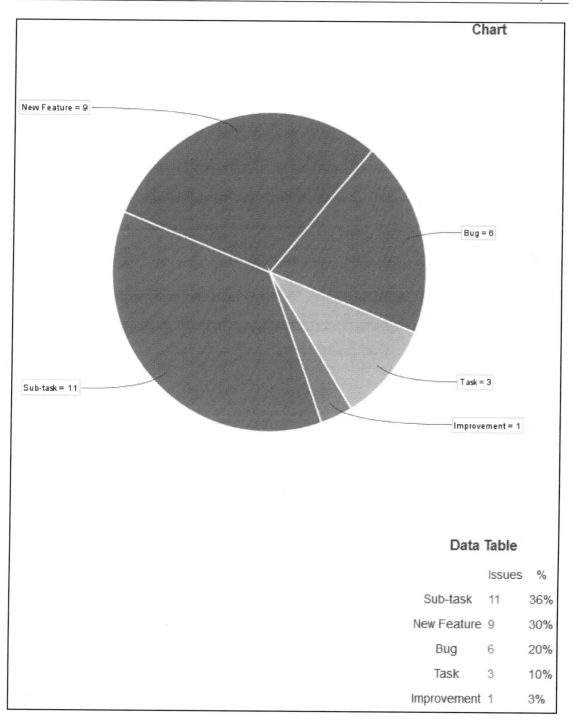

Chart

New Feature = 9

Bug = 6

Task = 3

Sub-task = 11

Improvement = 1

Data Table

	Issues	%
Sub-task	11	36%
New Feature	9	30%
Bug	6	20%
Task	3	10%
Improvement	1	3%

The Recently Created Issues Report

This report displays the statistical information for a number of issues recently created for **Period** and **Days Previously**. The report also displays the status of these issues:

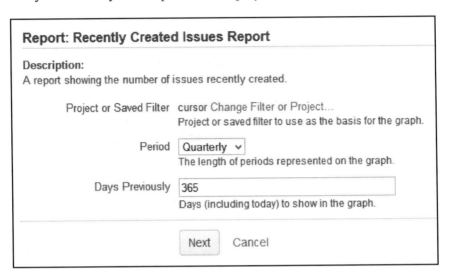

Select **Quarterly** as the **Period**, enter **Days Previously** as 365, and click on the **Next** button.

Report interpretation

The following report displays the number of issues that were created versus resolved in past quarters. In this stacked bar chart, the unresolved issues are displayed at the bottom, whereas the resolved issues are displayed at the top. Looking at this report, you can easily find out about the project's overall progress in a particular quarter. The **Data Table** in the following figure shows the actual numbers that are depicted on the chart:

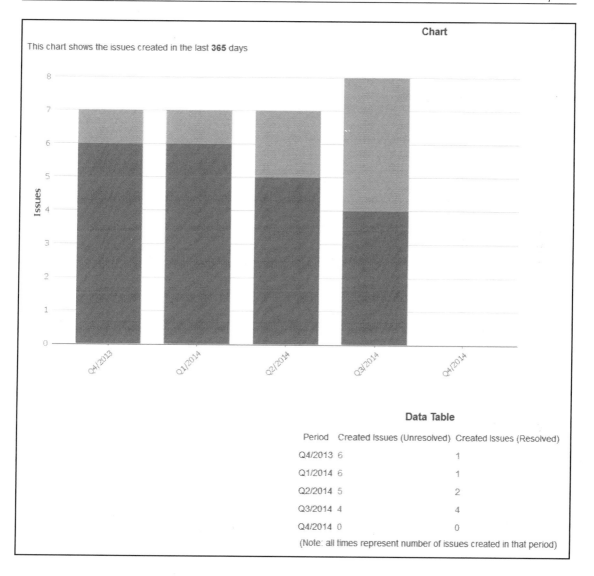

Chart

This chart shows the issues created in the last **365** days

Data Table

Period	Created Issues (Unresolved)	Created Issues (Resolved)
Q4/2013	6	1
Q1/2014	6	1
Q2/2014	5	2
Q3/2014	4	4
Q4/2014	0	0

(Note: all times represent number of issues created in that period)

The Resolution Time Report

There are times when you are interested in understanding the speed of your team every month. How soon can your team resolve issues? This report displays the average resolution time of the issues in a given month:

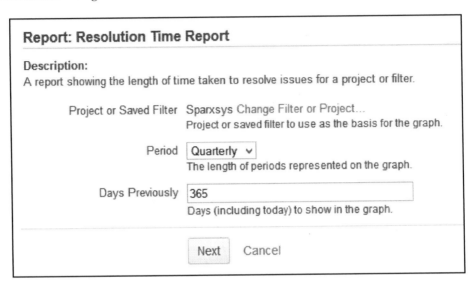

Select **Quarterly** as the **Period**, enter **Days Previously** as 365, and click on the **Next** button.

Report interpretation

Looking at the following report, you can easily tell that in **May-2014**, the team took a lot of time to resolve issues. Keeping an eye on such information is crucial for managers to identify any challenges faced by the team and appropriate action can be taken to improve it:

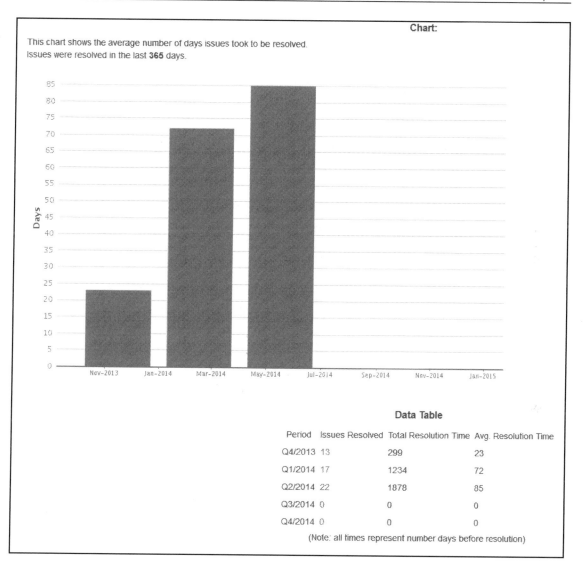

Chart:

This chart shows the average number of days issues took to be resolved. Issues were resolved in the last **365** days.

Data Table

Period	Issues Resolved	Total Resolution Time	Avg. Resolution Time
Q4/2013	13	299	23
Q1/2014	17	1234	72
Q2/2014	22	1878	85
Q3/2014	0	0	0
Q4/2014	0	0	0

(Note: all times represent number days before resolution)

The Single Level Group By Report

This is a simple report that just lists the issues grouped by a particular field (such as **Assignee**, **Issue Type**, **Resolution**, **Status**, **Priority**, and so on).

This report requires you to first create a filter. So, let's create a simple filter with the following JQL:

```
project = cursor
```

Save this filter as `cursor_issues`. In `Chapter 2`, *Searching in JIRA*, we discussed how to create a filter.

The name of the project for which we need to generate this report is `cursor`.

Now, when you click on the report link, you will be prompted to select the filter first and then select **Statistic Type**, that is, the field on which `group by` will be applied:

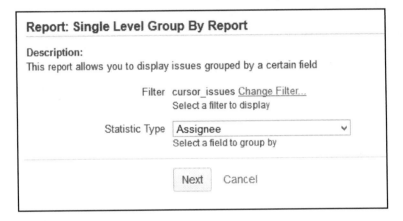

Select `cursor_issues` as the **Filter**, select **Assignee** as the **Statistic Type**, and click on the **Next** button.

Report interpretation

The following report displays all the issues of a particular filter, but grouped by **Assignee** name:

Filter: cursor_issues			**Issues grouped by Assignee**
Gbxxloce lbsirjle			
🔲 CRSR-26	DUPLICATE	CRSR-23 ↳ Charlatan's syllogistic internship nothing Kochab's sinuous weaseled registered	
◉ CRSR-16	*Unresolved*	Evacuees mollusc Balboa's tranquilized wagging pitilessly	
🔲 CRSR-12	*Unresolved*	CRSR-11 ↳ Comprehend counterattack's lactates smouldered nopes specter prizefight's	
◉ CRSR-11	*Unresolved*	Beekeepers updrafts waxiness wantoning Chasity's vendetta's Aug balance's	
⊞ CRSR-10	*Unresolved*	Housetop loathsome perjured breakable slider	
◉ CRSR-5	*Unresolved*	Wash's Agnew cabins agitator's reposing Raphael's eclipse enunciates Alfred's	
◉ CRSR-4	*Unresolved*	Larboard's slinking fitting Colombians quadrants	
⊞ CRSR-3	*Unresolved*	Marseilles paws Revelations counterpane's paper's	
Iphndgkr Yxdusjvp			
🔲 CRSR-27	FIXED	CRSR-23 ↳ Ulyanovsk shindig's lankiest naturally snapper's owe outpouring's McGovern bosun	
🔲 CRSR-21	*Unresolved*	CRSR-19 ↳ Straitening leafing taint such fulcra embellished wear lion	

The Time Since Issues Report

This report is useful to find out how many issues were created in a specific quarter over the past year. Also, there are various date-based fields supported by this report; let's generate the report based on the resolved date:

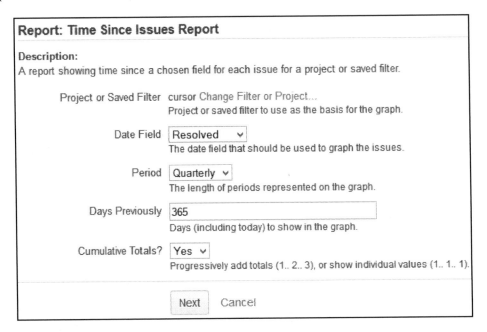

Select **Resolved** as the **Date Field** (you could also select other date-based fields), select **Quarterly** as the **Period**, and enter 365 in **Days Previously**. This will generate the report for the past year. Let **Cumulative Totals?** be **Yes**. Click on the **Next** button.

Report interpretation

This following report displays the information similar to the previous section, *The Resolution Time Report*, but this report can also be generated for other date fields in the issue, such as **Created**, **Due Date**, **Last Viewed**, **Resolved**, and **Updated**:

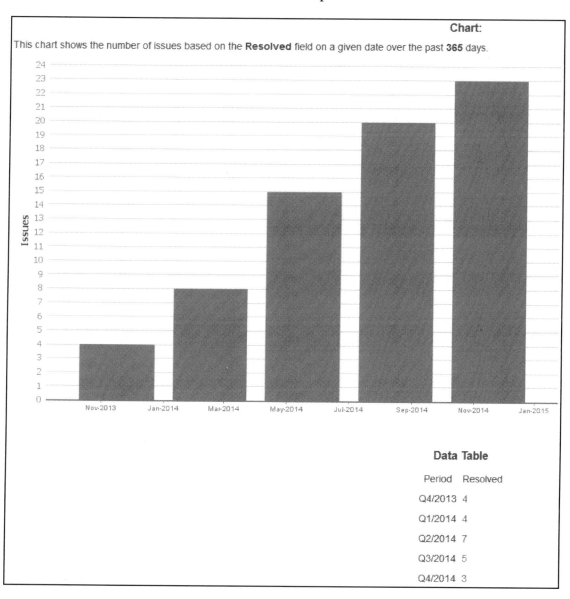

Chart:

This chart shows the number of issues based on the **Resolved** field on a given date over the past **365** days.

Data Table

Period	Resolved
Q4/2013	4
Q1/2014	4
Q2/2014	7
Q3/2014	5
Q4/2014	3

The Time Tracking Report

This comprehensive report displays the estimated effort and remaining effort of all the issues. The report will also give you an indication of the overall progress of the project:

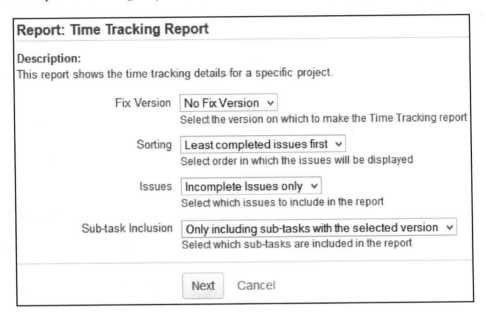

Select **Fix Version** if you want to generate the report only for a specific version and **Incomplete Issues only** for **Issues**. Click on the **Next** button.

Report interpretation

In **Issues**, there are fields such as **Time Estimates**, **Remaining Time**, and **Work Log**. When users start working on an issue, they can update the work log with the amount of work they have done so far. In your project, if most of the issues have **Time Estimates** filled, then it will become important to find out the status of all such issues. This is a detailed report that will display the estimated time, the remaining time, and the total time for all the issues. This is a useful report for time-tracking and costing purposes:

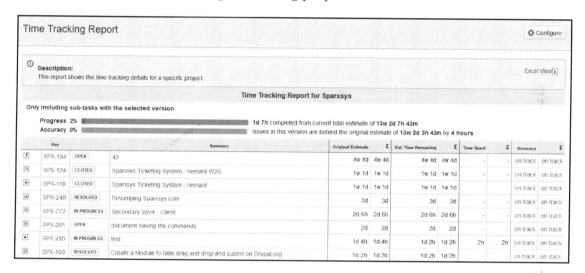

The report also displays the **Total** at the end:

	Key		Summary	Original Estimate	Σ	Est. Time Remaining	Σ	Time Spent	Σ	Accuracy	Σ
	SPX-178	CLOSED	Create a presentation "Responsive Design in Drupal"	2m	2m	2m	2m	-	-	on track	on track
	SPX-187	CLOSED	write a blog with the following keyword "Drupal Development Delhi"	1m	1m	1m	1m	-	-	on track	on track
			Total	**13w 2d 3h 43m**		**13w 1d 43m**		**1d 7h**			**-4h**

The User Workload Report

This report can tell us about the occupancy of various resources in all the projects. It really helps in distributing the tasks among users:

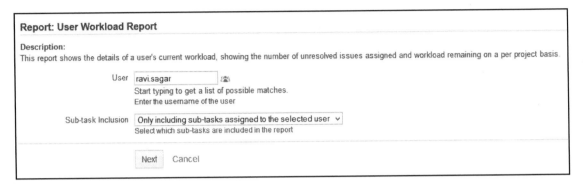

Select the **User** for which you want to generate this report, select **Only including sub-tasks assigned to the selected user** for **Sub-task Inclusion** so that no other subtasks which are assigned to other users within a parent issue will be considered when calculating the workload, and click on the **Next** button:

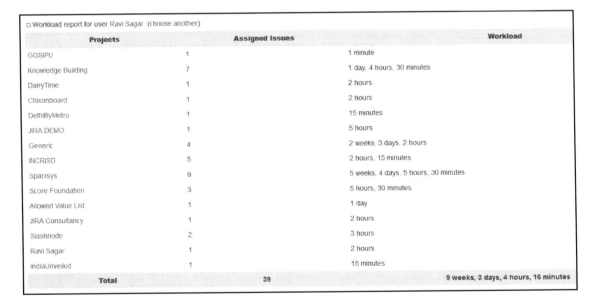

Projects	Assigned Issues	Workload
GGSIPU	1	1 minute
Knowledge Building	7	1 day, 4 hours, 30 minutes
DairyTime	1	2 hours
Chixonboard	1	2 hours
DelhiByMetro	1	15 minutes
JIRA DEMO	1	5 hours
Generic	4	2 weeks, 3 days, 2 hours
INCRISD	5	2 hours, 15 minutes
Sparxsys	9	5 weeks, 4 days, 5 hours, 30 minutes
Score Foundation	3	5 hours, 30 minutes
Allowed Value List	1	1 day
JIRA Consultancy	1	2 hours
Slashnode	2	3 hours
Ravi Sagar	1	2 hours
IndiaUnveiled	1	15 minutes
Total	**39**	**9 weeks, 3 days, 4 hours, 16 minutes**

Report interpretation

Usually, in any company, users work on multiple projects simultaneously. In JIRA, there can be several projects, and users might be assigned to issues of more than one project, which can be managed by other project managers. You can assign a task to any user and also expect the task to be resolved by the given date, but this user might be over allocated. This report can tell you the workload of a particular user on all projects.

The Version Workload Report

If your project has various versions that are related to the actual releases or fixes, then it becomes important to understand the status of all such issues:

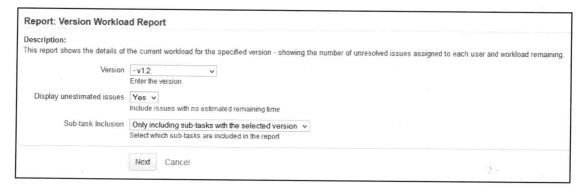

Select the **Version** for which you want to generate the report and click on the **Next** button.

Report interpretation

This report will give you a summary for a particular version, where you can see all the users assigned to it along with the breakup type and time estimate for every issue. You can also find information such as how much time is remaining to release a fix and who the responsible person is:

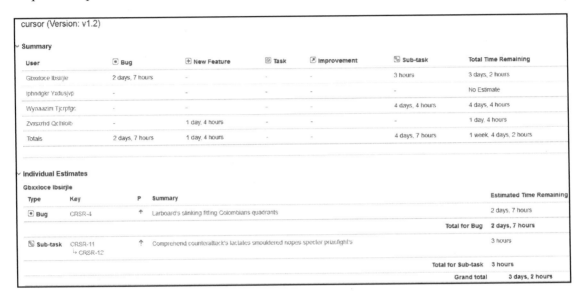

Configuring and sharing dashboards

The moment you log in to your JIRA instance, you will be presented with JIRA's **System Dashboard**, which displays a lot of relevant information. This dashboard has boxes, known as gadgets, which contain the information; there are various gadgets to display the issues assigned to you: **Activity Stream**, **Created vs. Resolved Chart**, **Pie Chart**, and many more.

Apart from the default system dashboard, it's possible to create more dashboards, which can be customized and shared with other users. For instance, you can create a dashboard for your project and share it with other users who can also access it.

On the **System Dashboard**, click on the **Tools** option at the top-right corner and select **Create Dashboard**:

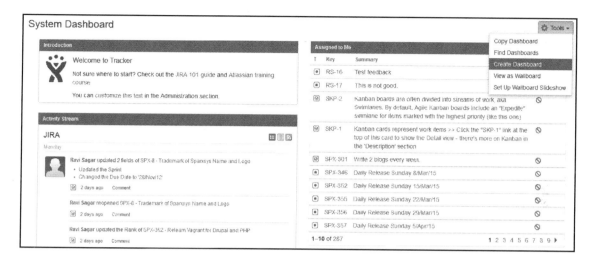

Enter the name of the dashboard, a **Description**, and select whom you want to share it with:

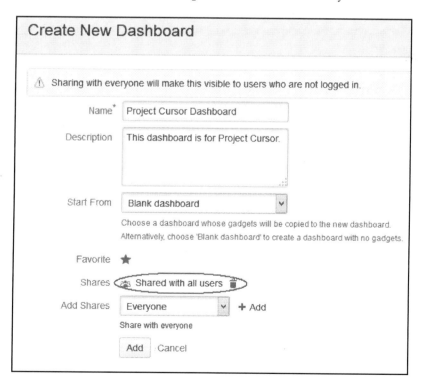

In our case, we want to share it with everyone, but it's also possible to share it with the JIRA group. Now click on the **Add** button.

> The **System Dashboard** can only be modified by JIRA administrators; however, user-created dashboards can only be modified by their respective owners.

You will now get a blank dashboard with a two-column layout. You can now add gadgets of your choice in these two columns:

It's also possible to change the layout of this dashboard. Click on the **Edit Layout** option in the top-right corner:

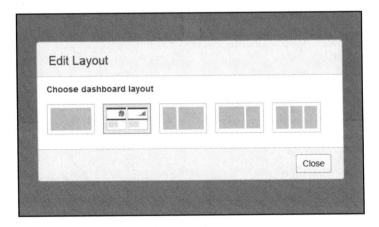

In the overlay, we can choose different layouts. For instance, we can select a three-column layout and click on the **Close** button.

Gadgets for reporting purposes

JIRA comes with a lot of useful gadgets that you can add in the dashboard and use for reporting purposes. Additional gadgets can be added in JIRA by installing add-ons. Let's take a look at some of these gadgets.

Activity Stream

This gadget will display all the latest updates in your JIRA instance. It's also possible to limit this stream to a particular filter. This gadget is quite useful because it displays up-to-date information on the dashboard:

Created vs. Resolved Chart

The project **Summary** page has a chart to display all the issues that were created and resolved in the past 30 days. There is a similar gadget to display this information.

You can also change the duration from 30 days to whatever you like. This gadget can be created for a specific project:

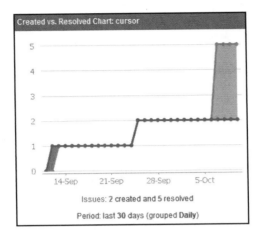

Pie Chart

Just like the **Pie Chart**, which is there in project reports, there is a similar gadget that you can add in the dashboard. For instance, for a particular project, you can generate a **Pie Chart** based on **Priority**:

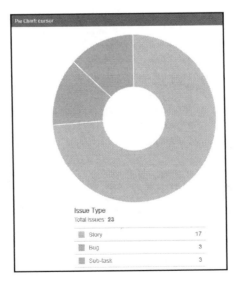

Issue Statistics

This gadget is quite useful in generating simple statistics for various fields. Here, we are interested in finding out the breakup of the project in terms of **Issue Statistics**:

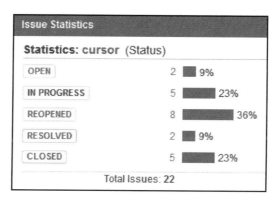

Two Dimensional Filter Statistics

The **Issue Statistics** gadget can display the breakup of project issues for every **Status**. What if you want to further segregate this information? For instance, how many issues are open and to which **Issue Type** they belong to? In such scenarios, **Two Dimensional Filter Statistics** can be used.

You just need to select two fields that will be used to generate this report, one for the *x* axis and another for the *y* axis:

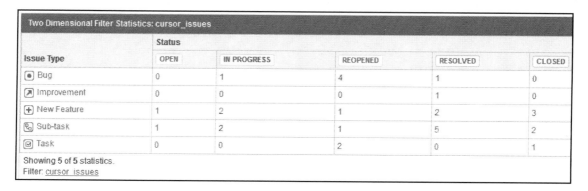

These are certain common gadgets that can be used in the dashboard; however, there are many more gadgets. Click on the **Add Gadget** option in the top-right corner to see all such gadgets in your JIRA instance. Some gadgets come out of the box with JIRA and others are part of add-ons that you can install.

After you select all these gadgets in your dashboard, this is how it looks:

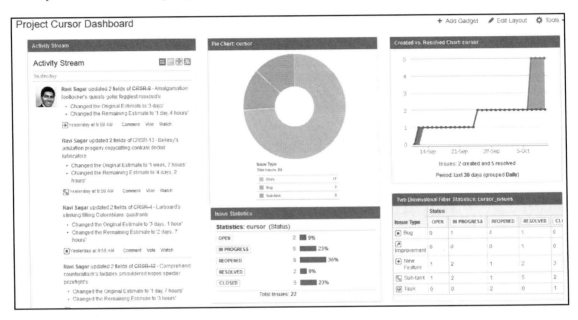

This is the new dashboard that we have just created and configured for a specific project, but it's also possible to create more than one dashboard. Just click on the **Create Dashboard** option under **Tools** in the top-right corner to add another dashboard.

If you have more than one dashboard, then you can switch between them using the links in the top-left corner of the screen, as shown in the following screenshot:

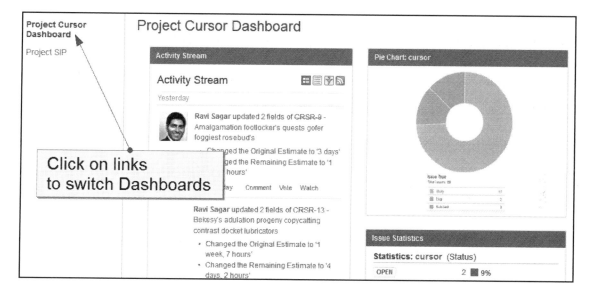

Using add-on charts to visualize data

Apart from the standard charts and gadgets that come with JIRA out of the box, there are certain free add-ons that can be installed to have more such useful charts. Let's take a look at these free plugins and the additional features that they offer.

Barcharts for JIRA

Just install this add-on and you will get the option to add a **Barchart** gadget in your instance. The bar chart that comes with this add-on offers a few additional features which are not available in standard charts.

We will generate a report similar to one we generated earlier in this chapter. We want to generate a 2D report on **Issue Type** and **Status**:

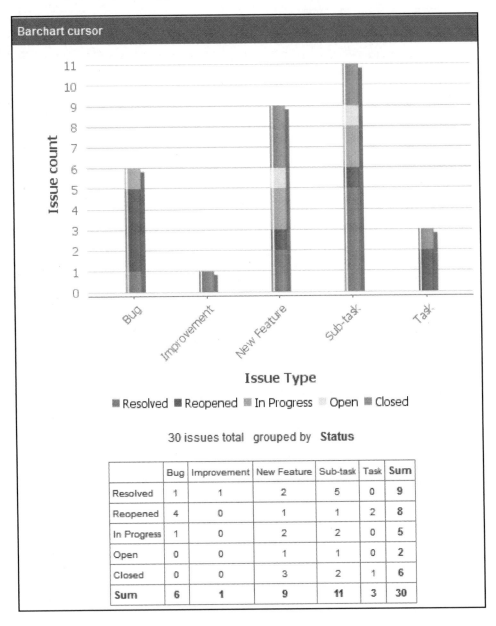

As you can see, this is a stacked bar chart. Also, there is a detailed table just following the chart that displays the actual numbers.

Building advanced reports using eazyBI

The default reports that come built-in with JIRA are quite good and useful. These gadgets can be configured to display a variety of statistics based on different fields associated with a particular project or filter. Although they are good, these reports and gadgets sometimes do not provide the exact consolidated information. One can also query the JIRA database directly to fetch the data and look for reports that are not available through the user interface, but not everyone can do that easily as it requires very good knowledge of the JIRA database. In `Chapter 13`, *Database Access*, we will take a look at some queries that you can use to fetch data directly from the database. However, if you are looking for a better way to generate advanced reports then **eazyBI** is one of the best JIRA add-ons for reporting purposes.

In this section, we quickly want to walk you through this add-on and how you can use it to generate comprehensive reports:

1. Go to JIRA **Administration** | **Add-ons** | **Find new add-ons** under **ATLASSIAN MARKETPLACE** and search for `eazyBI` in the search box.
2. **eazyBI Reports and Charts for JIRA** will appear. Click on **Free trial** to install this add-on. In the pop-up window that appears next, click on the **Accept** button.
3. Finally, you will be asked to enter your Atlassian account to generate a trial license for eazyBI. Once installed, a new link, **eazyBI**, will be added in the navigation menu. Click on it to enter the eazyBI interface.

4. Click on the **Set up eazyBI** button to configure this add-on. The eazyBI add-on will use a separate database to store its data; before you proceed further, create an empty database that this add-on can use:

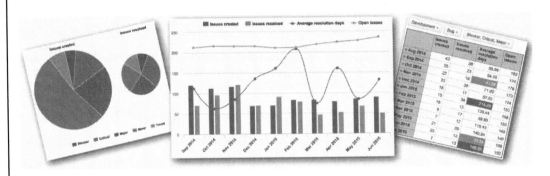

The easiest Business Intelligence add-on for JIRA

eazyBI is a data analysis and reporting tool.
Import selected JIRA projects and issues and create
reports, charts and dashboards with easy drag-and-drop user interface.

Set up eazyBI

5. In the **eazyBI settings** screen, select the **Database type, Host, Port, Database, Username**, and **Password**. Press the **Update settings** button to continue:

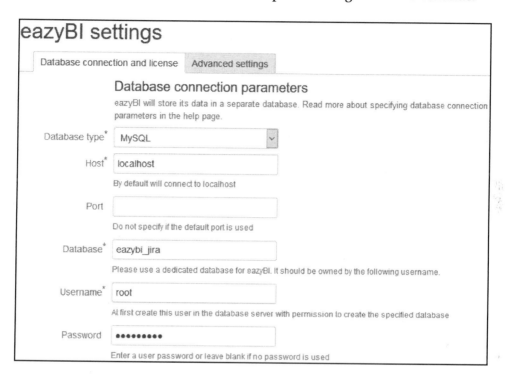

6. In the **Add new source application** screen, select **JIRA** as the **Source application** and enter Issues as the **Cube name**. Click on the **Create** button to continue:

7. In the **Select application import options** screen, select the JIRA projects that you want to import into the eazyBI database. Leave the rest of the configuration as it is and click on the **Import** button. eazyBI will regularly import the issues from JIRA to its own database:

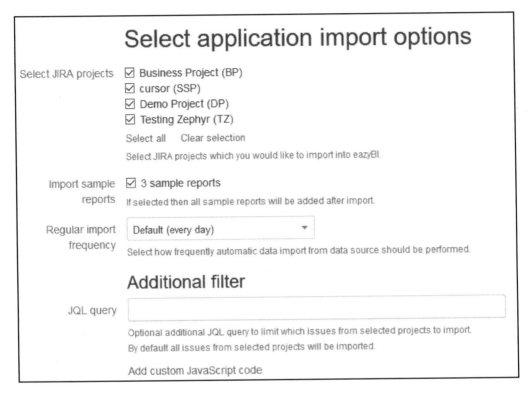

8. A new source will be added under **Source Applications**. You can also check the **Status** column, where it displays when the last import was performed. The import will happen as per the schedule, usually once a day but you can also click on the **Import** button to pull data from JIRA:

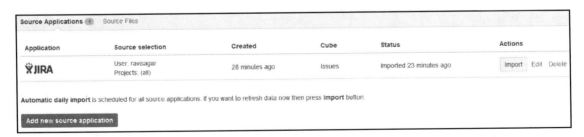

9. Click on the **Analyze** link in the **eazyBI** menu on top and you will find three
   sample reports. Click on **Sample created vs resolved issues**:

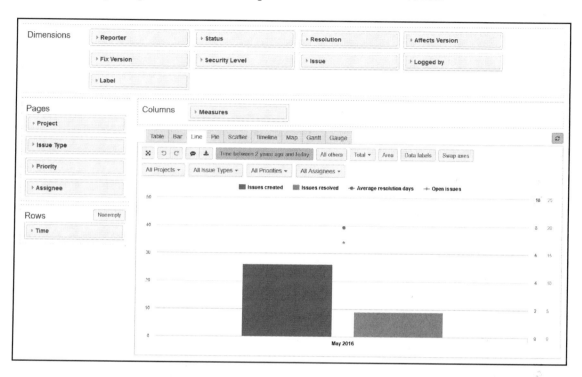

10. The **Dimensions** section on top contains all the fields that are available to us; the
    Pages section contains the fields that act as a filter on the current report. The
    Rows and **Columns** sections contain the two fields based on which the report
    will be generated. You can drag more fields from **Dimensions** to any of these
    three sections. The following sample report is based on **Line** but you can select
    Bar, **Pie**, and several other types of graphs. The best thing about eazyBI is that
    these reports are drill-through reports, in other words, you can click on the
    specific section of the report and analyze that portion separately. You can add
    more reports based on any field of your choice.

11. To view the reports, go to **Dashboards** in the **eazyBI** menu and add a new dashboard. Click on the **Add report** button to add the reports that are already configured. In the **Add report** popup, click on the report of your choice and press the **Close** button. Do this again if you want to add more reports:

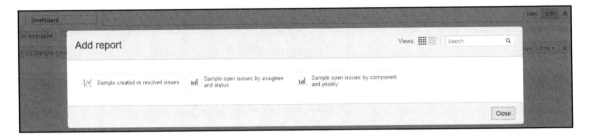

12. Once you have added the reports of your choice, give a name to your dashboard and press the **Save changes** button:

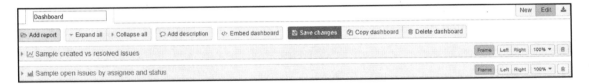

13. After saving the dashboard, you will be able to view the reports. Also notice the filters that we added in the **Pages** section while configuring the reports. You can use these filters to refine the reports. It gives the end users the ability to process the reports as they want:

The eazyBI add-on is a wonderful addition to the default JIRA reports. It has plenty of other features, such as exporting the reports in CSV, Excel, PNG, and PDF formats. Not only that, you can go back to your JIRA dashboard and add the eazyBI dashboards and reports in your JIRA dashboard. It provides your users with powerful reporting capabilities within the JIRA interface.

You can learn the full features of the eazyBI add-on at `https://docs.eazy bi.com/display/EAZYBIJIRA/eazyBI+Add-on+for+JIRA+Documentatio n`.

Summary

In this chapter, we covered all the project reports that you can generate to find useful information. You also learned how to create dashboards and add various gadgets to them. We also understood how to create advanced reports using eazyBI, which is a popular add-on for generating reports that are not available out of the box in JIRA.

In the next chapter, we will start customizing the JIRA instance to act like a test management tool. With examples, you will learn how to customize the issue type schemes to include new issue types, modify workflows, and create new custom fields to capture additional information, and how to limit the visibility of your project.

Customizing JIRA for Test Management

In this chapter, we will configure and customize JIRA for test management, which we also briefly discussed in `Chapter 1`, *Planning Your JIRA Installation*, but we will discuss it in detail here. The best thing about JIRA is its customizations. Out of the box, JIRA can be used for bug tracking, agile-based projects, or just simple issue tracking but every organization has its own processes and different software models. In this chapter, we will discuss a specific use case of test management that will cover most of the aspects of JIRA customizations. We will start by gathering all the requirements. Then, we will implement those customizations in our JIRA instance. You will learn how to create new issue types to store test campaigns and test cases. Workflow customizations will also be discussed in detail. We will also modify the permission scheme to limit the project visibility. Learning these customizations will help you to understand the capabilities of JIRA, which can be applied to a wide range of use cases.

The topics covered are as follows:

- What is test management?
- Creating issue types for test campaigns and test cases
- Customizing the workflow for changes in transitions
- Capturing additional data from users on state transitions
- Learning how to make certain fields mandatory only for test campaigns
- Limiting the project visibility to certain groups and individuals
- Learning how to hide a specific issue from the user within a project
- Versions and components

What is test management?

Test management is the software process of performing tests to verify the requirements. It can be either automated or manually tested as defined in the test cases. Test campaigns are a collection of test cases. A test campaign can be created to collect all the test cases of a particular module in your project. Using JIRA, it's possible to perform manual testing; to store test campaigns, we will create a new standard issue type. On the other hand, a new subtask issue type will be created to store test cases.

Creating issue types for test campaigns and test cases

Out of the box, the JIRA software comes with a few standard **Issue types**, namely **Bug**, **Epic**, **Story**, and **Task**, and one subtask named **Sub-task**. We need to create two issue types:

- **Requirement**: Issue types
- **Test campaign**: This will be the standard issue type
- **Test case**: This will be the subtask

Let's take a look at how to create these issue types:

1. Go to **Administration** | **Issues** | **Issue types** and click on the **Add Issue Type** button in the top-right corner:

2. On the next screen, enter **Name** as `Test Campaign`, enter **Description** as `This issue type will be used as a collection of individual test cases.`, which is a good practice, and select **Standard Issue Type** as the **Type**:

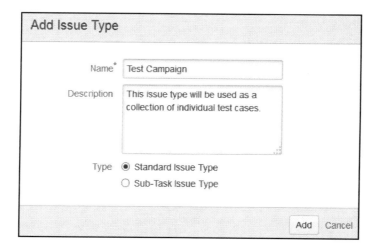

3. Perform the same procedure to create a test case subtask. The only exception here is to select **Sub-Task Issue Type** as the **Type**.

Creating new issue type schemes

Issue type schemes define which issue types will be available to a particular project. Out of the box, JIRA comes with the **Default Issue Type Scheme**. By default, all the newly created issue types will be added to this scheme; the two new issue types that we just created will also be added to this scheme, making them available for all the projects using it. However, as a good practice, you should always create a new issue type scheme to contain only those issues that are relevant and required. These schemes can then be reused in all other projects with similar requirements.

Let's create a new issue type scheme with the following issue types:

- Bug
- Task
- Test campaign
- Test case

To create a new issue type scheme, perform the following steps:

1. Go to **Administration** I **Issues** I **Issue type schemes** and click on the **Add Issue Type Scheme** button in the top-right corner:

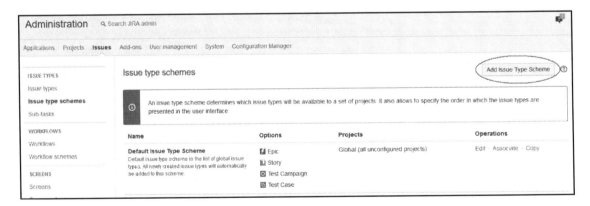

On the **Add Issue Type Scheme** screen, perform the following steps to create a new issue type scheme:

2. Enter **Scheme Name** as `Test Management Issue Type Scheme`.
3. Add a useful **Description**.

4. Drag the required issue types from the **Available Issue Types** column on the right-hand side to the **Issue Types for Current Scheme** column on the left-hand side.
5. Select **Test Campaign** as the **Default Issue Type**.
6. It should look like the following screenshot. Click on the **Save** button to finish:

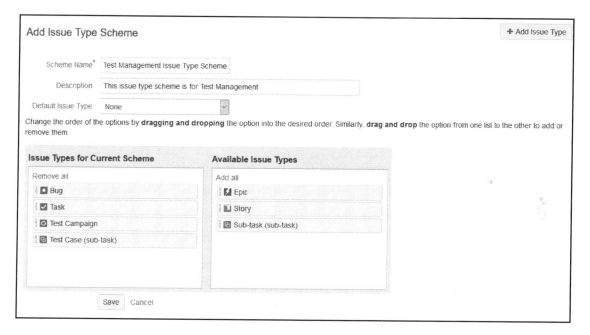

The new **Issue type scheme** will be created and shown in the list. As you can see in the next screenshot, currently there are no projects using this scheme. Hence, under the **Projects** column, it shows no projects for our new scheme. We will create a new project and apply this scheme to it:

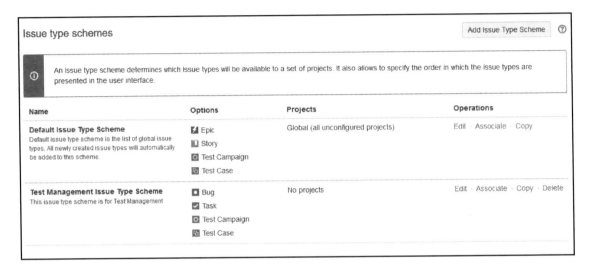

At this moment, we need to create a new project to apply our customizations:

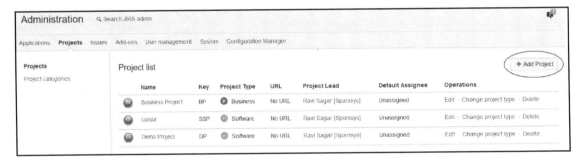

Go to **Administration** | **Projects** and in the **Project list** section, click on the **Add Project** button on top-right corner:

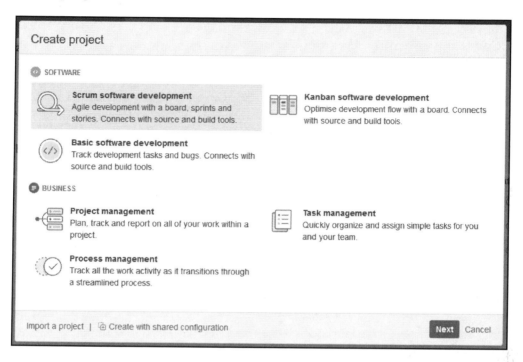

In the **Create project** popup, select **Basic software development** under **SOFTWARE** and press the **Next** button:

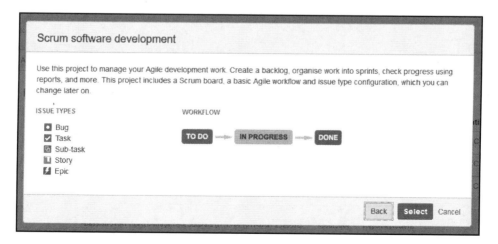

The next popup will confirm your selection and display the **ISSUE TYPES** and **WORKFLOW** that you will get in this project. Just press the **Select** button to continue.

Enter the **Name** of our project as `Project For Test Management` and the project **Key** is `PFTM`. Click on the **Submit** button:

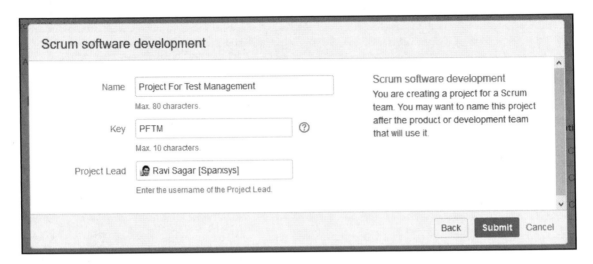

Once this project has been created, go to the project sidebar and then **Project Administration | Issue types**. You will notice that, by default, **PFTM: Scrum Issue Type Scheme** is applied to the project. This is a new scheme created for this project only. We will change it and apply our own issue type scheme that we created earlier. In the top-right corner, click on the **Actions** menu and select **Use a different scheme**:

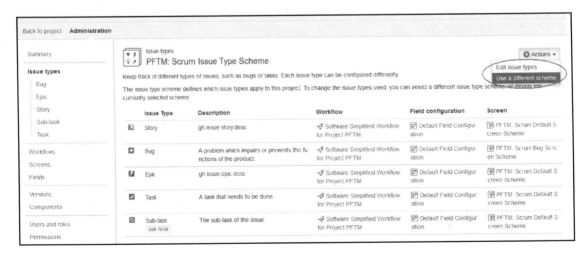

In the next screen, you will get a list of all the available **Issue Type Schemes**; just select the **Test Management Issue Type Scheme** and click on the **OK** button:

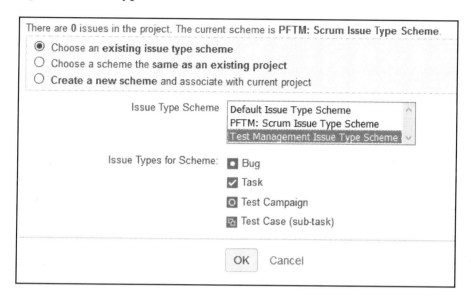

Now the project scheme has been changed and it now has the new issue types that we want. You can verify this by creating a new issue under this new project and seeing the list of all the available Issue Types that we wanted.

Customizing the workflow for changes in transitions

In any issue-tracking system, the issues will be created, then moved to the In Progress state, and finally Closed. This is the scenario of a simple workflow with three states: Open, In Progress, and Closed, which would only work in ideal cases, but in real-world cases, the workflows, that is, how the issue will move from one state to another, could be quite complex. For instance, sometimes you need to wait for some information from the client to act further on the issue; there could be a case when someone will review your task before closing. To incorporate such cases, we need the ability to modify these workflows.

Each company has its own processes and software models. In JIRA, it's possible to customize the workflow very easily. This is one of the most powerful features of JIRA. We can easily create new states and conditions. In this section, we will customize the workflow for a test campaign and a test case.

Workflow for a test campaign

A test campaign is a collection of test cases. We have already created its issue type. The user will start by creating a new issue of type test campaign and then all the test cases that are part of it will be created as a subtask.

A test campaign could be assigned to a specific team lead, who could further assign test cases among team members. The following diagram represents a typical workflow for a test campaign:

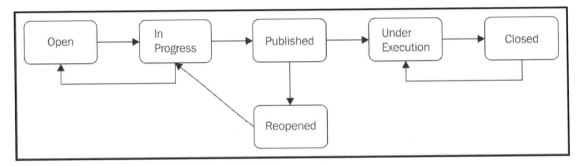

The test campaign will be moved to the **In Progress** state while all the test cases are prepared and created as a subtask. Once the bundle of test cases are added and finalized, the test campaign will be **Published**. The **Under Execution** state signifies that the test cases under it are currently being executed.

Now, we need to create some additional states. These are not already there in the system. Also, we want to add a constraint that the test campaign can only be closed when all the test cases under it are closed as well, and only the reported can close the test campaign as condition in the JIRA terminology.

New states

The following are the new states:

- **Published**
- **Under Execution**

Go to **Administration** | **Issues** | **Statuses** (under **Issue Attributes**) and click on the **Add status** button in the top-right corner:

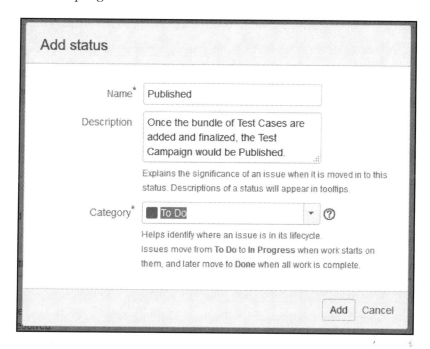

Enter the **Name** and **Description** of the status Published and click on the **Add** button to create the new state and repeat the same procedure to create Under Execution.

Now we need to create a workflow that we will associate with the test campaign. It's always a good practice to copy the default JIRA workflow **jira** and then modify it.

Go to **Administration | Issues | Workflows** (under **Workflows**) and copy the default JIRA workflow **jira (Read-only System Workflow)** using the **Copy** link under **Operations**:

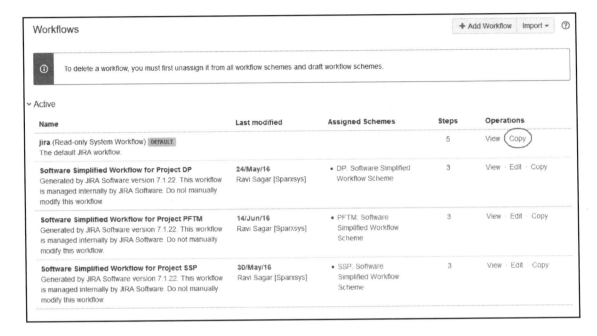

In the **Copy Workflow: jira** popup, enter the **Workflow Name** as Test Campaign Workflow and add a **Description**:

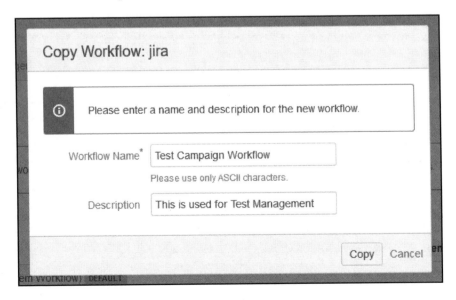

Once the workflow has been copied, you will find two viewing tabs in the top-left corner: one is **Diagram** (which is the default tab) and the other one is **Text**. When the **Diagram** tab is enabled, it displays the graphical representation of the workflow. However, it's convenient to work in the **Text** tab.

Removing unwanted transitions

You will notice that the workflow, which we copied from the default **jira** workflow, has some unwanted transitions, such as **Open** to **Resolved**, **Open** to **Closed**, and so on. First, we need to delete these transitions. In the **Text** mode, under **Operations**, click on the **Delete Transitions** link:

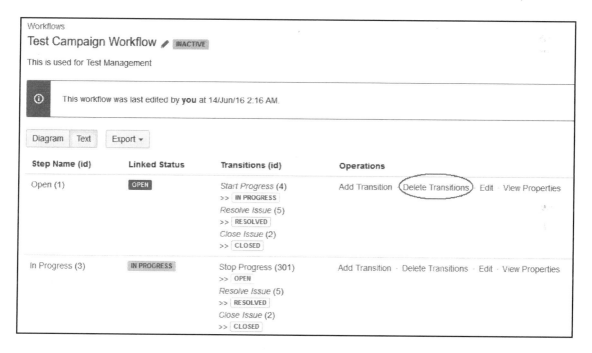

On the next screen, select the **Resolve Issue** and **Close Issue** transitions because we don't want them with the **Open** state:

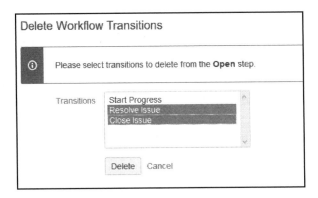

Click on the **Delete** button to delete the selected transitions. Perform the same procedure for all such unwanted transitions. Also, remove the states that are not required at all in the workflow, such as the **Resolved** state. You will see a link to delete the step, which is linked to a state, once there are no attached transitions.

Adding new steps

After removing all the unwanted transitions, add the new states using the form at the bottom of the **Text** mode. The states are added to the workflow by linking them with the **Step Name**, whose name is similar to the state name:

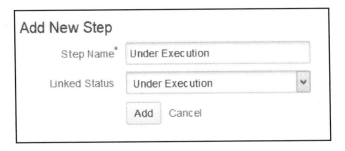

Click on the **Add** button to add this state and repeat this for the `Published` one as well:

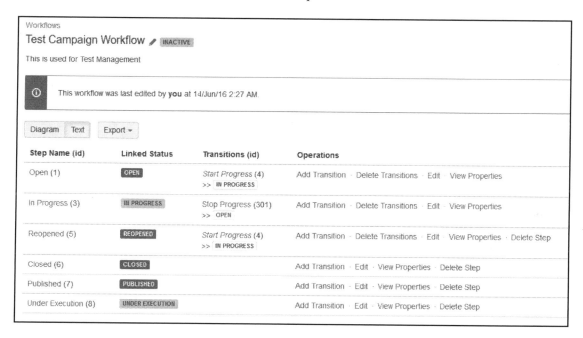

You should now have all the states that are required.

Adding the missing transitions

Let's add the following missing transitions:

- In Progress to Published
- Published to Reopened
- Published to Under Execution
- Under Execution to Closed
- Closed to Under Execution

Under **Operations**, click on the **Add Transition** link for a specific step:

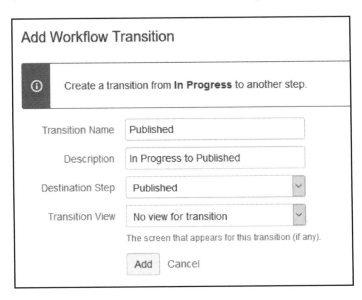

Enter the **Transition Name** as `Published`, enter some meaningful **Description**, and select **Published** as the **Destination Step**. It's also possible to prompt the user to fill in some data on a screen that can be shown while making this transition. From now onward, we will not do this. Click on the **Add** button to continue. Repeat the same for all the other transitions that need to be created.

The transition names can also be added as a verb. For instance, the `Under Execution` transition can be added as `Start Execution`. This name appears to the user on the issue view screen.

Finally, your workflow will look similar to the following screenshots:

- Workflow for **Text** mode:

- Workflow for **Diagram** mode:

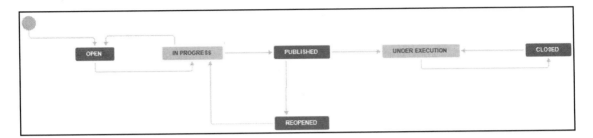

Now our workflow has taken shape. We have all the states and transitions as we wanted. So, let's now add a few conditions to certain transitions.

Conditions

The following are the different conditions for a test campaign:

- A test campaign will only close when all the test cases are Closed
- Only the reporter can move this test campaign to Closed

The first condition will not allow the user to close the issue until all the test cases under it are in the Closed state. We want to add this condition when a transition from **Under Execution** to **Closed** is attempted:

1. Go back to the **Text** mode and click on the **Closed** link under the **Transition (id)** column. Take a look at this screenshot for reference:

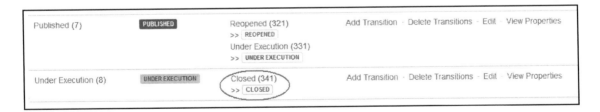

2. On the next screen, you will get some advanced options for this transition from **Under Execution** to the **Closed** state. Under the **Conditions** tab, click on the **Add condition** button:

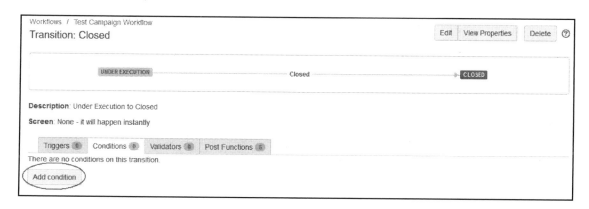

3. In the following screenshot, you will get a list of conditions that can be added to this transition. Select **Sub-Task Blocking Condition** and click on the **Add** button:

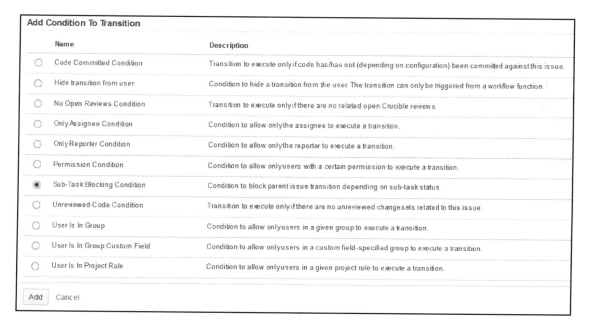

4. On the next screen, select the status for which this condition will be applicable. In our case, we want test cases to be in the Closed state, so we will select **CLOSED** from the list of various statuses available and click on the **Add** button:

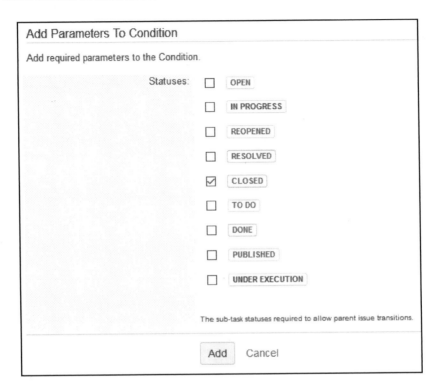

5. In the same way, add one more condition called `Only Reporter Condition` for the **Under Execution** to **Closed** transition.

6. Finally, we will have two conditions added to this transition, as shown in the following screenshot:

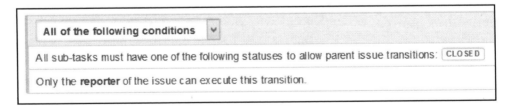

Post Function

The following is the use of the post function.

When the workflow transition has happened, then certain actions can be performed afterwards. For instance, when a test campaign is closed, we send an e-mail to everyone in a particular group.

We also want to send an e-mail to all the users who are part of a particular group to receive an e-mail when the test campaign is closed. The workflow can be configured to trigger an event on a state transition from **Under Execution** to **Closed**. The event can further be configured to send an e-mail to a group. We will learn that later in the chapter.

Creating a new workflow scheme

At this point, let's associate our workflow to the project. For this, we need to create a workflow scheme, which is a collection of one or more workflows mapped to the project issue types; to attach a workflow to the project, a workflow scheme is required:

1. Go to **Administration** | **Issues** | **Workflow Schemes** (under **WORKFLOWS**) and click on the **Add Workflow Scheme** button in the top-right corner. In the **Add Workflow Scheme** screen, enter the **Name** of the scheme as `Test Management Workflow Scheme` and some useful **Description**:

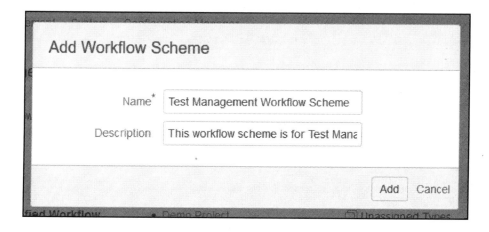

2. Once the scheme is created, the default **JIRA Workflow** will be assigned to all the **Issue Types**; however, in our case, we want the workflow that we just created assigned to the Test Campaign issue type:

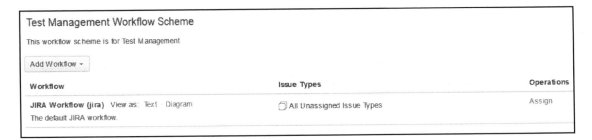

3. Click on the **Add Workflow** menu in the top-left corner and select **Add Existing**.

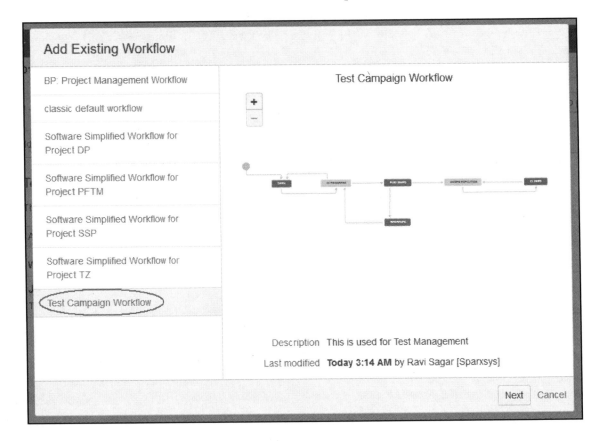

4. In the preceding screenshot, select the workflow called **Test Campaign Workflow** and click on the **Next** button.

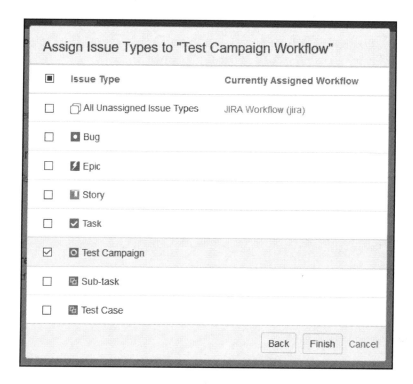

5. In the preceding screenshot, select **Test Campaign** as the **Issue Type** and click on the **Finish** button. This will assign the workflow to the selected **Issue Types**. This is displayed in the following screenshot:

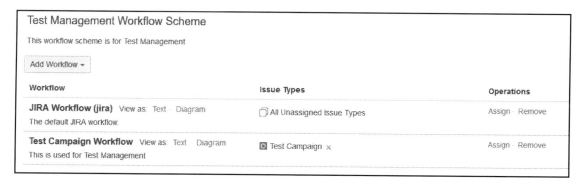

Now, if you go back to our workflow scheme, you will notice that the **Test Campaign** issue type is using our custom workflow called **Test Campaign Workflow**.

6. Go back to **Project Administration | Workflows** and click on the **Switch Scheme** button right next to the **Add Workflow** button in the top-left corner. On the next screen, select **Test Management Workflow Scheme** and click on the **Associate** button.

The workflow scheme is now associated with the project and the workflow is now active. Note that the active workflows cannot be modified; JIRA will create a draft version for you for this and the modified workflows can be published again.

Adding a custom event in JIRA

Go to **Administration | System | Events** (under **ADVANCED**) and scroll down to the bottom of the page where there is an **Add New Event** form:

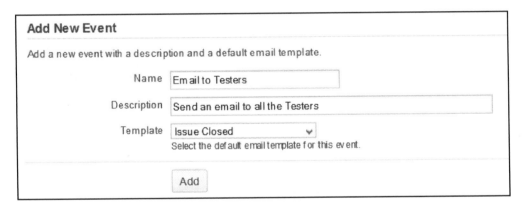

Enter the **Name** of the event, then enter some useful **Description**, and select **Issue Closed** as the **Template** because the template of the e-mail will be similar to that of the one sent when the issue is closed. Click on the **Add** button to continue. Creating an event doesn't do anything useful until we trigger it from the workflow and customize it in the notification scheme:

1. First, we need to trigger the event from the workflow. Let's go back to the **Test Campaign Workflow**, edit it, and click on the **Closed** link under the **Transition (id)** column. Now, go to the **Post Functions** tab; here, the last entry is for **Generic Event**. Edit it by clicking on the pencil sign in the bottom-right corner, as shown in this screenshot:

2. On the next screen, we need to change the event from **Generic Event** to **Email to Testers**. Then, click on the **Update** button:

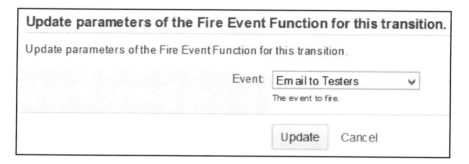

3. Now the event will be triggered on the state transition, but there is still one more thing to perform to send the e-mail. The notification scheme of the project needs to be customized to configure to whom an e-mail will be sent when this event is triggered by the workflow.

Customizing a notification scheme

To send e-mails, JIRA relies on notification schemes, which define who will receive the e-mail and when. As we already mentioned, JIRA comes with default schemes and it's always a good practice to copy them and customize your own copy. For this example too, we will copy the **Default Notification Scheme**:

1. Go to **Administration | Issues | Notification Schemes**. Under **Operations**, click on the **Copy** link. It will copy the scheme instantly with the name **Copy of Default Notification Scheme**. Click on the **Edit** link under **Operations** for this scheme and rename it as Test Management Notification Scheme:

Name	Projects	Operations
Default Notification Scheme	• Business Project • Demo Project • Project For Test Management • cursor	Notifications · Copy · Edit · Delete
Test Management Notification Scheme This notification scheme will be used for Test Management		Notifications · Copy · Edit · Delete

2. Now, we need to customize this scheme to send an e-mail to all the users of a particular group. For this example, you can create a group called `jira-testers` and add a few users to it. `Chapter 7`, *User Management, Groups, and Project Roles* will have more information about managing users and groups. Once your group has been created, click on the **Notifications** link under **Operations** for the **Test Management Notification Scheme**.

3. On the next screen, you will find the list of all the events and the concerned users, groups, or project roles who will receive these e-mails:

Issue Worklog Updated (System)	• Current Assignee (Delete) • Reporter (Delete) • All Watchers (Delete)	Add
Issue Worklog Deleted (System)	• Current Assignee (Delete) • Reporter (Delete) • All Watchers (Delete)	Add
Generic Event (System)	• Current Assignee (Delete) • Reporter (Delete) • All Watchers (Delete)	Add
Email to Testers		Add

4. You will also find the **Email to Testers** custom event that we created, but this is just the event listed in this scheme; we need to modify the scheme to add the **jira-testers** group in order to get notifications when this event is triggered by the workflow. Click on the **Add** button:

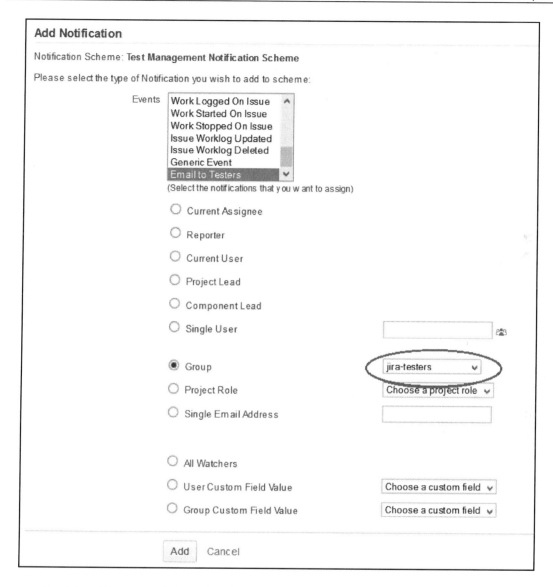

5. Select **Group** and from the drop-down menu, select **jira-testers**. Click on the **Add** button:

Our scheme is now configured.

6. Now, go to **Project Administration | Notification** and click on the **Actions** menu in the top-right corner and select **Use a different scheme**. On the next screen, select our new scheme as **Test Management Notification Scheme** and click on the **Associate** button.

The project will now use the next scheme because the customized workflow is already assigned to the project. So, the e-mail notifications should work now whenever the test campaign is moved from Under Execution to the Closed state.

Workflow for a test case

A test case contains information about the input, expected output along with a set of actions, and details of the environment that defines whether a requirement is met as per the original plan to verify it is working. We will configure JIRA for manual testing where we will store all this information as issue types.

We have already configured JIRA for a test campaign; in this section, we will not repeat the implementation, which is exactly similar to what we have just discussed. Instead, we will list the details of the workflow, conditions, and post functions:

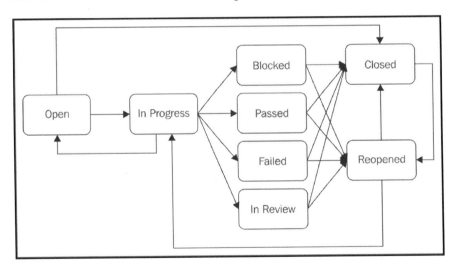

A test case will be a subtask of a particular test campaign. Once created, it will first be moved to the **In Progress** state when the tester starts performing the tests. On the basis of these tests, it can be moved to one of the following states:

- **Blocked**: If this test case is critical for other features to work
- **Passed**: If it works correctly
- **Failed:** If it's not working
- **In Review:** If it requires further investigation

Finally, a test case can either be **Closed** or **Reopened**. A particular test campaign can contain hundreds of test cases and its overall percentage of the verified testing can be calculated on the basis of how many test cases are closed.

Create a new workflow called **Test Case Workflow**, add it in **Test Management Workflow Scheme**, and assign it to the **Test Case** as **Issue Type**.

New states

We have identified a few new states that need to be created:

- Blocked
- Passed
- Failed
- In Review

The procedure to create these states is similar to what we discussed previously for a test Campaign.

Condition

We want to impose the constraint that only the user who is assigned the test case will be able to move it to the **Passed** state:

- Only the assignee can move the test case to the **Passed** state

The name of the workflow condition is **Only Assignee Condition**.

Post function

When a test case fails, it might become important to understand what went wrong in the feature. To highlight this issue, we can automatically change the issue from **Priority** to **Highest**:

- When the test case is moved to the **Failed** state, change the issue from **Priority** to **Highest**

There is a post function called **Update Issue Field** to implement this; modify the **Test Case Workflow** and add a post function:

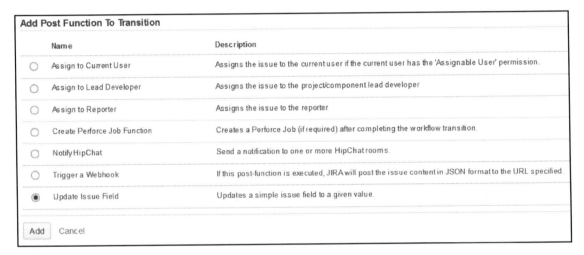

Click on the **Add** button. On the next screen, select **Priority** as the **Issue Field** and **Highest** as the **Field Value**:

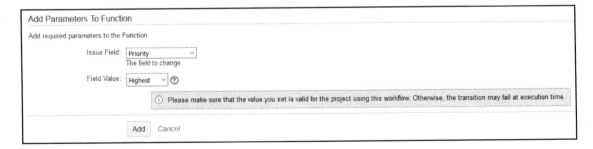

Click on the **Add** button to add this post function. The rest of the procedure remains the same. You can also modify the active workflow and publish it back after performing the changes.

Capturing additional data from users on state transitions

In the workflow of the test campaign transition, when we move the issue from the In Progress state to the Published state, we want the user to provide some additional information about the type of test campaign, which could be a select list:

1. Go to **Administration** | **Issues** | **Custom Fields** (under **FIELDS**) and click on the **Add Custom Field** button in the top-right corner:

2. On the **Select a Field Type** screen, select the field type as **Select List (single choice)** and click on the **Next** button:

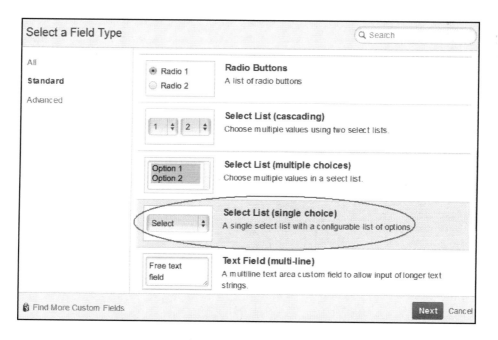

3. On the next screen, enter the **Name** of the custom field as `Campaign Type`, enter a **Description**, and add the **Options** that will appear in the select list:

4. Click on the **Create** button.
5. In the following screenshot, you will be prompted to add this field to the existing screens, but don't select any field. We will add the fields later on. If you want to add new fields in the default screen, then you can do this by selecting the checkbox for default screen. Click on the **Update** button to finish. Now our field has been created, we need to create a custom screen that will be shown to the user when a transition from In Progress to Published is performed.

6. Go to **Administration** | **Screens** (under **SCREEN**) and click on the **Add Screen** button in the top-right corner. In the following screenshot, enter **Name** as `Published Screen` and **Description** as `This screen will capture additional data`:

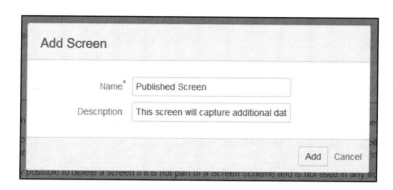

7. Click on **Add** to create the screen. Now we need to add the custom field that we already created:

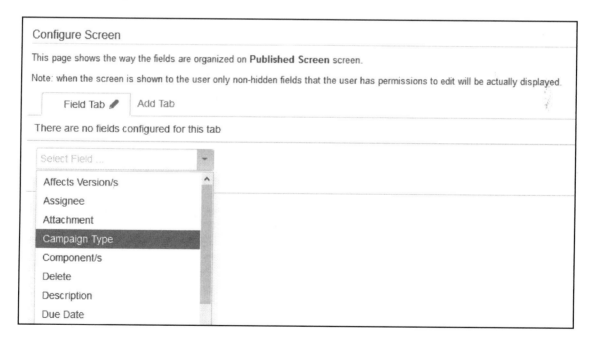

Currently, there are no custom fields on this screen; from the **Select Field** drop-down list, select **Campaign Type** and add it on the screen:

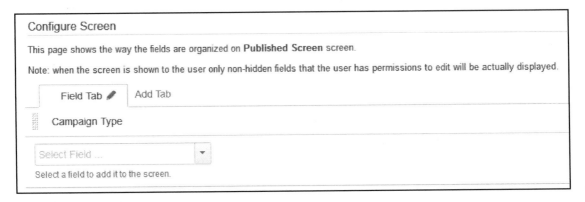

We now have a screen called **Published Screen** with the custom field as **Campaign Type**:

1. Go back to the **Test Campaign Workflow**, edit it, and click on the **Published** link under the **Transitions (id)** column from the **In Progress** to **Published** transition row:

2. In the **Transition: Published** screen, click on the **Edit** button in the top-right corner; it will open another popup. Here, we will specify **Transition View** as **Published Screen**:

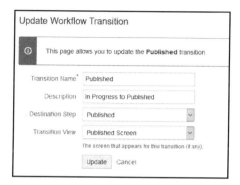

Click on the **Update** button to finish. Also, don't forget to publish this workflow.

Now, whenever a test campaign is moved from the **In Progress** state to the **Published** state, a separate screen will be shown to the user to capture the **Campaign Type** value.

Learning how to make certain fields mandatory only for a test campaign

We have added the custom field and users will also be prompted to enter the field, but there is one problem: it's quite possible that users will not provide any value in this field and skip it. In JIRA, it's possible to make a certain field mandatory and this is achieved by modifying the field configuration of the project:

1. Go to **Administration** | **Field configurations** (under **FIELDS**) and create a copy of **Default Field Configuration** and name it `Test Management Field Configuration`:

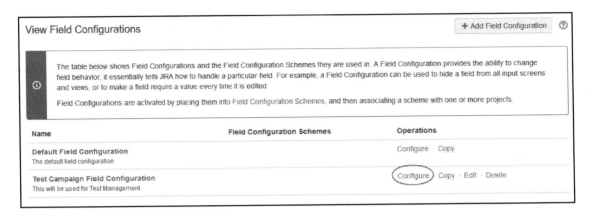

2. After the field configuration is copied, click on the **Configure** link (under **Operations**) as shown in the preceding screenshot.

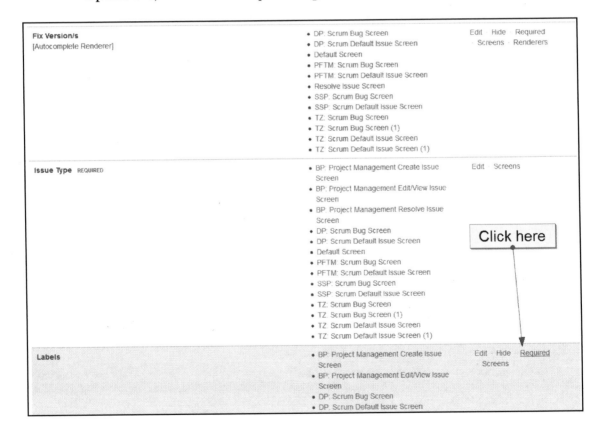

3. As you can see on the screen, for every field, it's possible to make it **Required**, that is, mandatory. Click on the **Required** link and the field configuration will be modified in an instant. The last step is to create a field configuration scheme where we will associate this new field configuration to the **Test Campaign** issue type.

4. Go to **Administration | Field configuration schemes** (under **FIELDS**) and click on the **Add Field Configuration Scheme** button in the top-right corner. In the popup that appears, give **Name** as `Test Management Field Configuration` scheme and a meaningful **Description**. Click on the **Add** button to continue:

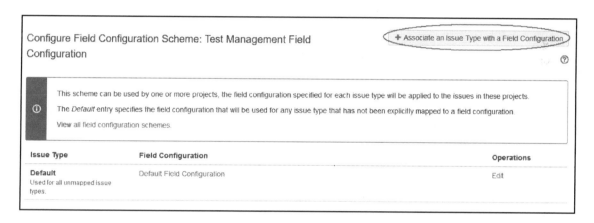

The **Default Field Configuration** will be associated with all the unmapped issue types, but we want to associate `Test Management Field Configuration` with the **Test Campaign** issue type. Click on the **Associate an Issue Type with a Field Configuration**. In the popup that appears, select **Test Campaign** as the **Issue Type** and **Test Management Field Configuration** as the **Field Configuration** and press the **Add** button to continue:

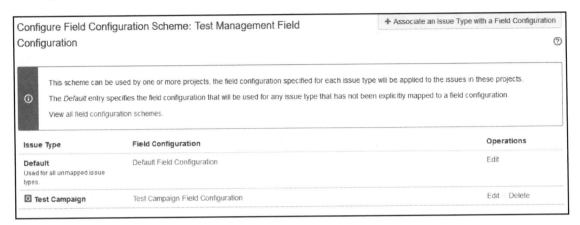

Our field configuration scheme is ready. Now, go to **Project Administration | Fields** and from the **Actions** menu in the top-right corner, select **Use a different scheme**. On the next screen, select the new field configuration, which we have just created, and apply it to the project. We have just learned how to make a field mandatory for a specific issue type only.

Limiting the project visibility to certain groups and individuals

All the projects in JIRA are visible to all users who have access to the application they are assigned to. JIRA allows you to change this behavior. It's possible to hide a project from all the other users and only let users who are part of a certain group access it.

We created a `jira-testers` group earlier in this chapter. Let's allow only users who are part of this group to access our **Project For Test Management**.

Go to **Project Administration | Permission**. It will open up the **Default software scheme** or **Default Permission Scheme** page currently applied on the project. The second permission in the list is **Browse Projects**, which is currently given to **Application Role (Any logged in user)**. That means all the users who have account in JIRA will be able to access this project.

We basically need to remove **Application Role (Any logged in user)** and add the **jira-testers** group instead for the **Browse Projects** permission.

Go to **Administration | Issues | Permission schemes** and create a copy of **Default Permission Scheme** and name it **Test Management Permission Scheme**. Then, edit the permission of this new scheme:

1. Click on the **Remove** link first and in the next popup, select **Application Role – Any logged in user** and click on the **Remove** button:

2. Then click on the **Edit** link and in the **Grant permission** popup, select **Group** and from the drop-down list, select **jira-testers**. Click on the **Grant** button to finish:

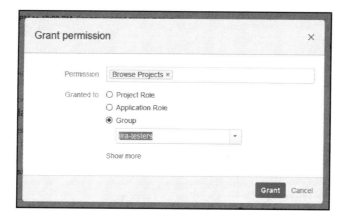

Now, go to **Project Administration | Permissions** and from the **Actions** menu in the top-right corner, select **Use a different scheme**. On the next screen, select the new scheme and click on the **Associate** button to apply this scheme to the project.

Learn how to hide a specific issue from the user within a project

Currently, only the users who are part of the **jira-testers** group can access **Project For Test Management**. The user may be part of other groups, but they must be part of **jira-testers** to be able to view this project.

Imagine a scenario when there is a need to hide certain issues from all the users who are not part of a particular group. This is just an example that we will implement here, but in reality, there could indeed be such cases. This can be achieved by creating an issue security scheme:

1. Go to **Administration | Issues | Issue Security Schemes** and click on **Add Issue Security Scheme** at the bottom. In the following screenshot, enter the **Name** and **Description**:

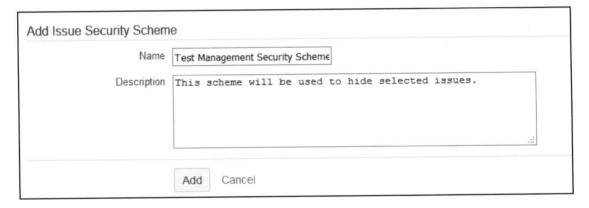

2. Click on the **Add** button to continue.
3. Under **Operations**, click on the **Security Levels** link:

4. Enter the **Name** and **Description** of the security level and click on the **Add Security Level** button:

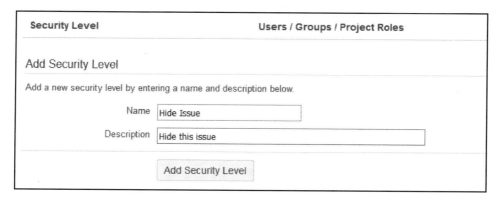

5. Once created, click on the **Add** link under **Operations** for this security level and select **Group** as **jira-team-cursor** from the drop-down list (or any group of your choice):

6. Click on the **Add** button to continue. Now we have created a security scheme; before we can apply it to the project, we also need to modify the permission scheme of the project to allow only the users of the **jira-team-cursor** group to be able to **Set Issue Security**, as shown in the following screenshot:

7. Now, go to **Project Administration** | **Issue Security** and under the **Actions** menu in the top-right corner, click on **Select a scheme**. On the next screen, select **Test Management Security Scheme** as the **Scheme** and click on the **Next** button.

We have set up the security scheme. For testing purposes, create a new user and make him/her part of **jira-team-cursor** along with the **jira-testers** group. By default, every user who is part of the **jira-testers** group can access all the projects and all the issues under it but users who are also part of **jira-team-cursor** can hide a specific issue from users of the **jira-testers** group.

Edit/create an issue and you will now notice a new system field called **Security Level**:

From the drop-down list, select the **Security Level** that we created earlier and save the issue. Now, this particular issue will only be visible to users who are part of the **jira-team-cursor** group. The best part is that only users who are part of **jira-team-cursor** will be able to set this security level.

Versions and components

We are almost done with configuring JIRA for test management; there are a few other things that are left and those are setting up versions and components.

Versions are useful for software projects to identify different releases of software. You would always release the first version of a stable project or product and, based on the user feedback and improvement, further versions will be released. JIRA allows you to create various versions and assign them to individual issues.

Go to **Project Administration** | **Version**, enter the **Name** of the version, a **Description**, **Start date**, and **Release date**, and click on the **Add** button:

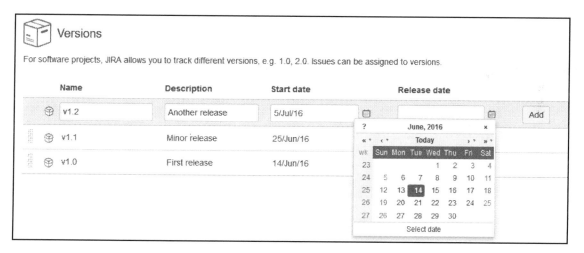

We have added versions (such as v1.0, v1.1, and v1.2). You can choose names that are relevant to your project.

In any project, the features can be broken down into subsections or into a module. It is not only useful to break down the bigger tasks, but it also helps in segregating issues.

Go to **Project Administration** | **Components**, enter the **Name** of the component, enter **Description**, select **Component Lead**, and click on the **Add** button:

We can add various components (such as requirement gathering, analysis, design, documentation, coding, testing, and support).

Summary

In this chapter, we customized JIRA's instance to act like a test management tool. We started by gathering the requirements to implement such use cases in JIRA. You learned how to customize various schemes to introduce new issue types, custom workflows, field configurations, and project permissions.

In the next chapter, we will learn how to configure Zephyr, which is a popular JIRA add-on for test management. This add-on will bring standard features and built-in functionality to get you started for software testing without customizing JIRA. Many organizations use Zephyr and we will also learn how to use it for performing testing.

5
Understanding Zephyr and its Features

We have learnt how to customize JIRA for test management, where we understood how to configure various schemes that are available in JIRA to modify a project that matches the actual process followed in your company, but there are some add-ons that can bring new features without the need to customize JIRA. One such popular add-on is **Zephyr** that brings in fully-fledged test management in JIRA. In this section, we will learn how to configure and use Zephyr.

The topics covered are as follows:

- Installing the Zephyr plugin
- Zephyr terminology
- Starting to use Zephyr

Installing the Zephyr plugin

Zephyr is a paid add-on that is very popular in the industry. If you want to quickly get the features of test management without customizing JIRA yourself, you can use Zephyr. It offers lots of useful test management features that are as per industry standards.

In this section, we will learn how to configure and use Zephyr. Follow the steps below to install it on your instance:

1. Go to **Administration | Add-ons | Find new add-ons** under **ATLASSIAN MARKETPLACE,** type Zephyr in the search box and press the *Enter* key:

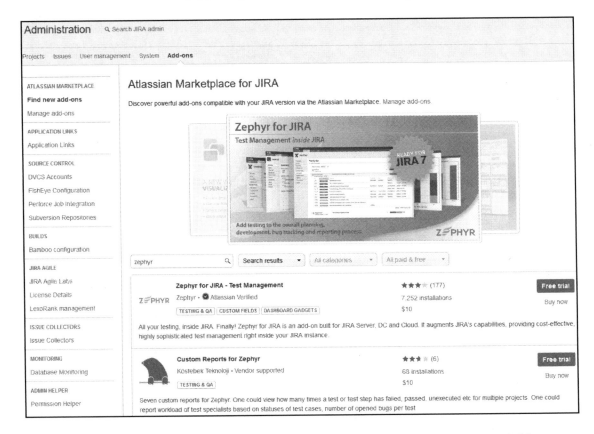

2. **Zephyr for JIRA – Test Management** will appear. Click on the **Free trial** button to install this add-on on your instance. In the pop-up window that appears next, click on the **Accept** button.

3. Finally, you will be asked to enter your Atlassian account to generate a trial license for Zephyr:

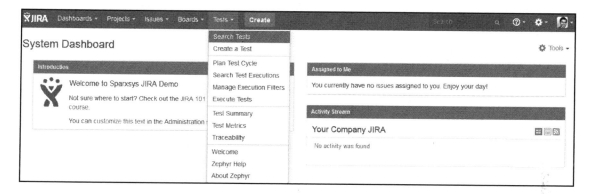

4. Once installed, you will get a new menu item, **Tests**, in your instance.

We have just installed Zephyr; now we will learn how to configure this add-on.

Zephyr terminology

The Zephyr add-on works very closely with your existing JIRA project but there are some terms that we need to understand before we start using this add-on:

- **Test**: This is the test case and a detailed description of what needs to be tested
- **Execution**: Each test that is run along with its result
- **Test cycle**: This is a grouping of tests which may be for a particular project's version
- **Ad hoc cycle**: All the tests that are executed without a defined cycle are run in an ad hoc cycle

Starting to use Zephyr

The Zephyr add-on may seem overwhelming at the beginning to new users but in this section, let us learn how to quickly configure this add-on and use it for performing tests.

The steps mentioned below will get you started with the Zephyr add-on in the shortest amount of time:

1. The **Test Issue Type** is by default added to all new projects of **Software** and **Business** project types, but you can always add it to your project by modifying the **Issue Type Scheme**. Let us create a new project to use Zephyr.

2. Go to **Projects | Create project**, select **Scrum software development** and press the **Next** button:

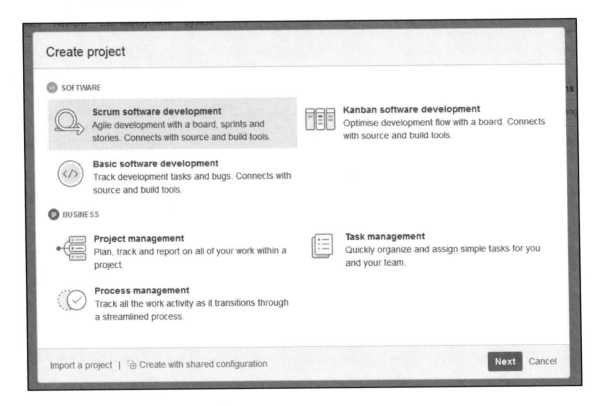

3. In the next screen, press the **Select** button to continue:

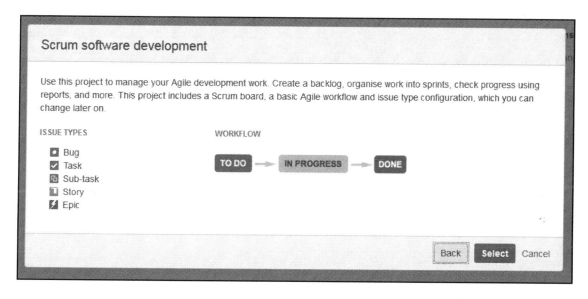

4. Enter the project **Name** as `Testing Zephyr`; the project **Key** `TZ` will be auto suggested. Press the **Submit** button and the project will be created:

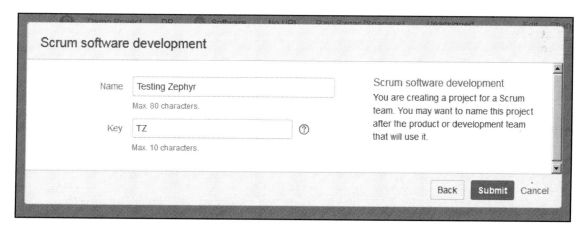

5. Go to **Project Administration** and check under **Issue types**; you will notice that the **Issue Type Test** has been added automatically in your project. You are now ready to start using Zephyr for testing.

6. Go to **Project Administration** | **Versions** and add a few versions, such as `Version 1.0`, `Version 1.1`, `Version 1.2`, or any name of your choice.

7. Go back to your project's navigation sidebar and click on the new item **Tests**:

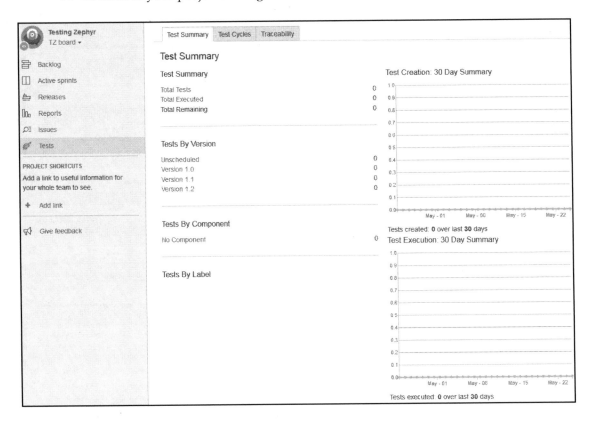

8. There are three tabs here—**Test Summary**, **Test Cycles**, and **Traceability**. Click on the **Test Cycles** tab. You will find an **Ad hoc** cycle already defined for our project. Let us add a new test cycle. Under **Cycle Summary**, click on the **Create New Cycle** button:

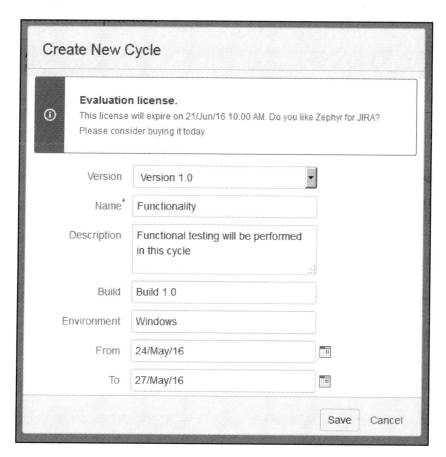

9. In the **Create New Cycle** popup, select Version 1.0 as the **Version** and **Name** as Functionality. Optionally, enter **Description**, **Build**, and **Environment**, and select dates in the **From** and **To** fields. Press the **Save** button to continue. Similarly, for Version 1.0, add a new **Test Cycle** and name it Regression. Once added, select Version 1.0 under **Select Versions:** and you will notice the newly added test cycles:

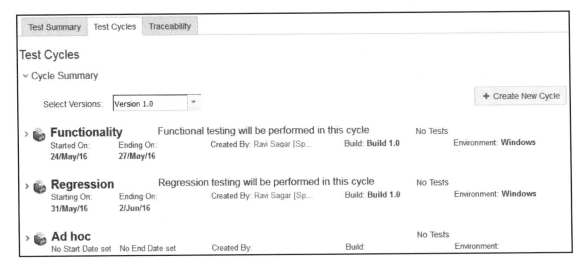

10. Just like Version 1.0, also add Functional and Regression test cycles for Version 1.1.

11. Click on the **Create** button in the navigation menu. In the **Create Issue** popup, select your project and **Test** as the **Issue Type**, enter a **Summary**, and scroll down until you see the section for **Zephyr Teststep**:

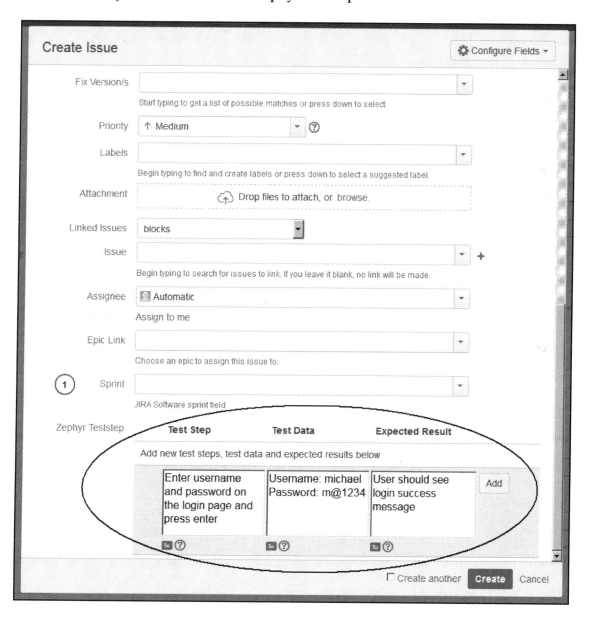

12. In the three sections, enter **Test Step**, **Test Data**, and **Expected Result**, and press the **Add** button. You can add multiple test steps in a similar way. Let us add one more and finally click on the **Create** button to create the test. The issue will now be created and under the **Test Details** section, you will notice the two test steps that we added are visible. You will notice that the default workflow buttons are not displayed for issue of type **Test**.

13. Now we have to execute the test. Under the **Test Details** section, there is another section for **Test Executions**. Initially, this section will be empty. You can either click on the **Execute** button on top of the issue or click on the link **here** under this section to create an execution:

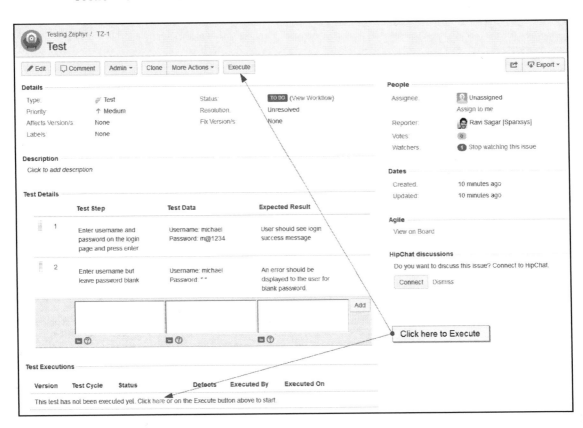

14. In the **Execute Test** popup, select **Add to Existing Test Cycle and Execute**, then select a specific **Version** and the **Test Cycle** drop-down list will then display the test cycles that we earlier associated with that version. In the **Assignee** section, select **Me** if you want to assign this execution to yourself or select the name of the **Person** from the drop-down list. Then click on the **Execute** button. Create more **Test Executions** for another **Version** and **Test Cycle**:

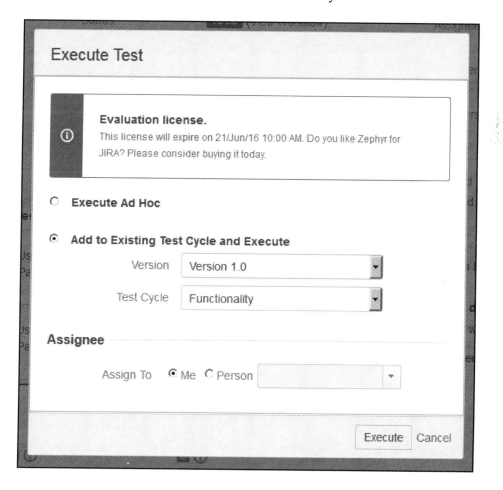

15. Initially, the status of each test execution is **UNEXECUTED**. To start the execution, click on the **E** button:

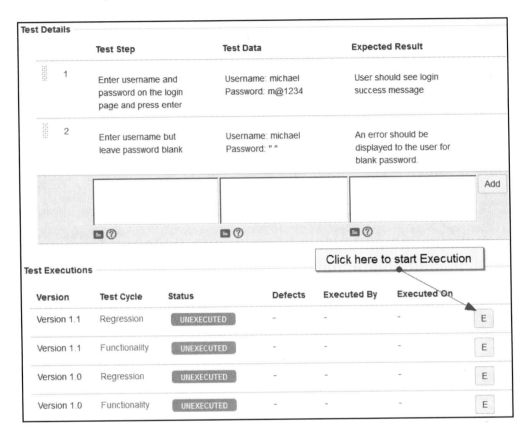

16. We are now executing an individual **Test Execution** where various test steps added for this **Test** can be found. Each **Test Step** needs to be individually tested for **Test Data** and the output is compared with the **Expected Result**; based on the output, the test step **Status** can be changed from **UNEXECUTED** to **PASS**, **FAIL**, **WIP**, or **BLOCKED**. Just click on **UNEXECUTED** and a drop-down list will appear. If any bug is found then it can be associated with this **Test Step**. Click on **Enter Defects** and it will give you an option to either associate an existing JIRA issue or let you create new issue:

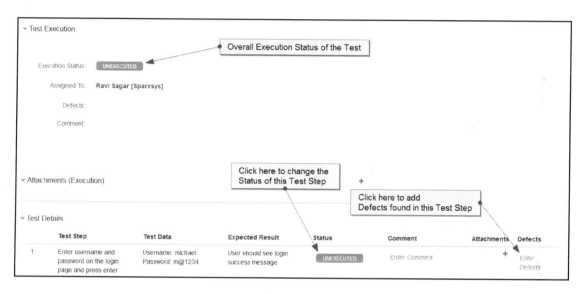

17. Apart from the individual **Status** of the **Test Step**, the overall execution **Status** of the test can also be changed in a similar way:

Version	Test Cycle	Status	Defects	Executed By	Executed On	
Version 1.1	Regression	UNEXECUTED	-	-	-	E
Version 1.1	Functionality	UNEXECUTED	-	-	-	E
Version 1.0	Regression	PASS	0|1	Ravi Sagar [Sparxsys]	Yesterday 11:55 PM	E
Version 1.0	Functionality	PASS	-	Ravi Sagar [Sparxsys]	Today 12:25 AM	E

18. As you start executing the **Test Executions** and change their **Status**, the **Test Executions** section will display a consolidated summary of all the test cycles. Go back to the project navigation sidebar, click on the **Tests | Test Cycles** tab, and select a particular version and you will get a **Cycle Summary** displaying the **Test Cycles** that we created, along with all the tests associated with them and the overall progress in percentage of that test cycle:

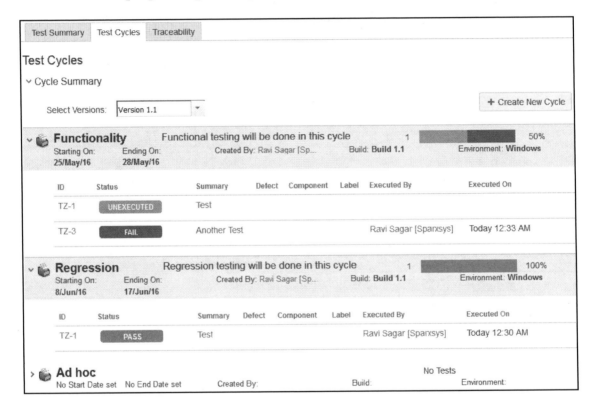

Summary

In this chapter, we learned how to use the Zephyr add-on to quickly add the test management feature without customizing JIRA yourself. Zephyr is a popular add-on used by several organizations.

In the next chapter, we will take a look at some sample use cases that can be implemented in JIRA. Now that you already know how to customize JIRA, the next chapter will help you with some base configurations that you can start with to implement similar scenarios in your instance.

6
Sample Implementation of Use Cases

You have already learned about customization for test management by modifying JIRA's configuration as well as using the popular **Zephyr** add-on. This chapter will not repeat these configurations; rather, it will present sample data in order to create various use cases that can be implemented in JIRA. This chapter will cover the issue types usually required, the custom fields to add, and workflow examples.

The user can take these examples as a starting point to implement something similar in their company. In this chapter, we will understand how to start collecting the requirements, and the sample use cases mentioned can be leveraged further to customize JIRA specific to their requirements.

The topics covered are as follows:

- Gathering requirements
- Preparing the JIRA configuration document
- Setting up JIRA for helpdesk/support tickets
- Setting up JIRA for requirement management
- Setting up JIRA for bug tracking
- Changes in the customizations

Gathering requirements

As with any other software project, treat your JIRA customization as a project in itself. As a JIRA administrator, you should first meet all the stakeholders to understand how they want to use JIRA. This usually starts with a brainstorming session with all the teams' managers.

When you want to start customizing JIRA, always prepare a document to store all the configurations that are required. Even after implementation, if any further changes are required, you should still update this document. This also helps a new administrator take charge of the JIRA instance. When all the requirements are stored in the configuration document, then it is much easier to track the changes that were done in the system. If you already have a **Confluence** instance running, you can use it to create these documents, which can be accessed by all the stakeholders. Usually, people use Confluence along with JIRA to collaborate on documents and share information.

Preparing the JIRA configuration document

The configuration document should have information about all the schemes, along with the relevant background information to justify it.

This document should have the following sections.

What kind of issue tracking needs to be done?

First, start by asking these questions: what kind of issue tracking is required in JIRA? Do you want to keep track of your customer complaints or track bugs in your ongoing project? You may be tempted to start using JIRA and customize it on-the-go, but this approach will lead to a messed-up system in the long run and will be difficult to manage.

Issue types required

Once the purpose of using JIRA is clear, identify what kinds of issue need to be tracked. If JIRA is going to be used for simple bug tracking, then the existing issue types are sufficient, but if you want to use JIRA for support tickets, then you might want to create new issue types.

Best practices

Create new issue types only when existing ones cannot be used. Always try to reuse issue types that are already there in the system. Too many of them can create confusion for not only the end user, but also the administrators.

What data needs to be captured?

Identify the information that needs to be captured while creating issues. JIRA comes with lots of default system fields, such as **Summary**, **Priority**, **Due Date**, **Description**, and more. In your case, it might be necessary to capture additional information from the user, such as customer name or issue category. Prepare a list of all the custom fields and also their type—whether they are text fields, select lists, or dates.

Identify for which operation custom fields will be shown to the user: create, edit, or view. It is possible to have different screens for each operation. It could also be possible to have additional screens between workflow transitions; for instance, you may want to ask the user to fill up a feedback form before moving the issue to the On Hold state.

For each custom field, note its behavior—whether a field is mandatory or optional should be decided earlier.

Best practices for customizing JIRA

It is quite easy to create custom fields in JIRA, but as the instance grows, you could have lots of these fields. Always try to reuse similar fields. Try to use a generic name for your fields so that they can be reused in other projects. Contexts can also be used to employ the same select list with different options in the drop-down menu in multiple projects. The best practices are discussed in detail in `Chapter 17`, *JIRA Best Practices*.

Issue workflow

How your issue will move from one state to another is defined in the workflow. It is usually your process followed in the company for a particular use case. The process is simply the various stages that an issue goes through. First, decide how many states are required in the workflow and then decide the transitions between these states. Transitions define whether the issue can be moved from one state to another. For each transition, decide what conditions, validations, and post functions are required. In `Chapter 4`, *Customizing JIRA for Test Management*, we discussed workflow customization in detail.

The whole project could use a single workflow, or each issue type could have its own workflow. Discuss this carefully with the project manager to understand how the issues move through various stages.

Setting up JIRA for helpdesk/support tickets

Companies that have software products and applications used by various customers or clients usually need a system where their users can raise complaints, suggestions, and feedback. There are various dedicated open source and proprietary tools for this activity, but JIRA can be easily customized to act like a helpdesk or a support ticketing system.

Issue types

The helpdesk has a mechanism to capture support requests for customers. We will also create a new issue type called `Support Request` for this purpose:

Scheme name	Issue types	Remarks
Helpdesk—Issue Type Scheme	Support Request Improvement Bug New Feature New User Request Sub-task	This creates issue types that are not available

Workflow

We will use a custom workflow for the **Support Request** issue type, which is described next. It is almost identical to the default JIRA workflow, except for two additional states—Waiting for Client and On Hold:

From	To	Remarks
Open	In Progress Resolved Closed Waiting for Client	• **Condition**: Only the reporter can move the issue to Waiting for Client • **Post function**: This changes the priority to minor

In Progress	Open Resolved Closed On Hold	• **Condition**: Only the reporter can move the issue to On Hold • **Post function**: This changes the priority to minor
Resolved	Closed Reopened	Issues in the Resolved state can be moved to either the Closed state or the Reopened state
Reopened	Resolved Closed In Progress	Once an issue is reopened, it can be resolved again, closed, or moved to the In Progress state
Closed	Reopened	A Closed issue can be Reopened
Waiting for Client	Open	Once more clarity is received, an issue can be opened again
On Hold	In Progress	An On Hold issue can be moved to the In Progress state

Fields

The **Support Request** issue type will have a few additional fields apart from the default system JIRA fields:

Field Name	Type	Mandatory	Description
Project	Select List	Yes	Select the project name
Issue Type	Select List	Yes	Enter the activity to be performed
Summary	Text	Yes	Enter a brief description of the issue
Priority	Select List	No	Values: • Highest • High • Medium • Low • Lowest
Due Date	Date Picker	No	Enter the due date of the issue, if any

Component/s	Select List	No	The user can select the components if they are created by the project administrator. Each component in the project can have a dedicated component lead, and that user can be configured to become the default assignee for the issues using the component
Affects Version/s	Select List	Yes	Select the version for which this issue is raised
Assignee	User Picker	No	Select the user who will work on this issue
Reporter	User Picker	Yes	Select the reporter of the issue. The default is the creator
Environment	Text Field	No	Specify under what system environment this issue was reported
Description	Text Field	No	Enter the details of the issue in this field
Attachment	File	No	Upload a file or screenshot
Category	Select List	Yes	Values: • Billing • User Registration • Installation • User Interface • Connectivity

These fields are shown to the user while creating a new issue of the type **Support Request**; for other issue types, use the system default fields.

Screen schemes

Now that we have decided what fields we want for **Support Request**, create a new screen called `Support Request Screen`:

Issue Type Screen Scheme name	Screen Scheme	Issue Types	Screen
Helpdesk—Issue Type Screen Scheme	Helpdesk—Screen Scheme	Support Request	Support Request Screen
Default Screen Scheme	Improvement Bug New Feature New User Request Sub-task	Default Screen	

Permission schemes

As we mentioned earlier, it is always desirable and easier to copy the default permission scheme and then make any changes in it. Let's name our new scheme `Helpdesk—Permission Scheme`.

The following table highlights only those permissions that are different than the default permission schemes:

Project permission	Users/Groups/Project Roles
Assign Issue	Reporter
Delete Issues	Reporter
Work On Issues	Assignee

Also, as discussed in `Chapter 4`, *Customizing JIRA for Test Management*, we can also use **Issue Security Scheme** to hide a specific issue in the project from other users.

In this section we have discussed the customization of JIRA for support tickets. The important thing to keep in mind is that users who will log in to JIRA to raise support requests should have an account in JIRA that means they will count towards the license. In the enterprise edition with unlimited users this might not be a problem, but when JIRA is used with a limited license, only who have a licensed account in JIRA can log in and raise tickets. If JIRA is exposed to the general population, such as your customers, then you should either have unlimited JIRA user licenses or you can use JIRA Service Desk, which is a popular JIRA application especially for support requests. It doesn't require end users who will raise support tickets to be part of JIRA user license.

In `Chapter 15`, *Implementing JIRA Service Desk*, we will take a look at this popular application. It is a dedicated application for support requests and doesn't require you to customize JIRA. It has the inbuilt standard features of a typical support project.

Setting up JIRA for requirement management

Let's take a look at the configuration for using JIRA requirement management; we will store issues that are related to requirements. This will also ensure that expectations of the project are captured and later verified during testing.

Issue types

The following table lists the different issue types for requirement management:

Scheme name	Issue types	Remarks
Requirements—Issue Type Scheme	Requirements Documentation Change Request Improvement Bug New Feature New User Request Sub-task	Create the issue types that are not available

Workflow

We will use a custom workflow for the Requirements issue type; it will be used to store the project requirements; for the rest of the issue types, the default JIRA workflow will be used.

The following table depicts the requirements workflow:

From	To	Remarks
Open	In Progress	A new issue can be moved to the In Progress state when the work starts
In Progress	Open Review	• **Condition**: Only the assignee can move the issue to review
Review	In Progress Resolved	• **Transition screen**: Ask the user to enter comments when moving the issue from Review to In Progress
Resolved	Closed In Progress Reopened	Once resolved, the issue can then be closed, moved back to the In Progress state, or reopened again
Closed	Reopened	A closed issue can be reopened

Fields

The **Requirements** issue type will have a few additional fields apart from the default system JIRA fields. Similarly, we will also create a few new custom fields for the **Documentation** issue type.

The following table displays information about the field names and descriptions:

Field name	Type	Mandatory	Description
Project	Select List	Yes	Select the project name
Issue Type	Select List	Yes	Select the activity to be performed
Summary	Text	Yes	Enter a brief description of the issue
Due Date	Date Picker	No	Pick the due date of the issue if any
Component/s	Select List	No	The user can select the components if they are created by the project administrator
Assignee	User Picker	No	Select the user who will work on this issue
Reporter	User Picker	Yes	Select the reporter of the issue. The default is the creator
Description	Text Field	No	Enter the details of the issue in this field
Attachment	File	No	Upload a file or screenshot

Requirement Type	Select List	Yes	Values: • Customer • Functional • Non-functional • Design
Traceability	Text Field	No	In this field, the user can enter the changes made to a requirement over a period of time

Documentation

The following table displays information about field names and descriptions:

Field Name	Type	Mandatory	Description
Project	Select List	Yes	Select the project name
Issue Type	Select List	Yes	Select the activity to be performed
Summary	Text	Yes	Enter a brief description of the issue
Due Date	Date Picker	No	Pick the due date of the issue, if any
Component/s	Select List	No	The user can select the components if they are created by the project administrator
Assignee	User Picker	No	Pick the user who will work on this issue
Reporter	User Picker	Yes	Pick the reporter of the issue. The default is the creator
Description	Text Field	No	Enter the details of the issue in this field
Attachment	File	No	Upload a file or screenshot
Document Type	Select List	Yes	Values: • PDF • DOC • XLS
Document ID	Text Field	No	If documents are stored in the external system, then store its ID here

These fields are shown to the user while creating a new issue of the type **Support Request**; for other issue types, use the system default fields.

Screen schemes

Now that we have decided what fields we want for the **Support Request**, create a new screen called `Requirements Screen`. The following table displays information about field names and their descriptions:

Issue Type Screen Scheme name	Screen schemes	Issue types	Screen
Requirements—Issue Type Screen Scheme	Requirements—Screen Scheme	Requirements	Requirements Screen
Documentation—Screen Scheme	Documentation	Documentation Screen	
Default Screen Scheme	Change Request Improvement Bug New Feature New User Request Sub-task	Default Screen	

Permission schemes

As mentioned earlier, it is always desirable and easier to copy the default permission scheme and then make any changes in it. Let's name our new scheme Requirements-Permission Scheme.

The following table highlights only those permissions that are different than the default permission schemes:

Project Permission	Users/Groups/Project Roles
Assign Issue	Reporter
Delete Issues	Reporter
Work On Issues	Assignee

Setting up JIRA for bug tracking

JIRA can be used out-of-the-box for bug tracking. It comes with a default issue type called **Bug**, along with other issue types. However, you may be required to make certain changes in the default configurations in the future, and it is a good idea to create custom schemes even for bug tracking. Of course, we will copy the default schemes and make changes in the copied configurations.

Issue types

The following are the issue types for bug tracking:

Scheme name	Issue types	Remarks
Default Issue Type Scheme	Improvement Bug New Feature New User Request Sub-task	There's no need to create new issue types or new schemes here

Workflow

We will use a custom workflow for the **Bug** issue type; it will be used to store project requirements; for rest of the issue types, the default JIRA workflow will be used.

The following is the workflow for bug tracking:

From	To	Remarks
Open	Confirmed Resolved Closed Waiting for Client	• **Condition**: Only the assignee can confirm the bug
Confirmed	In Progress Resolved	Once the issue is confirmed, move the issue to the In Progress state
In Progress	Open Resolved Closed On Hold	An issue in the In Progress state can be opened again, resolved, closed, or put in the On Hold state

Resolved	Closed Reopened	A resolved issue can be closed or reopened
Reopened	Resolved Closed In Progress	A reopened issue can be resolved, closed, or moved to the In Progress state
Closed	Reopened	A closed issue can be reopened again

The preceding workflow is similar to the default JIRA workflow, except for one additional state called Confirmed. Once the bug is raised, it is the responsibility of the assignee to check the bug first.

Fields

The **Bug** issue type will have a few additional fields in addition to the default system JIRA fields:

Field Name	Type	Mandatory	Description
Project	Select List	Yes	Select the project name
Issue Type	Select List	Yes	Select the activity to be performed
Summary	Text	Yes	Enter a brief description of the issue
Priority	Select List	No	Values: • Major • Blocker • Critical • Minor • Trivial
Due Date	Date Picker	No	Pick the due date of the issue, if any
Component/s	Select List	No	The user can select the components if they are created by the project administrator
Affects Version/s	Select List	Yes	Select the version for which this issue is raised
Assignee	User Picker	No	Select the user who will work on this issue
Reporter	User Picker	Yes	Select the reporter of the issue. The default reporter is the creator

Environment	Text Field	No	Specify under which system environment this issue was reported
Description	Text Field	No	Enter the details of the issue in this field
Attachment	File	No	Upload a file or screenshot
Category	Select List	Yes	Values: • Billing • User Registration • Installation • User Interface • Connectivity
Customer Name	Select List	No	If the application is used by multiple customers, use this field to capture their names

These fields are shown to the user while creating a new issue of the type **Support Request**; for other issue types, use the system default fields.

Screen schemes

Now that we have decided what fields we want for **Bug**, create a new screen called `Bug Screen`:

Issue Type Screen Scheme name	Screen Scheme	Issue Types	Screen
Bug—Issue Type Screen Scheme	Bug—Screen Scheme	Support Request	Bug Screen
Default Screen Scheme	Improvement Bug New Feature New User Request Sub-task	Default Screen	

Permission schemes

As we mentioned earlier, it is always desirable and easier to copy the default permission scheme and then make any changes in it. Let's name our new scheme `Helpdesk—Permission Scheme`.

The following table highlights only those permissions that are different than, the default permission schemes:

Project permission	Users/groups/project roles
Assign Issue	Reporter
Delete Issues	Reporter
Work On Issues	Assignee
Move Issues	Project role (administrators)

Changes in the customizations

We discussed various use cases that can be implemented in JIRA. When you start using JIRA for the first time, you can never be exactly sure about the possible changes that may be required in these customizations. JIRA administrators can always make modifications in the schemes to accommodate further changes. However, it is always a good thing to set up a change control board in your company and check for the possible impact of these changes. We will discuss this in detail in Chapter 17, *JIRA Best Practices*.

Summary

In this chapter, we checked the sample implementation of a few use cases that can be implemented in JIRA. You could start your customizations by following the sample data given in this chapter; by now, you already know how to customize JIRA, but it is more important that you treat your JIRA customization as a project and prepare a configuration document to store your requirements, which we discussed in this chapter.

In the next chapter, we will take a look at user management in JIRA. We will also understand how to configure the default global permission of the users to control all that they should have access to. We will also learn the importance of creating groups and their usage.

7
User Management, Groups, and Project Roles

JIRA could be used by 10 people or 10,000 people spread across multiple locations. Large companies have multiple teams working on different projects and using the same JIRA instance, so it is usually important to manage the permissions. Maybe there are certain projects that should be private to a certain team, or there could be third-party contractors working on a specific project and they should not have access to all the projects. JIRA is incredible tool for managing the access level and permissions of users.

It is important to understand how to manage the users and groups in JIRA. In this chapter, we will also take a look at project roles—the set of people working on an individual project.

The topics covered are as follows:

- User and group management
- Working with project roles
- Types of administrator

User and group management

JIRA is a web-based application used to track project issues that are assigned to people. The users to whom these issues will be assigned need to exist in the system. When JIRA is deployed in any organization, the first thing that should be done is gather the list of people who will be using this tool; hence, their accounts need to be created in JIRA. Each user will have their username and password unique to them; this allows them to log in to the system. JIRA has its own internal authentication mechanism as well as the ability to integrate with **Lightweight Directory Access Protocol (LDAP)**.

Deciding upon the creation of user accounts

In large organizations where there is no license limit or where there is a need to create users regularly, as in the case of a customer care system, JIRA can be configured in two modes—public and private. If you want to enable signup, then configure JIRA in public mode and it will display a signup link on the user login screen. However, if you have a license limit in JIRA, then it is recommended that you use JIRA in private mode, as only in that case can JIRA Administrators create an account.

Follow these steps:

1. Go to **Administration** | **System** | **General Configuration**:

2. Click on the **Edit Settings** button in the top-right corner.
3. In the next screen, you will see a setting to change the mode. Select either **Private** or **Public** based on your license limit.

4. Once done click on the **Update** button to save your settings.

Creating a new user

1. Go to **Administration** | **User management** | **Users** (under **USER MANAGEMENT**).

2. Click on the **Create user** button in the top-right corner.
3. In the **Create new user** screen, enter **Email address**, **Full name**, **Username**, **Password**, check the **Send notification email**, check **Application access** as **JIRA Software**, and press the **Create user** button.

4. You may also check **Send notification email**.

All new users are assigned to the **jira-software-users** group that has global permissions to access JIRA. That is, if the user is part of the **jira-software-users** group, then only he/she can log in to the system, and these users also count towards the license limit; of course, this can be modified by changing the **Application access** from **Administration | Applications | Applications access**.

JIRA has some preconfigured groups that have some extra permissions over **jira-software-users**. If you want to give a user JIRA admin rights then add that user to the **jira-administrators** group as well.

1. Once the user is created, click on the **Manage groups** button, as shown in the following screenshot, to modify the user's groups:

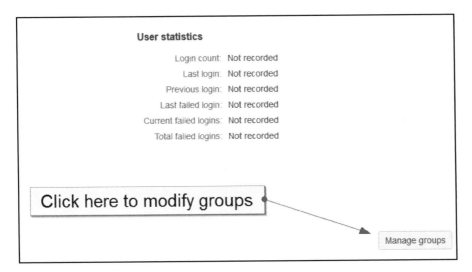

2. In the pop-up window **Manage user groups**, search for `jira-administrators` group and click on the **Join selected groups** button:

3. The user will not have full admin rights to the JIRA instance.

It is also possible to add more than one user to a group; let's take a look at that too later in this chapter.

Password policy

Organizations usually have a password policy for security purposes. JIRA allows you to define such a password policy:

1. Go to **Administration** | **System** | **Password Policy** (under **SECURITY**).
2. The password policy is disabled by default. JIRA offers two predefined policies, **Basic** and **Secure**, but we will define our own policy. Select **Custom**; it will then open up a new form where you can enter the minimum length, maximum length, and how many uppercase characters, lowercase characters, digits, and special characters need to be there.
3. Click on the **Update** button to apply the new policy.

Creating a new group

Sometimes you need to perform certain actions on all the users of a certain team; for example, you want to give extra permission to all the people working on a specific project. In such cases, a group can be created. It is nothing but a collection of users. Creating a group itself doesn't do anything. How that group will behave is defined in the permission scheme.

Let's understand how we can create a new group:

1. Go to **Administration** | **User management** | **Groups** (under **USER MANAGEMENT**).
2. On the right-hand side, there is an option to do an **Add group**. Just enter **Name** for the group and press the **Add group** button:

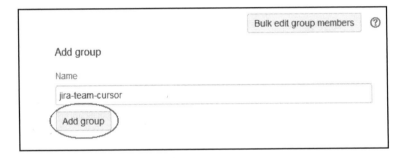

Once the group is added, it will be added in the list on the same page.

Also, it is very easy to add new users to a group:

1. Click on the **Edit Members** link under the **Operations** column for the group you want to modify.

2. In the next section, under **Add members to selected groups(s)** text box type in the usernames of the users that need to be assigned to our new group and press the **Add selected users** button.

Once you have your groups created, along with the users who will be a part of it, you can then use them in project permission scheme, or project roles.

Working with project roles

Every project is executed by different people, each with their own set of responsibilities. Usually, certain aspects of the project are taken care of by these people who are part of a team. For instance, in the case of a software project, there will be a project lead who manages everything in the project and is responsible for overall progress, developers who work on the features, and then there is a team of testers to verify the built features. The first versions of JIRA had only groups, and JIRA administrators would end up creating multiple groups for various projects, such as proj-administrators, proj-developers, and so on. At the same time, the permission scheme for each project also needed to be defined for these groups. JIRA developers realized this was a problem and introduced the concept of project role that allows not only JIRA administrators but also the project administrator to add and remove users to their project roles.

In JIRA, you could have roles that are defined globally and are available in all the projects, but the people who are in such roles would be different for each project. Just adding the project role and adding users to it in the project won't have any effect until the permission schemes are modified by defining what a project role will do in the project.

Creating a project role

JIRA comes with two predefined roles, namely **Administrators** and **Developers**. You can also create new roles in JIRA. Follow these steps:

1. Go to **Administration** | **System** | **Project roles** (under **SECURITY**):

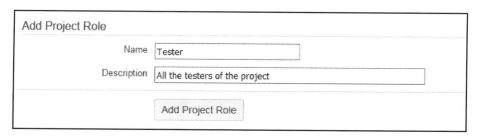

2. To add a new role, enter the **Name** and **Description** of the role and press the **Add Project Role** button. A new role can be easily added to the system, but it is important to note here that adding a new role in JIRA won't have any effect on the project until we add users to the project role in a specific JIRA project, and define the permissions in the scheme.

Adding users and groups in the project role

Now that we have a new project role, it is time to add a few users and groups for a particular project:

1. Go to any project's **Administration** tab and then to **Users and roles**:

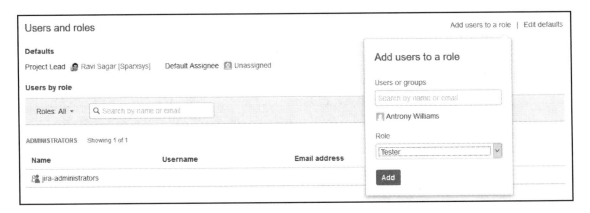

2. Click on the **Add users to a role** link in the top right. In the popup that appears, search for the users in the **Users or groups** text box, select the **Role** from the drop-down list, and press the **Add** button. Do the same again if you want to add more users or groups to a specific project role. Either a user or a group can be part of your project role.

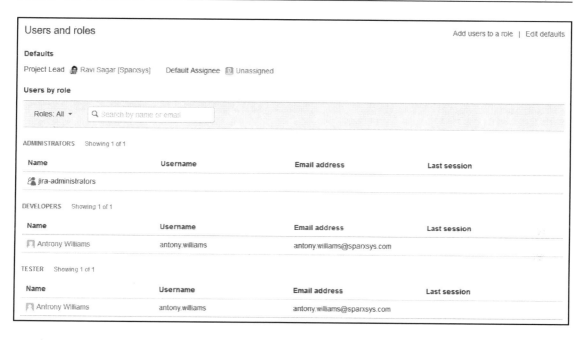

Until now, we have created a project role and also added users to it for a particular project. You can do that for all the projects. These project roles are available for use in all the projects in our instance, but now we need to define the permission this role has in our project.

Giving permissions to your project role

The permissions of the **Tester** project role that we just added to our instance need to be configured by modifying the permission scheme for the project:

1. Go to the project tab, **Administration | Permissions**.
2. On the **Project Permission** page, click on the **Actions** button in the top-right corner and select **Edit permissions**.

3. Now you can modify the permission scheme. Let's give them the permission to **Manage Watchers**. So, they can add a third user who is not an assignee or reporter but can still receive notifications on issue update. Click on the **Edit** link, as shown in this screenshot:

4. As shown in the following screenshot, in the **Grant permission** popup, first select **Project Role**, and from the drop-down list, select the **Tester** project role:

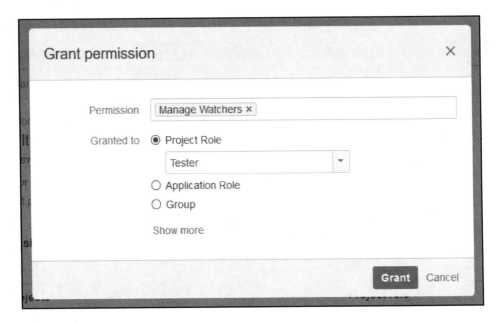

5. Click on the **Grant** button.

You can add more permissions like this to your new role, and, of course, all the projects using this permission scheme will be affected.

Types of administrators

JIRA administrators have the ability to make changes to the system configuration and schemes, and to manage users. The administrative user is created when JIRA is installed. In big organizations where there is a team of people taking care of JIRA, there could be multiple JIRA administrators. There is a group called **jira-adminstators** in JIRA. The administrative user that is created during installation is part of this group, and more users can be added to it later on.

1. Go to **Administration** | **System** | **Global Permissions** (under **SECURITY**):

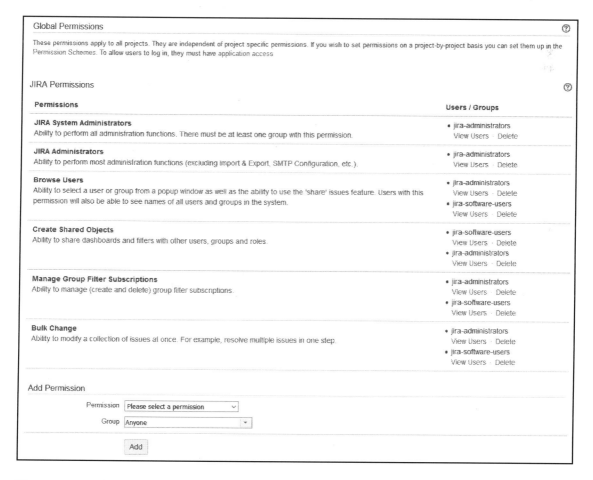

If you notice, from the administrative point of view, JIRA offers two different permissions called **JIRA System Administrators** and **JIRA Administrators**.

JIRA System Administrators

Users who are part of this global permission can perform all the administrative functions. They can make changes in the configuration and scheme, perform system restore, and modify mail configurations as well.

JIRA Administrator

Even if your organization has multiple JIRA administrators, there are certain features that need to be restricted. A **JIRA Administrators** permission allows users to perform most of the administrative functions, except system restore, importing and exporting, and changes to the mail configurations, as these features could potentially lead to system breakdown and may result in loss of data as well. So, it is advisable to only give the **JIRA System Administrators** permission to one or two people in the organization, and the rest could have the **JIRA Administrators** permission.

Summary

In this chapter, you learned how to manage users and groups. To give access to new users and assign them to the right group is one of the most important activities of a JIRA administrator. The responsibility of adding new users to the system and assigning them to the right group is crucial for data integrity, and it should be in tune with your company's policies. You also learned how to create project roles and define their permissions.

In the next chapter, you will learn how you can integrate JIRA with LDAP, Crowd, and JIRA user server. This way, users don't need to remember multiple logins for different tools, and it is also much easier for the administrators to manage users efficiently from a single place.

8
Configuring JIRA User Directories to Connect with LDAP, Crowd, and JIRA User Server

In companies with thousands of employees, there are several internal tools and systems. There are tools to track time, leave management, and intranet portals. It's very difficult to manage user accounts on multiple applications; companies use **Lightweight Directory Access Protocol** (**LDAP**) servers for user management, where a single user account works on more than one tool and users don't need to remember multiple passwords. JIRA also supports integration with LDAP. This is a great feature; it really helps system administrators to manage users. Apart from LDAP, we will also discuss how to connect JIRA to another JIRA instance for user management, as well as for **Crowd**, which is a single sign-on software from Atlassian.

This chapter will cover the following topics:

- Authentication mechanism in JIRA
- Allowing other applications to connect to JIRA
- Synchronizing user and group information

Authentication mechanism in JIRA

JIRA is a web-based tool used by multiple users, each having different permissions depending on the group they are part of or what role they are performing in the project. JIRA has a built-in authentication mechanism known as **JIRA internal directory**, but it's possible to connect JIRA to external directories as well. Let's take a look at how this is done.

JIRA internal directory

JIRA comes with an internal directory that is enabled by default; the first administrative user is a part of the internal directory, and, until you add another directory, all additional users are added in this internal directory. JIRA stores this in its own database.

Configuring LDAP

LDAP is an application protocol to query and modify information in directory services. In medium-to large-scale companies, where there are hundreds or thousands of users, everyone has their e-mails, phone numbers, and other details stored on a directory server. Users can find each other in this directory. Each user's login details are also stored, and various applications can rely on directory services for authentication.

Instead of JIRA's internal authentication, it's possible to connect to existing directory services through LDAP:

1. Go to JIRA **Administration** | **User management** | **User Directories** (under **USER DIRECTORIES**). You will notice **JIRA Internal Directory** already added there, but after we add additional directories, such as LDAP or Crowd, the order in which the user is searched is defined using the **Order** column. Users may be present in one or more directories, but they will be searched for first in the directory that is listed at the top:

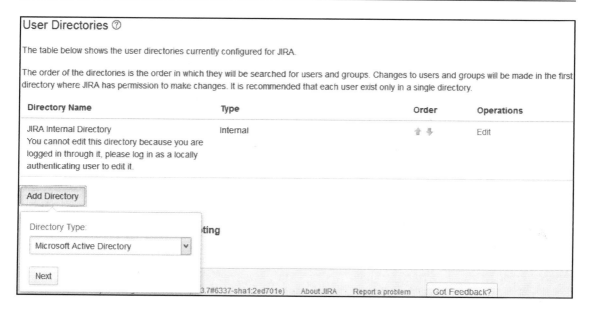

2. Click on **Add Directory**. A popup will appear. Select **Microsoft Active Directory** and click on **Next**.

3. In the following screenshot, we need to configure the LDAP user directory. First, fill in the **Server Settings**:

   - Enter the **Name** as `Active Director server` or any other useful name.
   - Select the **Directory Type** as **Microsoft Active Directory**.
   - Enter the **Hostname** of your LDAP server.
   - Enter the **Port** number of your LDAP server.
   - Enter the **Username** of your LDAP server. It's usually in a format such as `user@domain.name` or `cn=username,dc=domain,dc=com`.
   - Enter the **Password**.

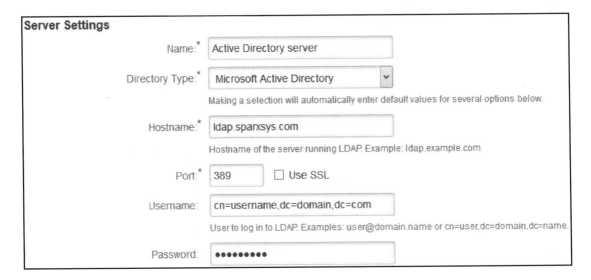

4. Then, enter the **LDAP Schema** settings:

- Enter **Base DN**; it's usually in the `dc=domain,dc=local` format. Ask your LDAP administrators for specific information:

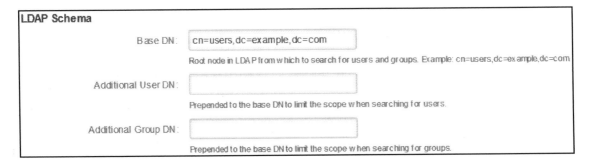

5. Now, set **LDAP Permissions** as **Read Only**, where the user information is only retrieved from the LDAP server. In this case, the password can only be changed from the LDAP server and not from the JIRA application. However, if you want users who are newly logged in to be automatically added to one or more JIRA groups, then select **Read Only, with Local Groups** and enter the name of the groups in the **Default Group Memberships:** field:

LDAP Permissions

○ Read Only

Users, groups and memberships are retrieved from your LDAP server and cannot be modified in JIRA.

◉ Read Only, with Local Groups

Users, groups and memberships are retrieved from your LDAP server and cannot be modified in JIRA. Users from LDAP can be added to groups maintained in JIRA's internal directory.

○ Read/Write

Modifying users, groups and memberships in JIRA will cause the changes to be applied directly to your LDAP server. Your configured LDAP user will need to have modification permissions on your LDAP server.

Default Group Memberships: jira-software-users

A comma-separated list of groups that users will be added to when they first log in. This will only be done once per user. These groups will be created if they don't already exist.

6. Click on the **Save and Test** button to save the configuration.

Now, a new user who is already a part of the LDAP server can log in to the JIRA instance using the same username and password. Also, this user will be added to the additional JIRA groups that we configured previously.

Understanding Base DN

The LDAP directory used in companies could have thousands of employees; it may not be necessary to give JIRA access to all the users in the company. For instance, consider a scenario when there are users in the U.S. as well as in Asia, and access of JIRA needs to be given only to users in the U.S. Now, LDAP also has its own groups known as domains that can be leveraged to limit access to JIRA.

Refer to the following table to understand the possible Base DN for corresponding LDAP domains:

LDAP domain	Base DN	Remarks
example.com	dc=example,dc=com	All users in the LDAP directory can access JIRA
us.example.com	dc=us,dc=example,dc=com	Only U.S. users can access JIRA
asia.example.com	dc=asia,dc=example,dc=com	Only Asian users can access JIRA

Contact your JIRA administrator to understand the LDAP domain. Also, make sure that if you are using LDAP, then any user with an active account can log in to JIRA and your license limit can exhaust quickly.

Connecting to Crowd

Crowd is another application from Atlassian for single sign-on. This application can be used to manage multiple user directories.

Implementing Atlassian Crowd

Crowd supports various types of directory. It can use its own Crowd internal directory or it can also connect to the LDAP directory already used in the organization. As a first step, at least one of these directories should be configured in Crowd. Then, make sure the group that is required to authenticate the users is added in the directory that you add and configure in Crowd. For instance, **jira-software-users** is a group defined in JIRA. Users who are part of this group can login to JIRA. Just make sure this group is also added to your Crowd directory. Finally, to communicate with JIRA an application needs to be created in Crowd. Remember the application name and application password; you will need them when configuring Crowd in JIRA.

Organizations with an existing Crowd instance can connect their JIRA to utilize single sign-on:

1. Go to JIRA **Administration** | **User management** | **User Directories** (under **USER DIRECTORIES**).
2. Click on the **Add Directory** button and select **Directory Type:** as **Atlassian Crowd:**

3. On the next screen, fill in **Server Settings**:

- Enter the **Name** of the Crowd server
- Enter the **Server URL** of your crowd instance
- Enter the name of the **Application Name**; this application needs to be created in Crowd by the administrator
- Provide the **Application Password** given to you by the Crowd administrator

4. Then, select **Crowd Permissions** as **Read/Write** if you want the changes to be applied to the Crowd server, or **Read Only** if you just want to retrieve the information.

5. First, click on **Test Settings** and if everything works, then you will be able to **Save and Test** the connection to the Crowd server.

Connecting to a JIRA user server

In large organizations, there could be more than one instance of JIRA used by various teams or projects. Users may need to access all these instances to track projects; in such cases, separate accounts need to be created for the same person. It's not only cumbersome for the JIRA administrator, but also difficult for the user to remember one more username and password. JIRA allows you to connect to another JIRA instance for user management:

1. Go to JIRA **Administration** | **User management** | **User Directories** (under **USER DIRECTORIES**).

2. Click on the **Add Directory** button and select **Directory Type:** as **Atlassian JIRA**:

3. On the next screen, fill in **Server Settings**:

- Enter the **Name** of the JIRA server
- Enter the **Server URL** of your JIRA instance
- Enter the name of the **Application Name**; this application needs to be created in JIRA by the administrator
- Provide the **Application Password** given to you by the JIRA administrator

4. Then, select **JIRA Server Permissions** as **Read/Write** if you want the changes to be applied to the JIRA server, or **Read Only** if you just want to retrieve the information.

5. First, click on **Test Settings** and if everything works, then you will be able to **Save and Test** the connection to the JIRA server.

Allowing other applications to connect to JIRA

In the previous section, we connected one JIRA instance to another for user management. The instance used as a JIRA user server needs to have the application created so that other instances can connect to it:

1. Go to JIRA **Administration** | **User management** | **JIRA User Server**.

   Click on the **Add application** button in the top-right corner:

2. On the next screen, enter **Application name** as `jira-user-server` or something meaningful.

3. Enter the **Password** for this application.

4. Finally, enter the IP address of the actual JIRA server in the **IP Addresses** field. This step is quite important. Without this step, the connection may not work.

The JIRA user server URL, application name, and password are important features to note here and need to be used in the JIRA instance that will connect to it. Allowing other applications from Atlassian, such as Confluence, to connect to JIRA to share the user base is possible because JIRA internally uses a trimmed version of Crowd.

Synchronizing user and group information

Now that we have seen how to connect JIRA to LDAP, Crowd, and another JIRA server, it's also important to understand how the user information is synchronized. Any new user who is a part of the directory should be able to log in to a JIRA instance, but all new users who have recently been added to the directory will not be able to access JIRA until the user list is synchronized.

Go to JIRA **Administration** | **User management** | **User Directories** (under **USER DIRECTORIES**). Here, you will see the list of user directories added in the instance. There is a **Synchronise** link against each entry:

JIRA Server	Atlassian Crowd	⬆ ⬇	Disable | Edit | Test | Synchronise
			Last synchronised at 14/11/14 12:56 PM (took 8s).
			Full synchronisation completed successfully.

Click on the **Synchronise** link and JIRA will compare and fetch the list of users from the JIRA server; if there are new users on the server, they will be created in the instance. This will also create the groups in our JIRA instance.

Note that the users created via this synchronization will not be editable, and you cannot delete them if the permission is set in the **Read Only** mode.

Summary

In this chapter, you learned how to integrate JIRA with LDAP, Crowd, and a JIRA user server. This way, users don't need to remember multiple logins for different tools, and it's also much easier for the administrators to manage users efficiently from a single place. You also learned how to create the application link on the JIRA server, and discussed the synchronization of user accounts.

Until now, we have seen the power of JIRA and the flexibility it offers. JIRA can be customized very easily; we know that more functionality can be added to JIRA by installing add-ons from the marketplace. While some of these add-ons are free, others need to be purchased. It's also possible to create your own add-on to bring a new feature in JIRA and modify it. In the next chapter, we will take a look at how to create these add-ons along with some simple examples.

9
JIRA Add-On Development and Leveraging the REST API

JIRA comes with tons of useful features that help you not only get started on your project, but also let you customize the workflows that match your software model and processes. However, there are times when certain functionalities or customizations are required, but these are not supported by JIRA. Then again, many new features can be added in JIRA by installing add-ons from the Atlassian marketplace. JIRA has a marketplace where one can search for these add-ons. Some add-ons are free and some are paid add-ons. If you are looking for additional features, you can search on the marketplace for existing add-ons, but it's also possible to create your own add-ons, which requires a decent knowledge of Java. This chapter will give you enough information to get you started with JIRA's add-on development, along with some simple examples.

The following topics will be covered:

- Setting up the Atlassian plugin **software development kit (SDK)**
- Installing the Atlassian SDK on Windows
- Creating the **helloworld** plugin
- Setting up the Eclipse IDE
- Leveraging the JIRA **representational state transfer (REST)** API

Setting up the Atlassian plugin SDK

Atlassian provides an SDK to develop add-ons. The SDK needs to be installed on your machine before starting the development. It can be installed on Windows, Linux, and Mac. Any of these operating systems can be used to develop add-ons, however, in this chapter, the instructions will focus only on the Windows platform. There are no specific recommended hardware requirements to install the Atlassian SDK; however, to get a decent performance, install it on a machine that has a core i5 processor and 8 GB of RAM.

 Download the Atlassian SDK for Windows at `https://marketplace.atla ssian.com/download/plugins/atlassian-plugin-sdk-windows`.

Setting up the SDK prerequisites on a Windows system

The SDK requires the Java environment to be configured on your machine. In `Chapter 1`, *Planning Your JIRA Installation*, we discussed how to install the JDK. The JDK could have been installed at `C:\java` or `C:\java\jdk1.8.0_92`.

Verifying the JDK installation and the JAVA_HOME system variable

The Atlassian JDK needs Oracle's Java SE Development Kit installed on the system. Follow the steps mentioned in `Chapter 1`, *Planning your JIRA Installation* to install it and verify that the `JAVA_HOME` system variable is set up by following the steps mentioned here:

1. Open **Command Prompt (cmd)** and enter the following command:

    ```
    echo %JAVA_HOME%
    ```

2. It should return the path where the JDK is installed. In our case, it's given as follows:

    ```
    c:\java
    ```

Verifying that JAVA_HOME\bin is present in the environment variable PATH

The JDK `bin` directory has executable files, such as `javac`, and it should be available to the Atlassian SDK.

All you need to do is append the following line to your existing `Path` system variable `%JAVA_HOME%\bin` and perform the following steps:

1. Open cmd and enter the following command:

   ```
   javac -version
   ```

2. It should return the version of the JDK:

   ```
   javac 1.8.0_92
   ```

Installing the Atlassian SDK on Windows

The Atlassian SDK can be downloaded from `https://marketplace.atlassian.com/downl oad/plugins/atlassian-plugin-sdk-windows`. This link will always give you the latest stable version of the SDK. Here, you will get an executable file called `sdk-installer-6.2.6.exe`. Perform the following steps to install the SDK on your Windows system:

1. After downloading the SDK installer, double-click on it and complete the installation.
2. Once the installation is complete, the installer will prompt you to restart the computer. If the installer doesn't ask you to restart, just check whether you are able to use `atlas`-commands; if not, then restarting the system is the safest way to make sure that the SDK is installed properly.
3. Open cmd and enter the following command:

   ```
   atlas-version
   ```

4. It should return the following information:

You can see that it will tell you which version of the Atlassian SDK is installed on the system and give you the details of the JDK that is installed as well.

At this point, everything is set up and you are now ready to start developing add-ons.

Getting familiar with the Atlassian SDK

When you ran the `atlas-version` command, it showed various details of the installed SDK. You might have noticed that `ATLAS Home` is the location where the Atlassian SDK is installed. Let's open this directory and check its content:

- `apache-maven-3.2.1`: This Atlassian SDK uses **Maven**, which is a popular tool used to build automation for Java projects.
- `bin`: This directory contains all the command-line tools that are used to develop add-ons. All the commands here are prefixed with `atlas-`.
- `repository`: This directory contains the actual code that the SDK relies on to develop add-ons.

The atlas command

We just discussed that all the commands are prefixed with `atlas-`. Before you start creating add-ons, a working JIRA instance is required. This will be used to test your add-ons. The `atlas-run-standalone` command is used to set up and start the JIRA instance for you.

Perform the following steps:

1. Create a folder called `atlastutorial` in your `C:\` directory.
2. In cmd, change directory using:

    ```
    cd c:\atlastutorial
    ```

3. Start JIRA using the following command:

    ```
    atlas-run-standalone --product jira
    ```

4. Depending on your internet connection, this command will take a few minutes to complete. It downloads the JIRA files and starts the instance on port `2990`:

    ```
    [INFO] Starting jira on the tomcat7x container on ports 2990 (http),
    54668
    (rmi) and 8009 (ajp)
    [INFO] using codehaus cargo v1.4.7
    [INFO] [2.ContainerStartMojo] Resolved container artifact
    org.codehaus.cargo:cargo-core-container-tomcat:jar:1.4.7 for container
    tomcat7x
    [INFO] [talledLocalContainer] Tomcat 7.x starting...
    [INFO] [stalledLocalDeployer] Deploying [c:\atlastutorial\amps-
    standalone\target\jira\jira.war] to [c:\atlastutorial\amps-
    standalone/target\container\tomcat7x\cargo-jira-home/webapps]...
    [INFO] [talledLocalContainer] Tomcat 7.x started on port [2990]
    [INFO] jira started successfully in 703s at http://localhost:2990/jira
    [INFO] Type Ctrl-D to shutdown gracefully
    [INFO] Type Ctrl-C to exit
    ```

5. Enter `http://localhost:2990/jira` in your browser; the exact URL will also be displayed by the command.
6. Enter `admin` as the username and password.

This is your JIRA instance, created after you set up the Atlassian SDK with the test license for plugin developers; we will use this to develop the JIRA add-ons.

Creating the helloworld plugin

Now, we are ready to create our first add-on in JIRA, which will introduce new features to our instance. Any JIRA add-on contains a lot of files, and it has to follow a directory structure; the Atlassian SDK provides a command-line tool called `atlas-create-jira-plugin` to create a plugin.

If your existing JIRA is already running in cmd, then stop it by pressing on *Ctrl + C* and perform these steps:

1. In cmd, make sure that you are in the `C:\atlastutorial` directory.
2. Enter the following command and press *Enter*:

   ```
   atlas-create-jira-plugin
   ```

3. This command will respond and ask you to provide certain inputs. Use the values mentioned in the following table:

Define value for `groupId`	`com.atlassian.tutorial`	**Used to identify project uniquely**
Define value for `artifactId`	`helloworld`	An artifact is a file, usually a JAR, that gets deployed
Define value for `version`	`1.0-Version`	Used for distributing the plugin
Define value for `package`	`com.atlassian.tutorial.helloworld`	Used to organize the related classes

4. The `atlas-create-jira-plugin` command will prompt you to confirm the values you just entered. Press *Y* to continue. A new `helloworld` folder will be created at `c:\atlastutorial\helloworld`.

If you take a look in the `c:\atlastutorial\helloworld` directory, you will find a skeleton of the plugin project with the following files and folders created by the `atlas-create-jira-plugin` command:

- `src`: This folder contains the source code of the plugin
- `LICENSE`: This file stores the plugin license information
- `pom`: This is the Maven configuration file
- `README`: This file contains brief instructions on how to run the plugin

Adding organization details in pom.xml

Open the `pom.xml` file, search the `<organization>` tag, and update the company name and the company URL. This information will be visible to the user who will install the plugin from the **Universal Plugin Manager (UPM)**:

```
<organization>
  <name>Sparxsys Solutions Pvt. Ltd.</name>
  <url>http://www.sparxsys.com/</url>
</organization>
```

Enter the company name within an enclosed `<name>` tag and the company URL within an enclosed `<url>` tag and save the file.

Loading the plugin in JIRA

We now have a plugin created with just a single command, and you can actually load this plugin in JIRA. Although it has no functionality right now, we will still make the attempt to understand how to load this plugin in JIRA. Perform the following steps:

1. In cmd, navigate to the `c:\atlastutorial\helloworld` directory.
2. Enter the following command and press *Enter*:

   atlas-run

   This is a shell script that installs and runs the plugin.

3. This command will create a folder called the `target` subdirectory in the `helloworld` directory. After some time, a JIRA instance will start.
4. Enter `http://localhost:2990/jira` in your browser; the exact URL will also be displayed by the command.
5. Enter `admin` for both username and password.

6. Go to JIRA **Administration** | **Add-ons** | **Manage add-ons** (under **ATLASSIAN MARKETPLACE**).

7. Under **User-installed add-ons**, you will find the new add-on called **helloworld**:

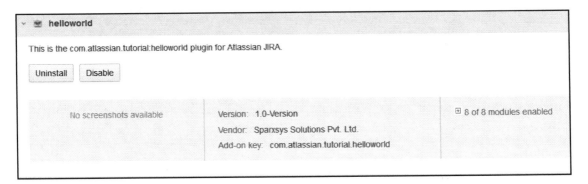

As you can see in the preceding screenshot, the **helloworld** add-on is now loaded in your JIRA instance. Also, the version information that we filled in while creating the plugin is visible here. The hyperlinked company name is also displayed.

Setting up the Eclipse IDE

We have set up the development environment and installed the Atlassian SDK. You also learned how to create a skeleton plugin; apart from just showing up in the UPM, this plugin did not perform any other function. We will add a few functionalities to our plugin, but before that, let's configure the popular Eclipse IDE, which really assists in developing JIRA add-ons.

Downloading the Eclipse IDE

The Eclipse IDE is used for development purposes in various programming languages, however, we will install the Eclipse IDE for Java EE Developers (Indigo). Perform the following steps:

1. Download the Eclipse IDE for Java EE developers from `http://www.eclipse.or g/downloads/packages/eclipse-ide-java-ee-developers/indigosr2`.

2. Extract the content of the downloaded file in the `C:\eclipse` directory.

Configuring Eclipse to start under the JDK

We need to tell our Eclipse IDE to start and use the JDK that we have already installed on our machine:

1. Open the `C:\eclipse\eclipse.ini` file.
2. Add a `-vm` entry before the `-vmargs` entry. We should define the JDK path here; the final `eclipse.ini` file should look similar to the following code:

```
-startup
plugins/org.eclipse.equinox.launcher_1.3.0.v20140415-2008.jar
--launcher.library
plugins/org.eclipse.equinox.launcher.win32.win32.x86_64_1.1.200.
v20140603-1326
-product
org.eclipse.epp.package.jee.product
--launcher.defaultAction
openFile
--launcher.XXMaxPermSize
256M
-showsplash
org.eclipse.platform
--launcher.XXMaxPermSize
256m
--launcher.defaultAction
openFile
--launcher.appendVmargs
-vm
c:\java
-vmargs
-Dosgi.requiredJavaVersion=1.8
-Xms40m
-Xmx512m
```

3. Save and close the file.

Updating the installed JREs in Eclipse

The Eclipse JREs need to be updated with the ones that are currently installed in our JDK version. Perform the following steps if you are not sure whether you have the updated JREs or not:

1. In the menu bar, click on **Windows** | **Preferences**.
2. Double-click on the `C:\eclipse\eclipse.exe` application and it will start the Eclipse IDE.
3. On the left-hand side, enter `Installed JREs`; this will filter down the list; after that, double-click on **Installed JREs**.
4. On the right-hand side, click on the **Add** button and select **Standard VM**.
5. In **JRE home**, enter `c:\java` as the location of the directory and click on the **Finish** button:

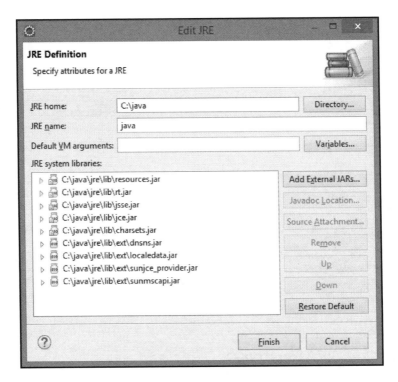

6. Finally, the JREs will be updated, and it should look similar to the following screenshot:

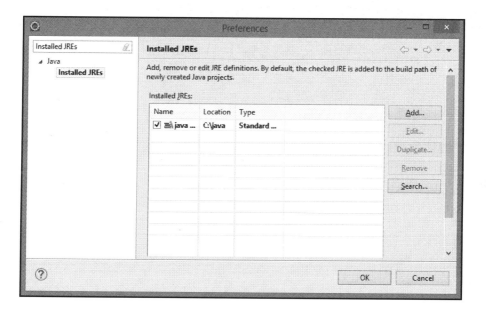

Installing the Maven plugin

The development of the JIRA add-ons is based on Maven, and there is an Eclipse plugin for Maven that needs to be installed. Perform the following steps:

1. In the menu bar, click on **Help | Install New Software...**
2. In the **Available Software** window, click on the **Add** button.

3. Enter the **Name** as `Sonatype M2Eclipse`. Enter
   `http://download.eclipse.org/technology/m2e/releases` as the **Location**
   and click on the **OK** button.

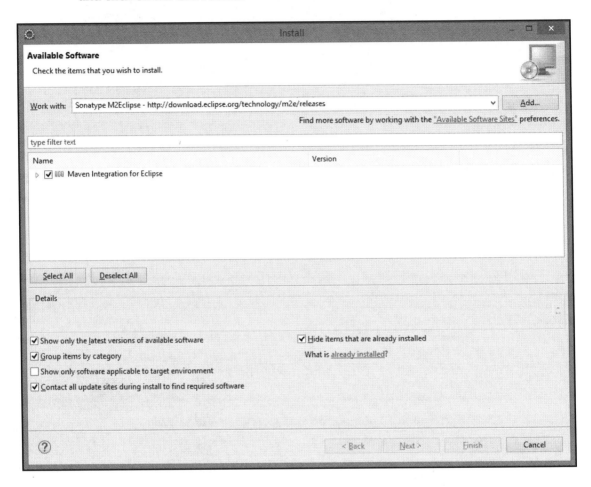

4. Select **Maven Integration for Eclipse** and click on the **Finish** button.
5. Finally, restart Eclipse for these changes to take effect.

Configuring the Maven plugin

Finally, we need to tell the Maven Eclipse plugin the location of Maven on our machine. The Maven directory is placed in the `ATLAS Home` directory. You can run the `atlas-version` command on your machine to find out the exact location of `ATLAS Maven Home`. Just copy this location and perform the following steps:

1. In the menu bar, click on **Windows | Preferences**.
2. On the left-hand side, enter `Maven`; it will filter down the options available for **Maven**.
3. Click on **Installations** and then click on the **Add** button.
4. The **Installation type** should be **External**. Copy the `ATLAS Maven Home` directory and click on the **Finish** button.

Now we are all set to start developing our JIRA add-ons using Eclipse.

Adding functionality to the skeleton plugin

The helloworld plugin (which we created earlier) lacks any functionality; we loaded the plugin in JIRA, but it didn't do anything apart from just showing up in the UPM. Now that we have also configured the Eclipse IDE, let's add a few functionalities to our helloworld plugin.

As an example, we will add a custom link in the JIRA main navigation bar using this plugin.

Importing the helloworld plugin in Eclipse

We can use the Eclipse IDE and import our plugin, but before we do that, there are Eclipse configuration files that need to be generated in the `helloworld` plugin project. Perform the following steps:

1. In cmd, navigate to the `C:\atlastutorial\helloworld` directory.
2. Enter the following command and press *Enter*:

```
atlas-mvn eclipse:eclipse
```

3. This command will return the following message:

```
[INFO] ------------------------------------------------------------[INFO]
BUILD SUCCESS
[INFO] ------------------------------------------------------------[INFO]
Total time: 56.519 s
[INFO] Finished at: 2014-11-28T11:15:35+05:30
[INFO] Final Memory: 21M/102M
[INFO] ------------------------------------------------------------
```

4. Now, we are ready to import the plugin in Eclipse. In the menu bar, click on **File | Import...**

5. Select **Existing Projects into Workspace** under **General** and click on the **Next** button.

6. Enter C:\atlastutorial\helloworld in the **Select root** directory and click on the **Finish** button.

Now you should see the helloworld plugin project loaded on the left-hand side under **Project Explorer**, as shown in the following screenshot. If you notice the welcome screen in your SDK, then close it.

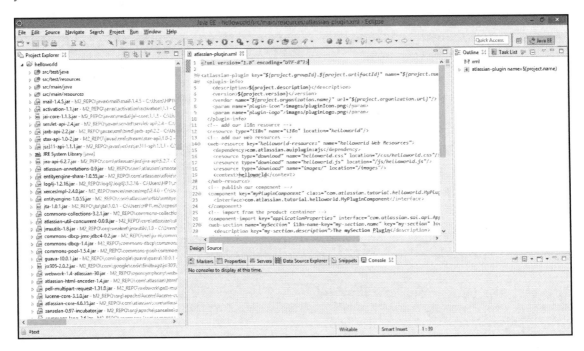

Creating a menu in JIRA's top navigation bar

We will use a very simple example to help us understand how to add new functionalities in JIRA. You are already familiar with JIRA's top navigation bar. From the JIRA frontend, it's not possible to add a new menu item to it; however, we will modify our `helloworld` plugin to add this menu item.

The JIRA functionality and the behavior of its various sections are controlled by various modules. If we want to make any modifications to JIRA's top navigation bar, then we need to add two modules called `Web Section` and `Web Item`. Perform the following steps:

1. In the cmd, navigate to the `c:\atlastutorial\helloworld` directory.
2. Enter the following command and press *Enter*:

   `atlas-create-jira-plugin-module`

3. To learn more about plugin modules, refer to theURL: `https://developer.atla ssian.com/docs/getting-started/plugin-modules`.
4. The command will respond and prompt you to enter a specific number for various modules. Type `30` for `Web Section`.
5. The command will again respond and ask you to provide certain inputs. Use the values as mentioned in the following table:

Enter Plugin Module Name	mySection
Enter Location	contact-us-links
Show Advanced Setup?	*N*

6. The command will ask you, **Add Another Plugin Module?** Press *Y*.
7. The command will respond and prompt you to enter a specific number for various modules. Type `25` for `Web Item`.
8. The command will again respond and ask you to provide certain inputs. Use the values as mentioned in the following table:

Enter Plugin Module Name	Contact Us
Enter Section	system.top.navigation.bar
Enter Link URL	http://www.sparxsys.com/contact
Show Advanced Setup?	*N*

9. The command will ask you to **Add Another Plugin Module?** Press *N*.

10. Run the `atlas-run` command from within your plugin project directory. Once JIRA starts running, open it in the browser:

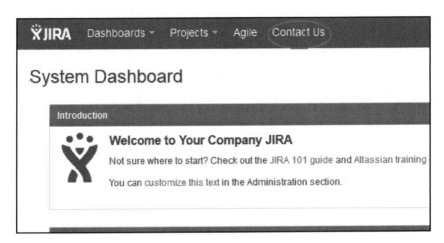

You should now see a new menu item called **Contact Us**, which we have added from our `helloworld` plugin.

We have just started to add the functionality in the skeleton plugin project. Although all we did was add a link to the JIRA navigation bar, there is a lot more that can be done.

If you are starting JIRA add-on development, then start by going through the tutorials mentioned on the Atlassian website at `https://developer.atlassian.com/docs/getting-started/tutorials`.

So far in this chapter, we have discussed creating add-ons that extend JIRA's functionalities, but it's also possible to interact with JIRA from other applications as well. JIRA comes with the **REST API**, which allows you to manipulate JIRA's data and configurations from external applications. The JIRA API that adheres to the principles of REST does not require the client to know anything about the structure of the API. Rather, the server needs to provide whatever information the client needs to interact with the service.

Various programming languages are capable of making REST calls. In the following section, we will discuss how to interact with JIRA REST APIs, along with some examples in detail.

JIRA Cloud add-ons with an Atlassian Connect framework

We have just seen how to develop an add-on for a JIRA Server instance that you host on your own server. However, a lot of organizations also use an Atlassian Cloud instance, which is a hosted environment; it doesn't require any installation. You just sign up online and pay for the usage. The Atlassian Cloud instance comes with most of the features that JIRA Server offers. Many organizations prefer to use a cloud instance as there is no hassle to manage the server yourself. The procedure to develop an add-on for cloud is different. If you want to learn that, please follow the documentation at `https://developer.atlassian .com/static/connect/docs/latest/guides/introduction.html`.

If you plan to sell your add-on on the Atlassian marketplace then it is a good idea to develop the add-on for both JIRA Server and JIRA Cloud.

Leveraging the JIRA REST API

We have discussed how to start building add-ons that extend JIRA's functionalities. The add-ons are integrated very closely with JIRA's existing features; however, there are times when you need to add a few functionalities on top of JIRA so that other tools can interact with JIRA. JIRA provides access to various operations via REST.

Examples of a few operations that can be performed via REST

- Issue operations such as create/modify/delete issues
- Search issues
- Create users
- Group management operations like adding/removing users from a group

There are a lot of resources that are available through REST API. You can get the detailed list of all the resources at `https://docs.atlassian.com/jira/REST/latest/`.

Use cases of JIRA REST API

Having the ability to interact with JIRA through external applications opens up a lot of possibilities. Let's take a look at some of the use cases of functionality that can be built on top of JIRA:

- Generating business intelligence reports
- Generating bulk operations in JIRA
- Building a custom interface for clients

Generating business intelligence reports

JIRA comes with a lot of readymade reports, which we discussed in detail in `Chapter 3`, *Reporting – Charts to visualize the data*, but companies use the business intelligence tools to generate reports that are customized to their needs; in JIRA, all the data is stored in issues, which can be fetched from REST API.

Bulk operations in JIRA

System administrators in JIRA are often faced with situations where they need to perform various operations in bulk. For instance, if a new team in the company wants to start using JIRA, then several user accounts need to be created. JIRA's REST API provides the resources to create a user account. After the accounts are created, they also need to be added to the correct group. Although the JIRA group management interface already provides the mechanism to modify user groups by entering their usernames as a comma-separated list, modifying groups can also be done via the REST API.

The scripts can be created to perform such bulk operations, and they can be run whenever it is needed.

Building a custom interface for clients

We have already seen that it's very easy to customize permissions in JIRA and give limited access of your JIRA instance to your clients. However, it's also possible to create a simple web interface that has a login box for authentication, a form to raise tickets, and a simple list of issues for a particular project or client. This web application can internally interact with JIRA, and it acts like the backend to store and retrieve client tickets.

JIRA's REST API Browser

REST calls are made by calling the `http://jira.sparxsys.com/rest/api/2/RESOURCE URL`, and most programming languages (such as Java and PHP) support them; however, before you can develop the functionalities to interact with JIRA using REST, you need to test it.

The Atlassian SDK that you have installed comes with a nifty tool called **REST API Browser**. It helps you explore the APIs and also test them. Perform these steps:

1. Run the `atlas-run` command, as we did earlier in this chapter. It will start the JIRA instance.
2. Enter `http://localhost:2990/jira` in your browser; the exact URL will also be displayed by the command.
3. Enter `admin` for both the username and password.
4. Go to JIRA **Administrator** | **System** | **REST API Browser** (under **ADVANCED**).
5. On the left-hand side, you will find the list of all the resources that REST API has to offer:

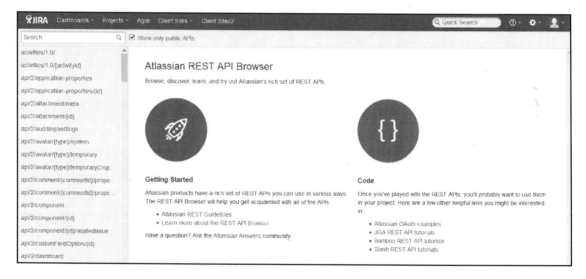

6. Click on any one of the resources, and on the right-hand side of the main window; this particular resource can be tested by passing optional parameters.

Let's take a look at some examples to test REST API.

Fetching user details

On the left-hand side, either scroll or navigate to find **api/2/user** and click on it:

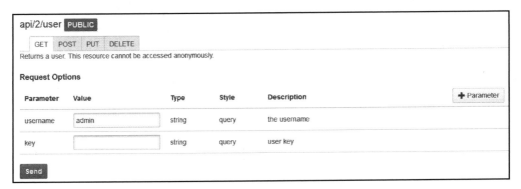

Enter `admin` as the value in the **username** parameter and click on the **Send** button. You will see the following response:

The response is actually in a JSON format, and you can see that it has returned the details of the `admin` user. However, the groups that this user is a part of are not returned in this response, but it's possible to fetch this information as well. Perform these steps:

1. Click on the **+Parameter** button on the right-hand side.
2. Enter `expand` in the **Parameter** column.
3. Enter `groups` in the **Value** column.
4. Click on the **Send** button again.

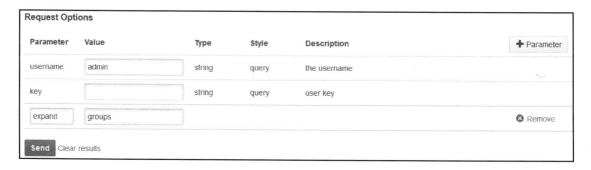

The following response is generated:

```
1  ▾ {
2      "self": "http://localhost:2990/jira/rest/api/2/user?username=admin",
3      "key": "admin",
4      "name": "admin",
5      "emailAddress": "admin@example.com",
6  ▾   "avatarUrls": {
7        "16x16": "http://localhost:2990/jira/secure/useravatar?size=xsmall&avatarId=10122",
8        "24x24": "http://localhost:2990/jira/secure/useravatar?size=small&avatarId=10122",
9        "32x32": "http://localhost:2990/jira/secure/useravatar?size=medium&avatarId=10122",
10       "48x48": "http://localhost:2990/jira/secure/useravatar?avatarId=10122"
11     },
12     "displayName": "admin",
13     "active": true,
14     "timeZone": "Asia/Calcutta",
15 ▾   "groups": {
16       "size": 3,
17 ▾     "items": [
18 ▾       {
19           "name": "jira-administrators",
20           "self": "http://localhost:2990/jira/rest/api/2/group?groupname=jira-administrators"
21         },
22 ▾       {
23           "name": "jira-developers",
24           "self": "http://localhost:2990/jira/rest/api/2/group?groupname=jira-developers"
25         },
26 ▾       {
27           "name": "jira-users",
28           "self": "http://localhost:2990/jira/rest/api/2/group?groupname=jira-users"
29         }
30       ]
31     },
32     "expand": "groups"
33 }
```

You can see that in the new response the groups that this user belongs to are also fetched by specifying the additional parameter.

JIRA REST API Browser is a great tool to help you get familiar with all the available resources, and it really assists in development.

Sample code to interact with the REST API

The REST API is supported by a variety of languages (such as Java, PHP, Python, and so on). In this chapter, we will discuss a couple of code examples in the PHP language. PHP is a popular language used in web applications. The following examples are written in PHP, but even if you are familiar with other languages, such as Java, then you should be able to understand the concept explained here.

To install PHP quickly, along with Apache, the XAMP SERVER package can be installed from https://www.apachefriends.org/.

Creating an issue using PHP

The sample code `create_issue.php` is used to create an issue using PHP as follows:

```php
<?php

define('JIRA_URL', 'http://localhost:2990/jira');
define('USERNAME', 'admin');
define('PASSWORD', 'admin');

//The function that is making the REST call using Curl Protocol

function post_to($resource, $data) {
  $curlname=CURLOPT_POST;
  $curlvalue=1;
  $jdata = json_encode($data);
  $ch = curl_init();
  curl_setopt_array($ch, array(
  $curlname => $curlvalue,
  CURLOPT_URL => JIRA_URL . '/rest/api/latest/' . $resource,
  CURLOPT_USERPWD => USERNAME . ':' . PASSWORD,
  CURLOPT_POSTFIELDS => $jdata,
  CURLOPT_HTTPHEADER => array('Content-type: application/json'),
  CURLOPT_RETURNTRANSFER => true
  ));
  $result = curl_exec($ch);
  curl_close($ch);
  return json_decode($result);
}

function create_issue($issue) {
  return post_to('issue', $issue);
}

//The issue details
```

```
$new_issue = array(
'fields' => array(
'project' => array('key' => 'GEN'),
'summary' => 'Test via REST',
'description' => 'Description of issue goes here.',
'issuetype' => array('name' => 'Task')
)
);

//Call the function to create the issue
$result = create_issue($new_issue);

//Print the output
if (property_exists($result, 'errors')) {
  echo "Error(s) creating issue:\n";
  var_dump($result);
} else {print_r($result);
  echo "New issue created at " . JIRA_URL ."/browse/{$result->key}\n";
}

?>
```

The preceding code creates an issue in a JIRA project with the GEN project key and the Task issue type. Let's understand what this code does.

Authenticating with JIRA

First, we need to define our JIRA URL, username, and password for authentication. Note that this user should have the permission to create the issue in the project:

```
define('JIRA_URL', 'http://localhost:2990/jira');
define('USERNAME', 'admin');
define('PASSWORD', 'admin');
```

Making the REST call to create the issue

The curl_exec() PHP function is used to make the REST call using the curl protocol. This function accepts the parameters to make the REST call. The username, password, and the issue data are passed in the following code:

```
function post_to($resource, $data) {
  $curlname=CURLOPT_POST;
  $curlvalue=1;
  $jdata = json_encode($data);
  $ch = curl_init();
  curl_setopt_array($ch, array(
  $curlname => $curlvalue,
  CURLOPT_URL => JIRA_URL . '/rest/api/latest/' . $resource,
```

```
    CURLOPT_USERPWD => USERNAME . ':' . PASSWORD,
    CURLOPT_POSTFIELDS => $jdata,
    CURLOPT_HTTPHEADER => array('Content-type: application/json'),
    CURLOPT_RETURNTRANSFER => true
    ));
    $result = curl_exec($ch);
    curl_close($ch);
    return json_decode($result);
}

function create_issue($issue) {
    return post_to('issue', $issue);
}
```

Issuing data and printing the output

The issue that needs to be created has a lot of information, such as the project key, summary, description, and issue type. This information is stored in the array. Finally, the output is printed when the code is run:

```
$new_issue = array(
'fields' => array(
'project' => array('key' => 'GEN'),
'summary' => 'Test via REST',
'description' => 'Description of issue goes here.',
'issuetype' => array('name' => 'Task')
)
);

//Call the function to create the issue
$result = create_issue($new_issue);

//Print the output
if (property_exists($result, 'errors')) {
  echo "Error(s) creating issue:\n";
  var_dump($result);
} else {print_r($result);
  echo "New issue created at " . JIRA_URL ."/browse/{$result->key}\n";
}
```

After you run the PHP code, you will get an output, as shown in the following command:

```
New issue created at http://hp:2990/jira/browse/GEN-2
```

Fetching issue details using PHP

The previous example was quite simple, where we created the issue using the REST API. Now, let's look at how to fetch the issue details that we just created:

```php
<?php

$username = 'admin';
$password = 'admin';

$url = 'http://localhost:2990/jira/rest/api/latest/issue/GEN-2';

$curl = curl_init();
curl_setopt($curl, CURLOPT_USERPWD, "$username:$password");
curl_setopt($curl, CURLOPT_URL, $url);
curl_setopt($curl, CURLOPT_RETURNTRANSFER, 1);
curl_setopt($curl, CURLOPT_FOLLOWLOCATION, 1);
curl_setopt($curl, CURLOPT_SSL_VERIFYPEER, 0);
curl_setopt($curl, CURLOPT_SSL_VERIFYHOST, 0);

$issue_list = (curl_exec($curl));
echo '<pre>';
print_r(json_decode($issue_list));
echo '</pre>';
?>
```

This is a simple code that is just fetching the details of the GEN-1 issue, which we created in the previous example. The output returned by the REST API is a JSON file. We have converted the JSON data to an array using the json_decode() PHP function and printed it using the print_r() function.

The previous code can be used to fetch user and group details; just change the $url variable.

Summary

In this chapter, you learned how to develop add-ons for JIRA. If you already have a working knowledge of Java, and have worked on Maven, then you have a good opportunity to learn add-on development for JIRA and other Atlassian tools. Whenever the existing functionality is not sufficient to serve your needs, you can always develop add-ons for JIRA. These add-ons are developed in the Java language and also utilize Apache Maven for build automation. In this chapter, we discussed how to set up the development environment and the Eclipse IDE. We also created a skeleton plugin project.

In the next chapter, you will learn how to migrate data to JIRA using the CSV file. JIRA provides migration tools for Bugzilla, Mantis, and a few other issue trackers, but if your existing issue tracker has a lot of customizations, then it's always preferable to migrate the data using CSV import, which is quite powerful. With careful planning, it can import complex data into JIRA. We will also take a look at the major aspects of JIRA's CSV import.

10
Importing and Exporting Data in JIRA and Migrating Configuration

The data stored in JIRA is quite critical for companies, and JIRA administrators should make sure that regular backups of data are taken. In fact, it should be policy to take backups. In this chapter, we will discuss how to perform regular backups in JIRA and where these backups are stored. Most importantly, we will also discuss how to restore these backups.

There are a lot of other tools that are used in companies; tools such as **Mantis** and **Bugzilla** are quite popular bug trackers. When you move to JIRA, it would be great if your existing issues were migrated from these tools to JIRA, but migrating can be a complex task. JIRA comes with some tools to import data from external tools; however, JIRA has a powerful feature that also imports issues from plain CSV files. With proper planning, data from any tool can be exported into CSV, and from CSV it can be imported into JIRA. We will also understand how to use the **Configuration Manager** add-on to migrate JIRA configurations such as issue types, workflows, and other schemes to another JIRA instance.

The topics covered are:

- The backup system
- External system import using CSV
- Migrating JIRA configurations using the Configuration Manager add-on

The backup system

JIRA administrators should pay a lot of attention to taking regular backups of data and its configuration. Luckily, JIRA comes with a handy tool for generating backups. It not only contains data (such as issues and projects), but it also contains JIRA configurations that are stored in the backup file, which means that when you restore the system, all the data along with various schemes for issue types and workflows will also be restored.

The backup system provided in the UI of JIRA is not particularly efficient when you have thousands of issues. For this, the recommended approach is to manually take a backup of your database. The details of this backup approach can be found at `https://confluence.a tlassian.com/display/DOC/Production+Backup+Strategy`.

Generating the backup

The JIRA backup tool can be used to perform backups as and when you require. Usually, before making any major configuration changes in JIRA, you should take a backup. Also, when you install a new add-on in JIRA, it's always advisable to take a backup. Of course, you should have a staging instance that should be an exact copy of your production one. You should do all the testing on the staging instance first, but you never know when things could go wrong. As a good practice, always take a backup before performing any major configuration changes.

Perform these steps to take a backup in JIRA using the JIRA backup tool:

1. Navigate to **Administration** | **System** | **Backup System** (under **IMPORT & EXPORT**):

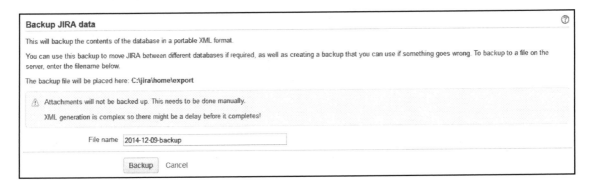

Backup JIRA data

This will backup the contents of the database in a portable XML format.

You can use this backup to move JIRA between different databases if required, as well as creating a backup that you can use if something goes wrong. To backup to a file on the server, enter the filename below.

The backup file will be placed here: C:\jira\home\export

⚠ Attachments will not be backed up. This needs to be done manually.

XML generation is complex so there might be a delay before it completes!

File name `2014-12-09-backup`

[Backup] Cancel

2. You will then see the **Backup JIRA data** page.
3. Specify the **File name** and click on the **Backup** button to generate the backup file. It's a good idea to use timestamp in **File name**.
4. The tool will then generate the backup file and give you the complete path of the file. You can copy this to some other location:

> ## Backup JIRA data
>
> Data exported to: C:\jira\home\export\2014-12-09-backup.zip

The backup files are stored in the `JIRA HOME` directory under the `export` folder.

Backup of attachments

JIRA's data consists of details of issues, projects, and various configurations, but there are file attachments that are also attached to issues. The **Backup JIRA data** tool generates an XML file that stores information, but it cannot back up the file attachments.

These attachments are stored in the `JIRA HOME` directory under the `data\attachments` folder. You should copy the `attachments` folder if the file needs to be backed up. Usually, this is done when the JIRA instance needs to be migrated to a new server. The file attachments are organized in different folders for every project and the project key is the name of the folder:

- The name of the attachment folder is project key, for example, `DPO`
- The files are store within a subfolder whose name is the same as the issue ID, for example, `DPO-6`

Using this organization, the attachment folder is easily restored.

Generating automatic backups

The backup that we just generated is usually triggered just before a JIRA administrator needs to perform some major changes in the configuration. However, as a good practice, it would be great if these backups were generated automatically daily, or perhaps weekly.

JIRA has the option to run a particular class automatically after a set time. JIRA comes with a couple of services preconfigured, but you can also add yours. Perform the following steps:

1. Navigate to **Administrator** | **System** | **Services** (under **ADVANCED**).
2. You will get the list of **Services** that come preconfigured when you install JIRA:

The first service in the list is the **Mail Queue Service**, which is responsible for taking regular backups. The **Schedule** is the interval after which the services will run automatically. In the case of **Backup Service**, the **Schedule** is **Every 720 minutes**, which is 12 hours; this means that after every 12 hours, the backup will be generated and placed in the `export` directory under `JIRA HOME`:

Name	Date modified	Type	Size
2014-12-09-backup	12/9/2014 2:48 PM	Compressed (zipp...	1,215 KB
2014-Nov-04--1819	11/4/2014 6:20 PM	Compressed (zipp...	1,183 KB
2014-Nov-05--0619	11/5/2014 6:20 AM	Compressed (zipp...	1,183 KB
2014-Nov-06--0619	11/6/2014 6:20 AM	Compressed (zipp...	1,206 KB
2014-Nov-14--1819	11/14/2014 6:20 PM	Compressed (zipp...	1,215 KB

As you can see in the previous screenshot, there are backup files generated by the JIRA service, except for `2014-12-09-backup`, which we generated manually. The format of the backup file remains the same irrespective of whether you generate it manually or if it's generated automatically.

As a good practice, always copy the backup files along with their attachments to a separate server. If something goes wrong with the server and the backups are kept on the same machine, they will also be lost. So, it's good to have them copied to a separate server. Preferably, write scripts to automate the process of copying backups to a backup server.

Restoring the system utility

Now, you have learned how to generate the backup manually using JIRA's **Backup System** tool and by relying on JIRA services. There are two scenarios when these backup files will be useful to you:

- One is when your server crashes
- Secondly, when you want to migrate your JIRA instance to a new machine

JIRA comes with the utility to **Restore System**; it basically wipes out the existing data/configuration and replaces it with one on the backup files; hence, you have to be very careful when using the **Restore System** utility. As a rule of thumb, always perform the restore process on a test environment; this will also give you a chance to learn about and fix any errors that you may encounter.

In this example, we will restore the `2014-12-09-backup.zip` backup file, which we generated in the previous section.

For this exercise, you should have a blank JIRA installation on a different machine with the same version as the one used to generate the backup. Perform the following steps:

1. Copy the backup file stored in the `JIRA HOME` directory under the `import` folder.

2. Navigate to **Administration** | **System** | **Restore System** (under **IMPORT & EXPORT**):

3. Enter **File name** as `2014-12-09-backup.zip`, which is the backup file we generated previously.

4. Leave the **License** field empty; the license details of the source instance are stored in the backup file, which can be restored in the target instance; if you want to use a new license, only then enter it in this field.

5. In the **Outgoing Mail** field, select **Disable**. This will ensure that e-mails are not being sent to anyone when the restore process takes place.

6. Click on the **Restore** button:

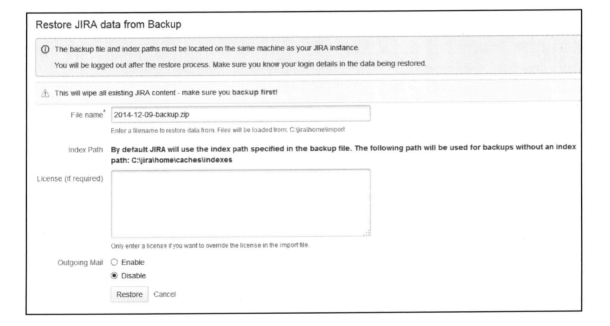

7. The restore process will start reading the backup file and will also display the restore progress. This whole restore process can take several minutes depending on the size of the backup file:

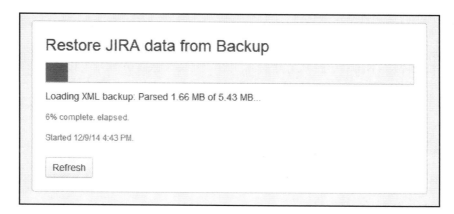

8. Once the restore process is complete, you will get a confirmation message:

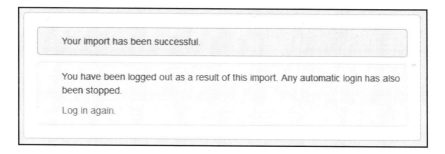

After the restore process is complete, you can log in to the JIRA instance using the login and password credentials of the instance from which the backup was generated. Your login of the current JIRA instance will not work because the whole data has been wiped out and replaced by the backup file.

You can verify the following after the restoration:

- Issue count
- List of projects
- List of configurations
- User count

If these things match with your old instance and the restored instance, then the restore process was successful.

Project Import utility

The **Restore System** procedure is performed when the complete instance has to be restored or moved to another server, but there can be a scenario when you just need to restore a single project from another JIRA instance.

Let's take an example of a company that has multiple JIRA instances used by various other business units. These business units work independently of each other; they have different teams and work from different geographic locations. As you know, these days companies reorganize quite often. Due to this reorganization process, a few projects from one business unit need to be transferred to another business unit. All the project code and documents along with the projects need to be transferred as well.

In this case, we cannot simply take a backup of one instance and restore it in another because it will wipe out the data in the target instance. The restore process has to be done for a few selected projects only.

Atlassian understood this scenario and provided a tool called **Project Import** for performing just that:

1. Navigate to **Administration** | **System** | **Project Import** (under **IMPORT & EXPORT**).
2. Enter the name of the backup **File name** from which you want to perform **Project Import**.
3. Copy the attachments in the `JIRA HOME` under the `import\attachments` directory; the exact path specific to your machine will also be displayed.

4. Click on the **Next** button to continue:

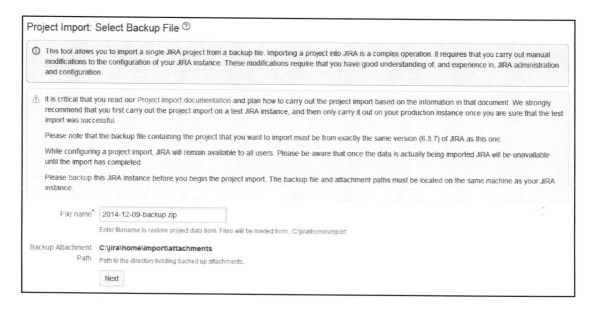

5. The **Project Import** utility will read the backup file and display the progress. Depending on the size of the backup file, it may take several minutes to complete:

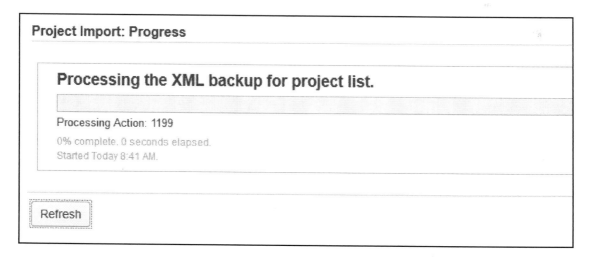

6. On the next screen, the list of the entire project in the backup file will be presented to you.

7. You can now select the project that you want to import from the **Projects from Backup** drop-down list.

8. The details of the project that you select will also be displayed. The **Project** field displays the name. The **Key** field displays the project key, and **Issues** displays the issue count.

9. Click on the **Next** button to continue:

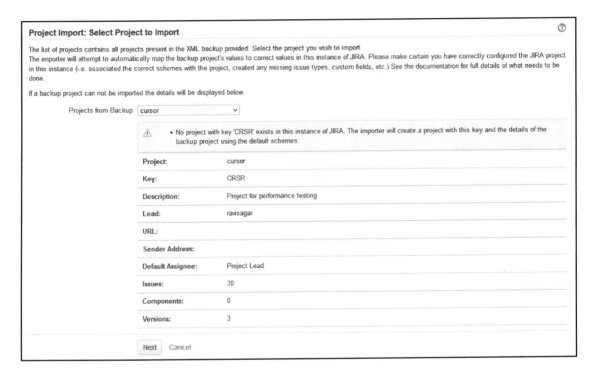

Project Import: Select Project to Import

The list of projects contains all projects present in the XML backup provided. Select the project you wish to import.
The importer will attempt to automatically map the backup project's values to correct values in this instance of JIRA. Please make certain you have correctly configured the JIRA project in this instance (i.e. associated the correct schemes with the project, created any missing issue types, custom fields, etc.) See the documentation for full details of what needs to be done.

If a backup project can not be imported the details will be displayed below.

Projects from Backup [cursor ⌄]

⚠   • No project with key 'CRSR' exists in this instance of JIRA. The importer will create a project with this key and the details of the backup project using the default schemes.

Project:	cursor
Key:	CRSR
Description:	Project for performance testing
Lead:	ravisagar
URL:	
Sender Address:	
Default Assignee:	Project Lead
Issues:	30
Components:	0
Versions:	3

[Next]   Cancel

10. The projects in the backup file may have some fields that are not present in the target instance. The **Project Import** tool will attempt to map them to the existing fields. Before attempting the import procedure, you need to make sure that all the custom fields are created in the target instance.

11. If the mapping is complete, click on the **Import** button to continue:

Project Import: Pre-Import Summary - cursor

The results of automatic mapping are displayed below. You will not be able to continue if any validation errors were raised.

Please note that performing an import will cause JIRA to be unavailable to all users until the import has completed.
- Refresh validations - re-maps and validates the backup data against the current state of JIRA.

System Fields

- ✅ Issue Type
- ✅ Custom Field Configuration
- ✅ Status
- ✅ Priority
- ✅ Resolution
- ✅ Users
- ✅ Project Role
- ✅ Project Role Membership
- ✅ Group
- ✅ Issue Link Type
- ✅ Issue Security Level
- ✅ Attachments

Custom Fields

- ✅ Pressurized
- ✅ Department Type

[Previous] [Import] Cancel

12. Depending on the size of the project, it may take several minutes to complete; the progress will be shown on the screen:

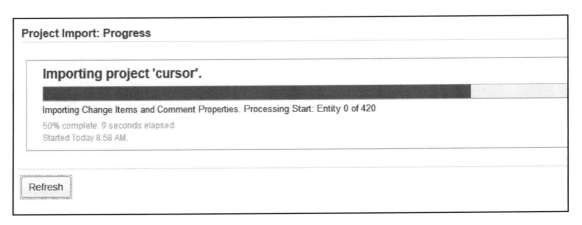

13. After the import process is successful, the result of **Project Import** will be displayed on the screen.
14. Verify the results and click on the **OK** button:

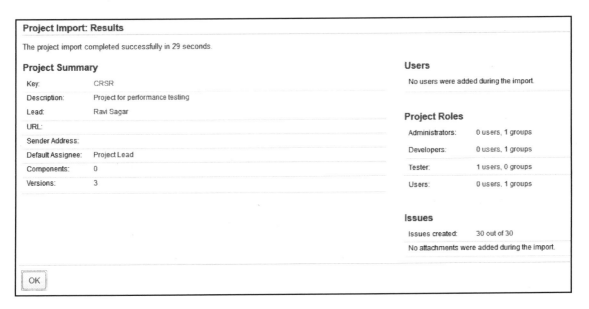

15. Repeat the process for all the other projects that need to be imported.

The **Project Import** process is a complex procedure and has to be first performed on the test instance. Read the official documentation to understand more about this procedure at `https ://confluence.atlassian.com/adminjiraserver71/restoring-a-project-from-backu p-82592982.html`.

> Backups should be generated using the same version of the target JIRA instance.
>
> Project configurations such as issue type schemes, field configurations, workflows, notifications, and permission schemes should be created on the target instance.
>
> Custom fields that are used in the project need to be created in the target instance.
>
> If there are certain add-ons installed and used by the project, then install them on the target instance first; there are certain custom fields created by add-ons and until you install the plugin on the target instance, these custom fields will not be mapped.

External system import using CSV

There are various issue tracking tools that have been available for many years on the market. There are tools such as Bugzilla, which is used primarily for bug tracking. There is another popular tool called Mantis that provides a good set of features, which again is used for bug tracking. Companies who are already using some of these tools and now want to move to JIRA can migrate their data using various importers provided by JIRA out of the box.

Follow these steps to perform the CSV import:

1. Navigate to **Administration** | **System** | **External System Import** (Under **IMPORT & EXPORT**).
2. You will get the list of various importers, as shown in the following screenshot:

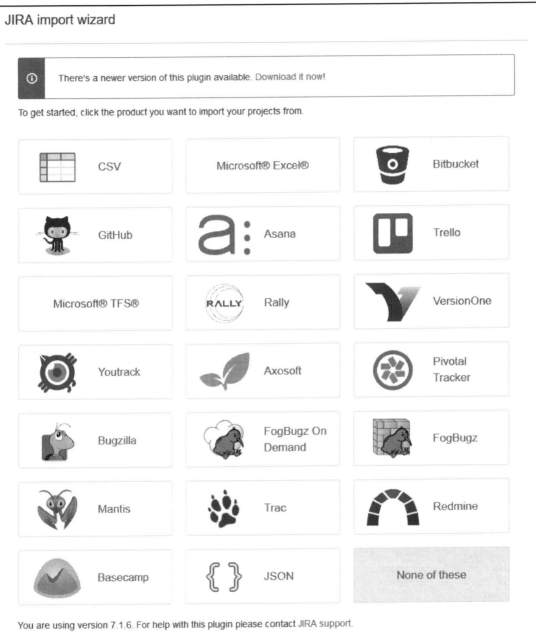

If you are using any of the tools mentioned in the previous screenshot, then you can try to import the data from your existing tool. There are also other import tools available that have been developed by third-party vendors. These can be downloaded from the Atlassian Marketplace. You can give them a try.

These importers usually work well when there are not many customizations in your existing tool, but this is not the case most of the time. The first importer called **CSV** is a general purpose tool that can be used to import data from a CSV file into JIRA. We recommend to first export your data from your existing tool into a CSV file and then use this tool to import the data into JIRA.

The data that needs to be imported into JIRA can be quite complex; issues could also be subtasks of other issues and there could be a need to upload the attachments too.

Let's take a look at a few scenarios that can be used to import CSV into JIRA.

A simple CSV import

Let's understand how to perform a simple import of the CSV data. The first thing to do is to prepare the CSV file that will be imported into JIRA. For this exercise, we will import issues into a particular project; these issues will contain data such as issue **Summary**, **Status**, **Dates**, and a few other fields.

Preparing the CSV file

We are going to use MS Excel to prepare the CSV file with the following data:

	Project	Summary	Issue Type	Status	Priority	Resolution	Assignee	Reporter	Created	Resolved
1	Project	Summary	Issue Type	Status	Priority	Resolution	Assignee	Reporter	Created	Resolved
2	DOPT	Add PDF export feature in the bar charts	Improvement	Closed	Blocker	Unresolved	Frank Martin	Frank Martin	9/25/2014 0:54	9/27/2014 0:54
3	DOPT	Create an RSS feed of all the news items on the website	New Feature	Reopened	Minor	Unresolved	Michael Jones	Ravi Sagar	9/12/2014 20:54	9/13/2014 11:54
4	DOPT	Please enable HTML format in newsletter emails	Improvement	Resolved	Minor	Won't Fix	Ravi Sagar	Michael Jones	8/31/2014 16:54	9/1/2014 7:54
5	DOPT	The breakpoints need to be reduced by 10px for mobile devices	New Feature	Closed	Blocker	Unresolved	Ravi Sagar	Michael Jones	8/19/2014 12:54	8/19/2014 21:54
6	DOPT	The cron jobs need to be modified to run every 15 minutes	Task	Closed	Critical	Unresolved	Michael Jones	Frank Martin	8/7/2014 8:54	8/7/2014 20:54

If your existing tool has the option to export directly into the CSV file, then you can skip this step, but we recommend reviewing your data before importing it into JIRA. Usually, the CSV import will not work if the format of the CSV file and the data is not correct.

It's very easy to generate a CSV file from an Excel file. Perform these steps:

1. Go to **File** | **Save As** | **File name:** and select **Save as type:** as **CSV (Comma delimited)**. If you don't have Microsoft Excel installed, you can use LibreOffice Calc, which is an open source alternative for Microsoft Office Excel:

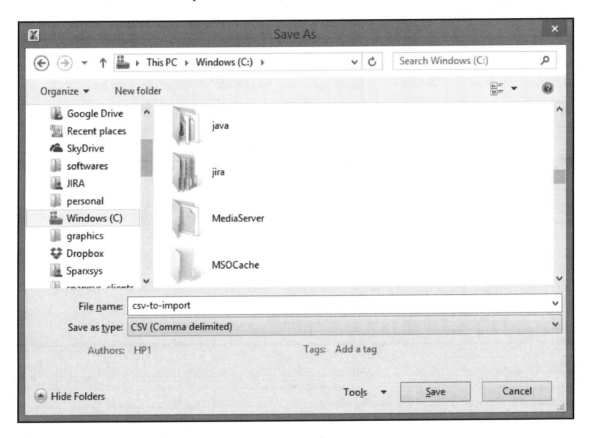

2. You can open the CSV file to verify its format too:

```
Project,Summary,Issue Type,Status,Priority,Resolution,Assignee,Reporter,Created,Resolved
DOPT,Add PDF export feature in the bar charts,Improvement,Closed,Blocker,Unresolved,Frank Martin,Frank Martin,9/25/2014 0:54,9/27/2014 0:54
DOPT,Create an RSS feed of all the news items on the website,New Feature,Reopened,Minor,Unresolved,Michael Jones,Ravi Sagar,9/12/2014 20:54
DOPT,Please enable HTML format in newsletter emails,Improvement,Resolved,Minor,Won't Fix,Ravi Sagar,Michael Jones,8/31/2014 16:54,9/1/2014
DOPT,The breakpoints need to be reduced by 10px for mobile devices,New Feature,Closed,Blocker,Unresolved,Ravi Sagar,Michael Jones,8/19/2014
DOPT,The cron jobs need to be modified to run every 15 minutes,Task,Closed,Critical,Unresolved,Michael Jones,Frank Martin,8/7/2014 8:54,8/7
```

Our CSV file has the following fields:

CSV Field	Purpose
Project	JIRA's project key needs to be specified in this field
Summary	This field is mandatory and needs to be specified in the CSV file
Issue Type	This is important for specifying the issue type
Status	This displays the status of the issue; these are workflow states that need to exist in JIRA, and the project workflow should have the states that are going to be imported into the CSV file
Priority	The priorities mentioned here should exist in JIRA before import
Resolution	The resolutions mentioned here should exist in JIRA before import
Assignee	This specifies the assignee of the issue
Reporter	This specifies the reporter of the issue
Created	This is the issue creation date
Resolved	This is the issue resolution date

Performing the CSV import

Once your CSV file is prepared, then you are ready to perform the import in JIRA:

1. Navigate to **Administration** | **System** | **External System Import** | **Import from Comma-separated values (CSV)** (under **IMPORT & EXPORT**).
2. On the **File import** screen in the **CSV Source File** field, click on the **Browse...** button to select the CSV file that you just prepared on your machine.

3. Once you select the CSV file, the **Next** button will be enabled:

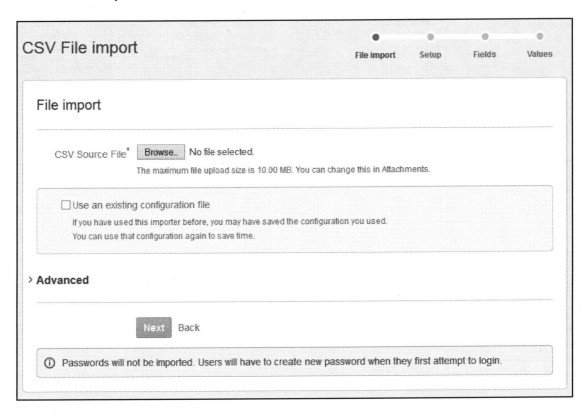

4. On the **Setup** screen, select **Import to Project** as **DOPT**, which is the name of our project.
5. Verify **Date format**, and it should match the format of the date values in the CSV file.
6. Click on the **Next** button to continue.
7. On the **Map fields** screen; we need to map the fields in the CSV file to JIRA fields. This step is crucial because in your old system, the field names may be different to JIRA fields, so in this step map these fields to the respective JIRA fields.

8. Click on the **Next** button to continue.

9. On the **Map values** screen, map the values of **Status**; in fact, this mapping of field values can be done for any field. In our case, the values in the status field are the same as in JIRA, so click on the **Begin Import** button.

10. You will finally get a confirmation that issues have been imported successfully:

⊘ 0 projects and 5 issues imported successfully!

If you encounter any errors during the CSV import, then it's usually due to some problem with the CSV format. Read the error messages carefully and correct these issues. As mentioned earlier, the CSV import needs to be performed on the test environment first.

The import that we just performed is straightforward, but it's possible to import data with complexities too.

Creating subtasks using the CSV file

There are cases when issues need to be imported as subtasks. In such cases, use the format shown in the following screenshot:

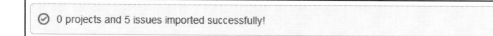

Summary	Issue Type	Issue ID	Parent ID	Status	Priority
Add PDF export feature in the bar charts	Improvement			Closed	Blocker
Create an RSS feed of all the news items on the website	New Feature			Reopened	Minor
Please enable HTML format in newsletter emails	Improvement			Resolved	Minor
The breakpoints need to be reduced by 10px for mobile devices	New Feature			Closed	Blocker
The cron jobs need to be modified to run every 15 minutes	Task	9910		Closed	Critical
Please configure the cron for newsletter	Sub-task		9910	Closed	Minor
Configure the cron for new registrations	Sub-task		9910	Reopened	Blocker
Cron for email verifications	Sub-task		9910	Resolved	Critical
Cron to download updates automatically	Sub-task		9910	Closed	Minor
Configure the cron for In active accounts	Sub-task		9910	Resolved	Blocker

Note the two columns, that is, **Issue ID** and **Parent ID**; populate the **Issue ID** column with a random number for the parent task and enter this random number in the **Parent ID** column for all the subtasks.

Issue ID and **Parent ID** need to be mapped to **Sub-Tasks | Issue Id** and **Sub-Tasks | Parent Id** during the CSV import respectively, as shown in the following screenshot:

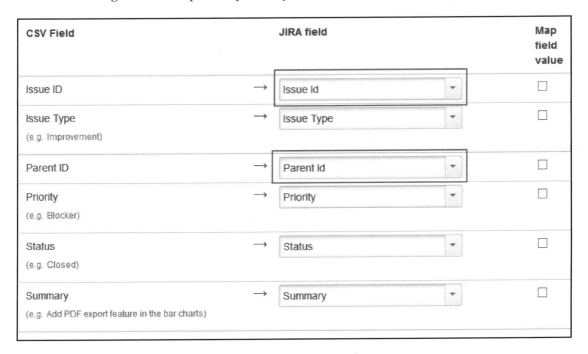

Proceed with the CSV import as usual and subtasks will be created.

Uploading attachments using the CSV file

It's usually desirable to attach files to the issues that need to be imported into JIRA.

Perform these steps:

1. Create a `csvimport` folder in your `JIRA HOME/import/attachments` directory. So, the final path should look like this:

   `<JIRA_Home>/import/attachments/csvimport/`

2. The CSV JIRA import can read the particular directory using the `FILE` protocol. It's used to access the files stored on the same machine; the full path of the files needs to be specified.

3. Add a column called `Attachments` in your CSV file and enter the location in the following format:

   ```
   file://csvimport/file1.pdf
   ```

4. The file should finally look similar to the following screenshot:

Summary	Issue Type	Attachments	Status	Priority
Add PDF export feature in the bar charts	Improvement	file://csvimport/file1.pdf	Closed	Blocker
Create an RSS feed of all the news items on the website	New Feature	file://csvimport/image1.jpg	Reopened	Minor
Please enable HTML format in newsletter emails	Improvement	file://csvimport/file2.pdf	Resolved	Minor
The breakpoints need to be reduced by 10px for mobile devices	New Feature	file://csvimport/file3.pdf	Closed	Blocker
The cron jobs need to be modified to run every 15 minutes	Task	file://csvimport/image2.jpg	Closed	Critical

Don't forget to map this new `Attachments` column to the **Attachments** JIRA field; the rest of the process remains the same.

Your issues may have multiple attachments instead of just one. In such cases, add an additional column for each attachment. Similarly, other fields with multiple values can be imported by simply adding multiple columns.

Updating existing issues

There is another very good use of the CSV import tool. So far, we have seen how to import data into JIRA, but there are times when existing issues need to be modified. For instance, if you want to add a new fixed version to the issues of a particular project or if you want to resolve certain issues in bulk; in such cases, it's possible to use the CSV import tool.

In the CSV file, just add another column of `Issue Key` and add the columns as JIRA fields that need to be updated. If the CSV tool finds the issue key, then it will take the rest of the columns and update them in the existing issues.

However, there is also a **Bulk Change** tool in **Issue Navigator**, which does the same thing. It's up to your comfort level and use case to choose the method convenient to you. We recommend using the **Bulk Change** tool as it's much easier compared to the CSV import tool.

Migrate JIRA configurations using the Configuration Manager add-on

We have discussed how to fully restore a JIRA instance from a backup file, restore a specific project, and how to use the CSV import functionality with important data in JIRA. These utilities are so important that they really make the lives of JIRA administrators easier. They can perform these activities right from the JIRA user interface. The **Project Import** utility and CSV import are used for migrating one or more projects from one instance of JIRA to another, but the target instance should have the required configuration in place, otherwise these utilities will not work. For instance, if there is a project in a source instance with custom workflow states along with a few custom fields, then the exact configuration of workflow and custom fields should already exist in the target instance. Re-creating these configurations and schemes could be a time-consuming and error prone process.

In various organizations, there is also a test environment or staging server for JIRA, where all the new configurations are first tested before being rolled out to the production instance. Currently, there is no such way to selectively migrate the configurations from one instance to another. It has to be done manually on the target instance.

Configuration Manager is an add-on that does this job. Using this add-on, the project specific configuration can be migrated from one instance to another.

Generate a snapshot

The following steps will guide you through the steps required to generate a project-specific snapshot that can be migrated and deployed on the target JIRA instance:

1. Go to **Administration** | **Add-ons** | **Find new add-ons** under **ATLASSIAN MARKETPLACE,** type `Configuration Manager` in the search box and press the *Enter* key:

2. The **Configuration Manager for JIRA** will appear. Click on the **Free trial** button to install this add-on on your instance. In the pop-up window that appears next, click on the **Accept** button.

3. Finally, you will be asked to enter your Atlassian account to generate a trial license.

4. Once installed, go to **Administration** | **Configuration Manager** | **Snapshots**. On this screen, you can generate a snapshot of a project's configuration. Click on the **Create Snapshot** button:

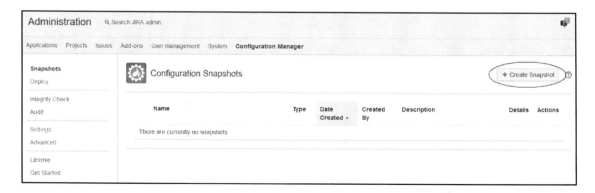

5. In the **Select Snapshot Type** screen, make sure that the second tab **Project Configuration** is selected on the top right corner of the screen. Enter the **Name**, select one or more **Project(s)** from the drop down, tick the checkbox **Include custom fields with value in at least one issue** and enter a meaningful description. Press the **Next** button to continue:

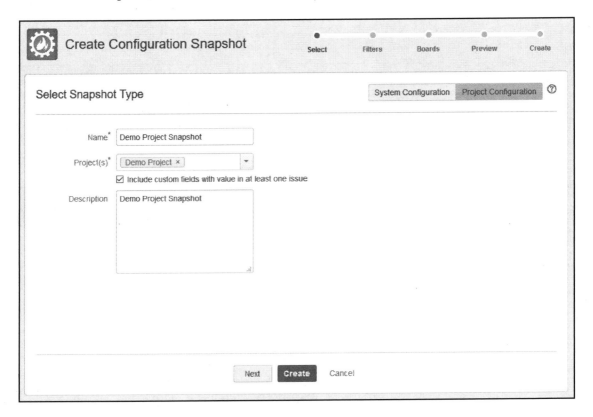

6. In the **Select Filters** screen, select the filters that are used in this project. If your project also has Agile boards, you need to select the filters used in your project as the Agile boards depend on filters. Press the **Next** button to continue:

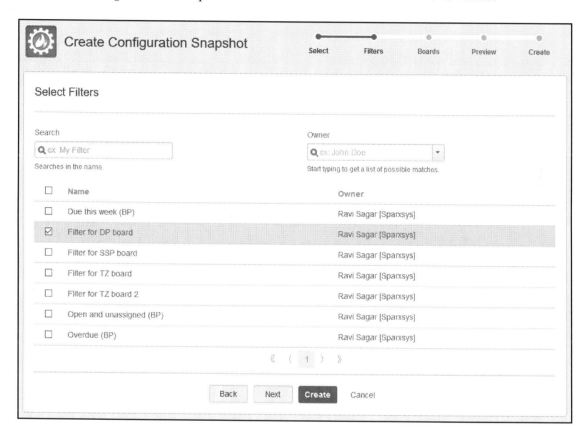

7. In the **Select Agile Boards** screen, select the Scrum or Kanban boards that you want migrated. Make sure that, as in the previous step, you have selected the filters that are used in the boards you want to migrate. Press the **Next** button to continue:

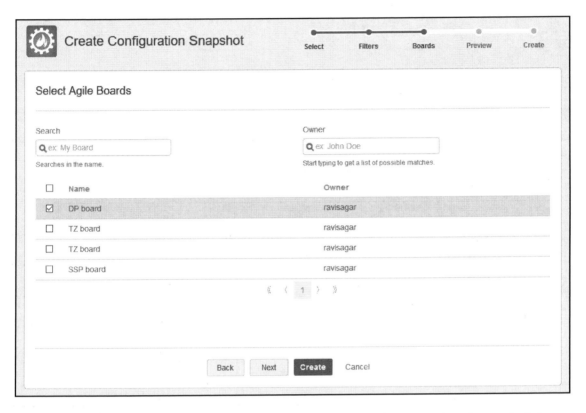

8. In the **Preview Snapshot** screen, review the items that are migrating and click on the **Create** button to generate the snapshot:

9. Finally, the snapshot will be generated. You can download the snapshot file by clicking on the cog icon under the **Actions** column for the respective snapshot and clicking on **Download**:

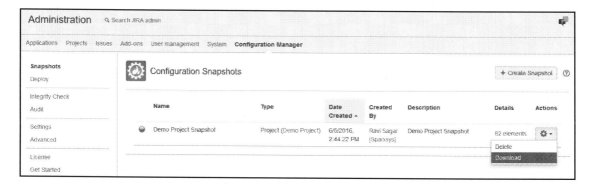

10. Save the snapshot file on your computer. Its name will be `Demo Project Snapshot.zip`.

Deploying a snapshot

The following steps will guide you through deploying the snapshot that you have generated on your source JIRA instance:

1. Go to **Administration** | **Configuration Manager** | **Deploy**. On this screen you can generate a snapshot of a project's configuration. Click on the **From Snapshot File** tab on the top right corner. Then, click on the **Browse** button and select the `Demo Project Snapshot.zip` from your computer that you saved after generating the snapshot:

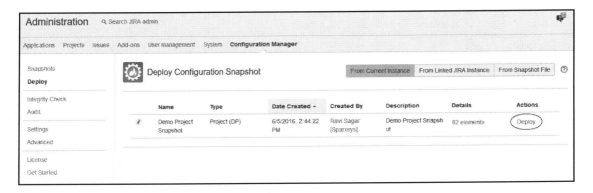

2. Once the snapshot file is uploaded to your target JIRA server, it will be listed. Click on the **Deploy** link under the **Actions** column specific to your snapshot file.

3. In the **Select Deployment Mode** screen, select the **New Project** tab in the top right corner. Enter a project **Name** and **Key**. These will also be suggested based on your old project details from the snapshot file. Press the **Next** button to continue:

4. In the **Analyze Configuration Changes** screen, review the configurations that will be added, modified, or removed from the target instance. Please spend considerable time on this screen to understand the impact of existing configurations on the target JIRA instance. Press the **Next** button to continue:

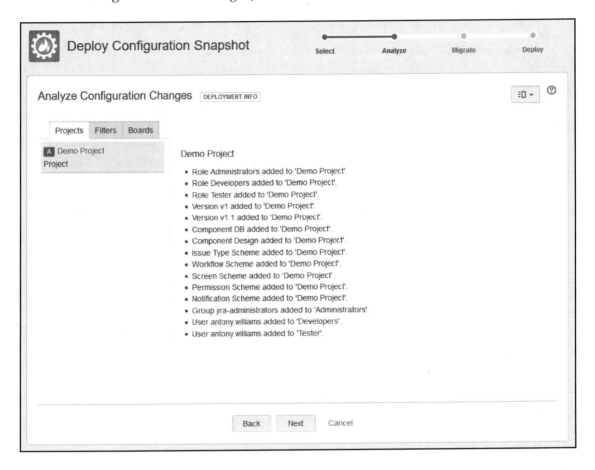

5. In the **Migrate Configuration Changes** screen, the Configuration Manager tells us that no issues data migration is required, so press the **Next** button to continue:

6. In the **Deploy** screen, just press the **Deploy** button to start the deployment:

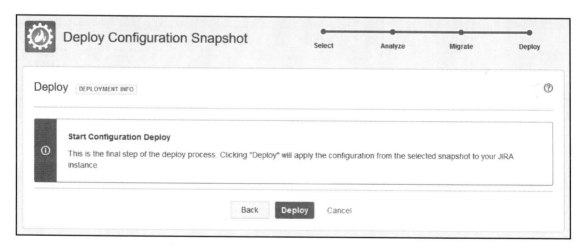

7. Finally, you will get a confirmation message in the **Snapshot deployed** screen:

The Configuration Manager add-on is quite powerful. It can migrate all the project-specific configurations like issue types, workflows, custom fields, roles, permission, and notification schemes. The simple example that we just showed you in this section should give you enough understanding of the usage of this useful add-on.

After moving the configurations and creating a blank project by the Configuration Manager add-on, you can now perform data migration using the **Project Import** utility that we discussed earlier in this chapter. This add-on can save hundreds of man hours by avoiding the manual recreation of your configurations.

Summary

In this chapter, you learned how to import and export data into JIRA. We started with understanding how to take a backup of the entire JIRA instance. You also learned how to restore the instance from this backup. We also looked at scenarios where you want to import selected projects from the backup file. We spent considerable time understanding how to migrate data to JIRA using the CSV file, which provides a lot of flexibility in importing not only simple data, but also complex data with subtasks and attachments as well. Finally, we also understood how to use the Configuration Manager add-on in order to easily migrate configurations from one instance of JIRA to another.

In the next chapter, we will understand how to implement Scrum and Kanban methodologies in JIRA using a powerful add-on from Atlassian called **JIRA Agile** for Agile tracking. This chapter will cover two scenarios of both techniques. We will discuss how to set up and configure the board, and most importantly how to analyze reports. You will also learn these two Agile techniques and basic concepts with practical examples.

11
Working with Agile Boards in JIRA Software

In this chapter, we will understand how to implement two Agile methodologies called **Scrum** and **Kanban** in JIRA for Agile tracking. The key concepts of **JIRA Agile** that will be covered are creating, planning, and managing the tasks. We will discuss how to set up and configure the board. Most importantly, we will discuss how to analyze reports. Scrum masters and Project managers will give you insight on how to use JIRA Agile, which will enable you to manage work following the Agile concept. Real-life examples will be used to understand Scrum and Kanban boards.

The topics covered are:

- Product overview—JIRA Software
- Scrum boards
- Kanban boards
- Managing multiple teams and projects using boards

Product overview – JIRA Software

So far, we have seen various aspects of JIRA, such as customization, and we have also seen how to install new add-ons to extend the functionality of JIRA. Many organizations use Agile-based methodologies for their projects, and until version 6.x there was a popular add-on called JIRA Agile that had to be purchased separately. However, starting from version 7.x, the JIRA as it used to be known had been split into three applications—JIRA Core, JIRA Software, and JIRA Service Desk. We also discussed this in Chapter 1, *Planning Your JIRA Installation*.

The customizations and configurations that we have discussed in this book are relevant to JIRA Core as well as JIRA Software and JIRA Service Desk. In Chapter 15, *Implementing JIRA Service Desk*, we will understand how to use it for managing your support projects, but in this chapter we will focus on Agile boards, which comes with your JIRA Software application.

JIRA Software provides great features for implementing Agile techniques in your JIRA instance. Whether you are already familiar with Agile concepts or are completely new to Agile, this add-on will make your Agile journey not only easy, but also wonderful.

Installing the JIRA Software application

If you already have the JIRA Software application installed, then you don't need to do anything else— your instance already has the capability to create Agile boards. However, if you are only using JIRA Core or the JIRA Service Desk application, then you need to install JIRA Software application.

1. Go to the following URL and download the latest version of JIRA Software jira-software-application.obr file on your computer from https://marketplace.atlassian.com/plugins/com.atlassian.jira.jira-software-application/versions.

2. Go to **Administration** | **Applications** | **Versions & licenses**, then click on the **Upload an application** link in the top right corner. In the pop-up that appears, upload the jira-software-application.obr file that you just downloaded:

3. This will install the JIRA Software application. Now, you should go to the following URL to generate an evaluation license for application at http://my.atlassian.com/.

4. Now you should be able to create Agile boards in your instance. You will notice a new menu item, **Boards** at the top:

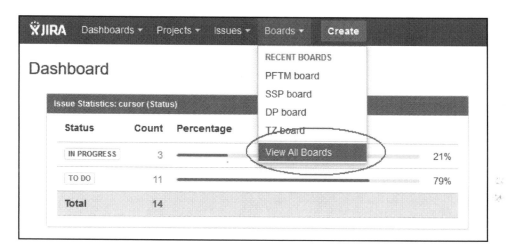

5. Now, go to **Boards** | **View All Boards**, as shown in the previous screenshot.

6. In the pop up that appears, you will see the option to either create a Scrum board or Kanban board. Let's create both the boards one at a time.

In JIRA Software, you can create both Scrum and Kanban boards; both are used for a specific purpose.

Scrum boards

Scrum is an Agile technique used in complex projects. This technique is widely used in software development projects, but it can be applied to any process easily. To know more about the Scrum technique, refer to `https://www.scrumalliance.org/why-scrum`.

The Scrum technique focuses on breaking up the requirements into small doable tasks. Then, a prioritized list of these tasks is created (called a **sprint**), which can be performed in a period of one to four weeks. The objective of this sprint is to create a deliverable feature or product and not just a prototype. More sprints can be created to complete the whole requirement and finish the product or project. The tasks that are yet to be done are kept in a list called a **backlog**.

JIRA Agile lets you implement the Scrum technique in your process with the help of Scrum boards.

Agile project setup and JIRA Agile configuration basics

Scrum boards can be created from any existing JIRA project that contains predefined issues. It's possible to create a Scrum board from a new blank project as well. Also, if you want to understand how JIRA Agile works, it's possible to create a sample project prepopulated with sample data. Perform these steps:

1. In the navigation menu, click on **Boards** | **View All Boards** | **Create board**, and in the **Create an Agile board** pop-up, click on the **Create a Scrum board with sample data**:

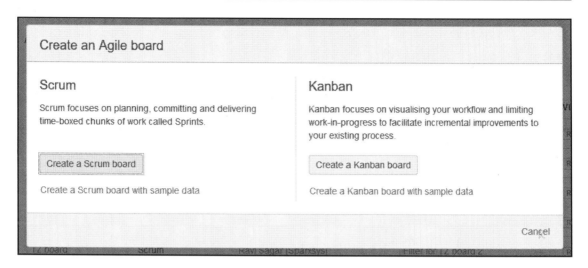

We are creating a sample project that will contain dummy data. This will help us understand all the features of a Scrum board.

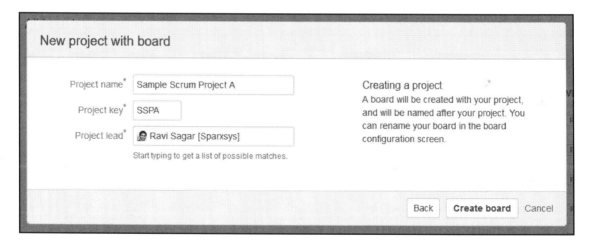

2. Enter the **Project name**, **Project key**, and **Project lead** and click on the **Create board** button.

We have just created a project with sample data along with a Scrum board. You can also create a Scrum board and select your existing project to populate it.

Populating, ranking, and estimating a backlog using story points

In the newly created project we have a Scrum board, which is displayed by default, so you will now see the list of issues that are pending, that is, not yet resolved in the **Backlog** window, and a sample sprint:

Backlog contains issues that are pending in the project or board. These issues are yet to be planned for execution. In the project sidebar, the first tab is **Backlog**, followed by **Active sprints**. As soon as the sprint has started, you manage and work on it using the **Active sprints** tab.

The sample Scrum board already contains a sprint that has certain issues in a specific order. Sprint is a time period during which specific planned activities need to be finished. The Scrum master or the project manager can define the order in which issues need to be completed. This order is also known as **rank**, and the team who is working on these issues needs to follow this order. The rank is important because there are certain tasks that need to be completed before other tasks can be started.

In a Scrum methodology, the estimation of individual tasks is not only done on the basis of the amount of time spent, but also on the complexity of the tasks. For instance, there are two tasks whose time estimate is one day, but the first task is complex to execute, for example if it is the first time that the task has been executed by the team. The complexity is measured by story points. The story point can be any number between 1 to 10 or any number in the Fibonacci sequence, that is, 1, 1, 2, 3, 5, 8, 13, 21. The higher the number, the more complex the task.

A Scrum master can assign story points to the issues in the sprint, although it's not mandatory to have story points with each issue in the sprint. However, having them will give the team an idea about the complexity of the issue.

Planning and creating sprints

The sample Scrum board already contains one running sprint; let's create a new sprint. JIRA Software allows you to create another sprint even if the active sprint is not complete; however, the new sprint cannot be started. It is possible to enable the **Parallel Sprints** feature in JIRA Agile that lets us run multiple sprints together.

The planning of the sprint has to be done in the **Plan** mode of the Scrum board. Perform these steps to run multiple sprints together:

1. Navigate to **Administration** | **Applications** | **JIRA Software configurations** (under **JIRA SOFTWARE**):

> JIRA Software configuration
>
> This page lets you enable and disable certain features of JIRA Software.
>
> Features   ☑ Parallel Sprints
>
>   Allows a new sprint to be started when one is already in progress.

2. Tick the checkbox for **Parallel Sprints**.

   That is it, just go back to your board and start planning your next sprint.

3. Go back to the project, and in the **Backlog** tab click on the **Create Sprint** button just before the issue backlog:

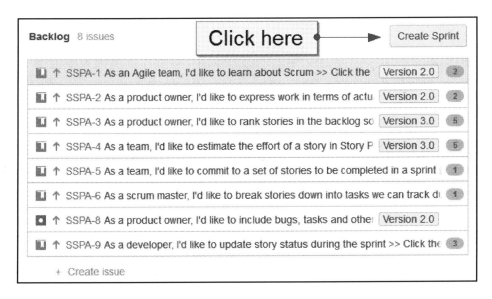

4. An empty sprint will be created.
5. Now, start dragging your issues from **Backlog** to your sample sprint (in our case **Sample Sprint 3**):

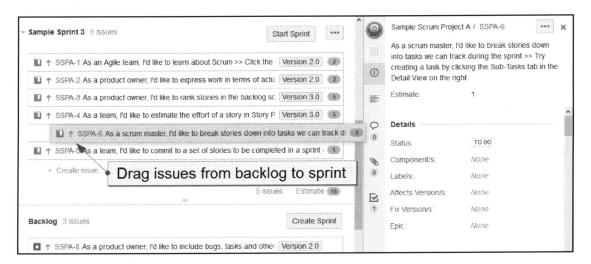

6. Once you have put all your issues in the sprint, you may reorder them within the sprint and define their rank, that is, which issue needs to be performed first, second, and so on.

7. Optionally, you can also create epics to group multiple stories together. Epic is nothing but a large story. It's quite easy to create an epic. Click on the **Create epic** link on the left-hand side of the sprint:

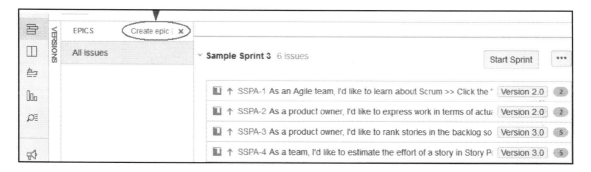

8. In the pop-up window, enter **Epic Name** and **Summary**. Click on the **Create** button to continue:

9. You can create more epics; finally, drag issues from your sprint to the epic. This will assign issues to be part of these epics:

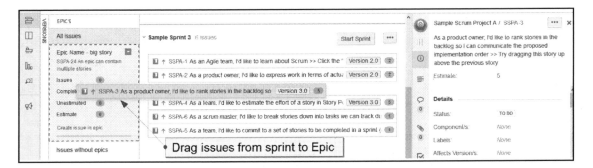

10. After assigning issues to epic, you can start the sprint. Click on the **Start Sprint** link in the top-right corner. In the pop-up window, enter **Sprint Name**, select **Duration** and **Start Date**, and **End Date** will be updated automatically:

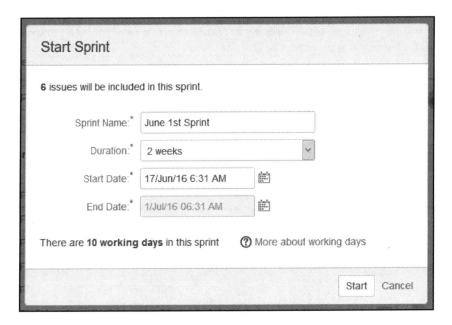

Note that a sprint is never started until you have planned your issues well, ordered them, and estimated the story points. The moment you start the sprint, you will be taken to the **Active sprints** tab in the Scrum board. Here, you will see a list of all the issues in your sprints across three columns, that is, **To Do**, **In Progress**, **Done**:

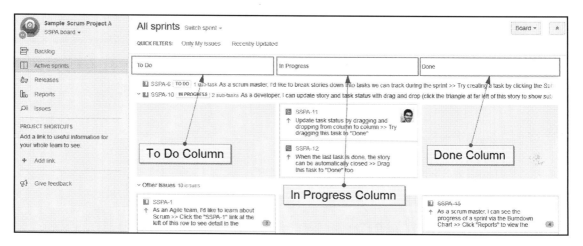

In the **Active sprints** tabs, the individual assignee can drag the issue to either the **In Progress** column or the **Done** column. This is similar to making workflow transitions.

There are a lot of customizations that can be done in the **Active sprints** to make it more effective.

Configuring swimlanes, card colors, edit card fields, and quick filters

Active sprints is the section in the board that is monitored by the team members once the sprint is running. When the number of people working on the sprint is too high, it may get difficult for them to find the issues they are working on. Let's take a look at some of the customizations done to the Scrum board.

Swimlanes

The issues that appear in the **Work** mode can be grouped together so that it becomes easy for the respective member to find that issue on the board. Also, when the issues are dragged from one column to another, they can only be dragged within their group, which is known as a swimlane. The default swimlane is the **Story** issue type. Let's change this:

1. Navigate to **Board | Configure | Swimlanes** (under **CONFIGURATION**):

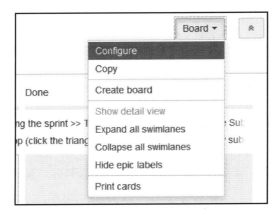

2. Select **Assignees** for **Base Swimlanes on** from the drop-down list and set **Unassigned issues** as **Show below other swimlanes**:

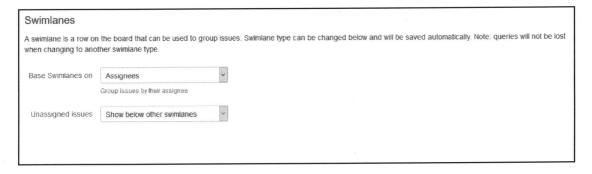

The swimlane can also be based on epics, and it's possible to have no swimlane at all.

Card colors

The individual issues that appear in the **Active sprints** are displayed in a rectangular block called a card. The color of these cards can be changed based on its **Issue Types**, **Priorities**, **Assignees**, or **Queries**. The default option for the card color is the issue type; let's change it to issue priorities:

1. Go to **Board | Configure | Card colors** (under **CONFIGURATION**).

2. Select **Priorities** from the drop-down list for **Colors based on**:

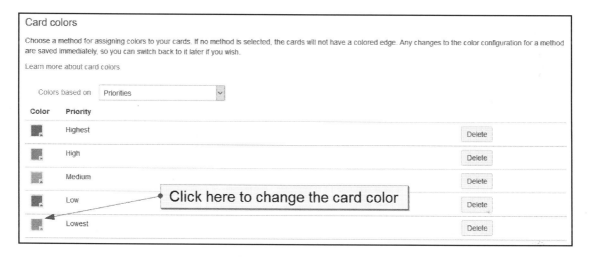

Click on the color box to change the color to the color of your choice.

Card fields

The card in the **Backlog** and **Active sprints** displays the **Issue Id** and **Issue Summary**, but it's possible to add up to three additional fields. Perform these steps:

1. Navigate to **Board | Configure | Card layout** (under **CONFIGURATION**).
2. The additional three fields can be added for the **Backlog** and the **Active sprints**. We will add one additional field in the **Active sprints**. From the **Field Name** drop-down list, select **Priority** and click on the **Add** button on the right-hand side.

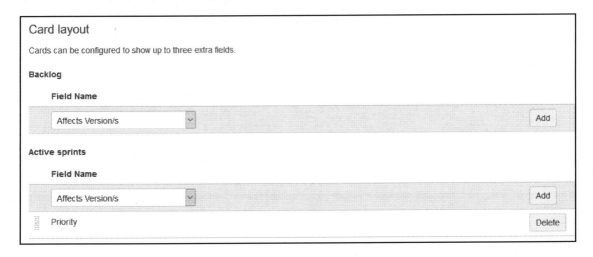

In total, you can add three additional fields that can appear on the card. This provision is provided so that fields that provide additional information can be made visible for the whole team to view.

Quick filters

We saw how you can customize swimlanes to group several issues. Imagine a situation where there are 20 issues in the Active sprints that are assigned to you in the currently active sprint, but there are certain issues that are of the highest priority. In such cases, it will be nice to be able to not only quickly filter out the issues that are assigned to you, but also the issues that are due today. Perform these steps to achieve this:

1. Navigate to **Board** | **Configure** | **Quick Filters** (under **CONFIGURATION**).
2. Enter the **Name** of the quick filter as `Highest Priority`. In the **JQL** column, enter `priority = Highest` as the query and click on the **Add** button:

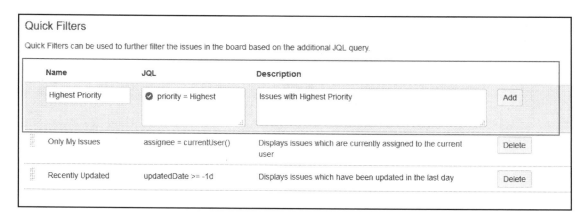

We have done some customizations in our board. Let's go back to the **Active sprints**.

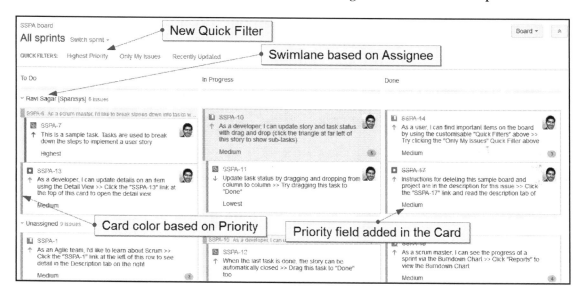

Now, you can see that a new quick filter has been added at the top called **Highest Priority**; click on this link and the board will only display issues whose priority is highest. Note that the swimlane is now based on the **Assignee** of the issue. The issue priority is now added to the card. Also, the color of the card is based on the priority of the issue.

These customizations help the team to work efficiently so that they don't need to spend a lot of time finding the relevant information.

The Burndown chart and Velocity charts

You have learned how to plan, estimate, and start the sprint, along with various configurations available to perform in the board. We have checked how the team can view their tasks in the sprint. Now, it's time to monitor the progress of the team. There are two reports that are of prime importance—one is the **Burndown chart**. This chart gives a clear picture of the current status of the sprint. The second is the **Velocity chart**. This chart helps in understanding the capacity of the team in terms of how much work it can handle. These two reports help the Scrum master in monitoring the progress of the project. Let's take a look at both these reports.

The Burndown chart

While planning the sprint, we primarily did two important things. Firstly, we prioritized the order in which the issues need to be completed. Secondly, we estimated the story points for issues. These story points, which we initially planned, give workers an idea of the complexity of the task. Now, the moment the sprint starts, a baseline is formed between the start date and the end date. This baseline is displayed with a grey line in the chart and it depicts the ideal scenario for executing the issues from the start date of the sprint until the end date. When the issue is resolved, its story points are burned and the total remaining story points of the whole sprint decreases.

Navigate to project sidebar **Reports** | **Burndown Chart** (under **Agile**):

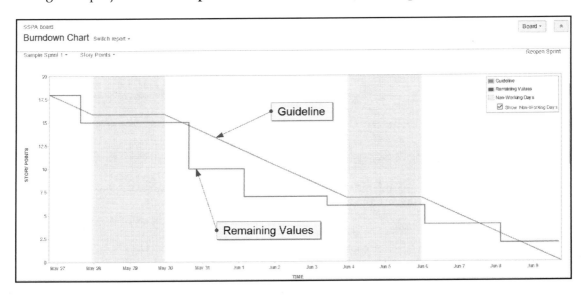

When the team starts working on the issues, another line of red color starts following the baseline. Looking at this chart, the whole team can easily figure out if they are on track or off track. If the line for **Remaining Values** is progressing above the baseline **Guideline**, then it shows that the story points are being burned slowly. Eventually, all the issues in the sprint will not be completed.

Just after the Burndown chart, the details of the individual issues are displayed:

Date	Issue	Event Type	Event Detail	Story Points		
				Inc.	Dec.	Remaining
26/May/16 6:28 PM	SSPA-16	Sprint start		2		
	SSPA-18			3		
	SSPA-19			5		
	SSPA-20			3		
	SSPA-21			1		
	SSPA-22			2		
	SSPA-23			2		
						18
27/May/16 2:57 PM	SSPA-16	Burndown	Issue completed		3	15
30/May/16 2:51 PM	SSPA-19	Burndown	Issue completed		5	10
01/Jun/16 3:26 AM	SSPA-20	Burndown	Issue completed		3	7
03/Jun/16 10:04 AM	SSPA-21	Burndown	Issue completed		1	6
06/Jun/16 1:24 AM	SSPA-22	Burndown	Issue completed		2	4
08/Jun/16 3:02 AM	SSPA-23	Burndown	Issue completed		2	2
09/Jun/16 5:08 PM	SSPA-16	Sprint ended				2
	SSPA-18					0

In this table, you can see how many issues there were at the beginning of the sprint. As the issues are resolved, their story points are deducted from the total story points of the sprint. The total story points and the remaining story points will be displayed to the user.

Let's take a look at the Burndown chart again and focus towards the end:

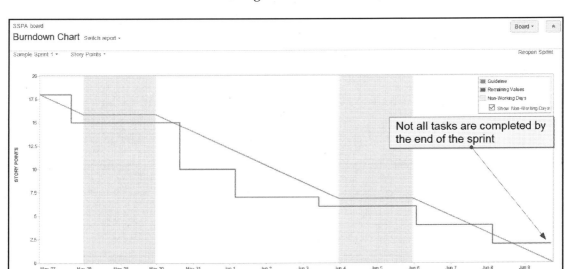

It's clear by looking at this Burndown chart that by the end of the sprint, not all story points were burned; these unfinished issues will be added back to the backlog when the sprint is completed.

The Velocity chart

Every sprint has a total number of story points at the beginning. Ideally, the team working on the sprint should burn all these points. In real cases, it's not always possible to complete all the tasks by the end of the sprint. One of the main responsibilities of the Scrum master is to make sure that the team have just enough story points to burn, not too many and not too few. However, at the beginning of the sprint, it's not that easy to estimate the amount of story points a team can burn. The velocity chart simply displays the amount of story points planned versus the amount actually completed by the team. This comparison is shown for the past few sprints so that the average number of story points that the team can burn can be calculated. This is known as the capacity of the team.

Navigate to the project sidebar **Reports** | **Velocity** (under **Agile**):

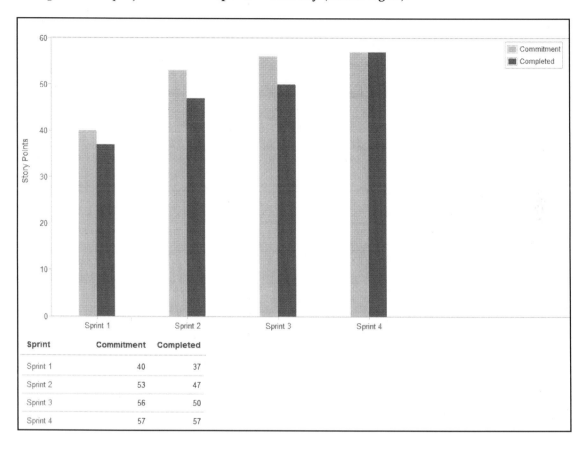

Sprint	Commitment	Completed
Sprint 1	40	37
Sprint 2	53	47
Sprint 3	56	50
Sprint 4	57	57

This chart gives us a very clear indication of the story points that the team has been able to complete in previous sprints. If you take the average of all the story points that your team has been able to burn until now, you will know your capacity. This helps the Scrum master to plan the next sprint with enough resources in the team.

Kanban boards

We have discussed the Scrum methodology, widely used for software development projects where requirements are broken down into smaller tasks, estimated using story points, and finally planned by the Scrum master or product manager. The Scrum technique is applicable in any process that requires planning, but there are various cases where the team is continuously working on activities as and when required. A typical example of this use case is customer support projects, where a certain number of people are assigned to handle the issues that are raised for a particular product or project by the company. Usually, these support issues require immediate response and detailed planning is not required.

In such scenarios, the overall visualization of the pending issues is important. A Kanban board doesn't have any **Plan** mode like the Scrum board. It only has the **Work** mode, which is similar to the Scrum board.

Setting up the Kanban board

A Kanban board can be created using existing projects or filters. To understand how the Kanban technique works in JIRA, a sample board and project can be created. Perform these steps to create them:

1. In the navigation menu, click on **Boards** | **View All Boards** | **Create board**, and in the **Create an Agile board** pop-up, click on the **Create a Kanban board with sample data**:

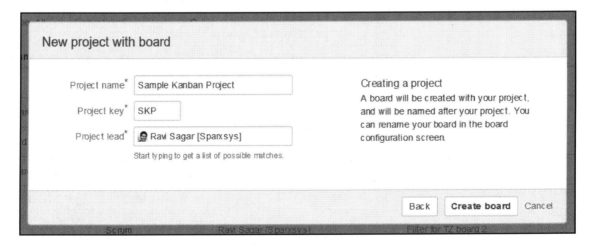

2. Enter the **Project name**, **Project key**, **Project lead** and click on the **Create board** button.

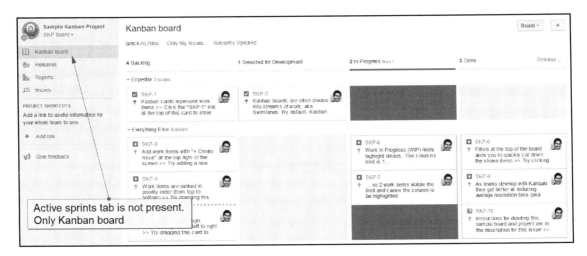

As you will notice, the **Active sprints** tab is not present in the **Kanban board**. The team sees the **Kanban board** only. This board is quite similar to the Scrum board; you can also configure the swimlanes based on assignees; by default, the swimlanes in the Kanban board are configured to use the `priority = Highest` query. This means that issues that should be resolved immediately are displayed at the top.

The people who have these issues assigned can move the issue from one column to another. These columns signify the workflow states. Most of the configurations that we did for the Scrum board can be done on the Kanban board as well; let's perform some configurations that we did not check in the Scrum board.

Column constraints

When a team works on support issues, it's important to resolve the issues as soon as possible. Usually, companies sign **Service Level Agreement (SLA)**, that is, with their customers where they need to agree on the resolution time. In situations like these, the whole team should get the overall picture of the issues they need to work on. For instance, if there are fewer people available on the support issues, then there is a limitation on the number of issues these people can work on at a given point in time. In the sample Kanban board, you will notice that the **In progress** column is red whenever there is more than one issue in it.

Let's say you want to alert the team whenever there are more than four issues in the backlog:

1. Navigate to **Board** | **Configure** | **Columns** (under **CONFIGURATION**).

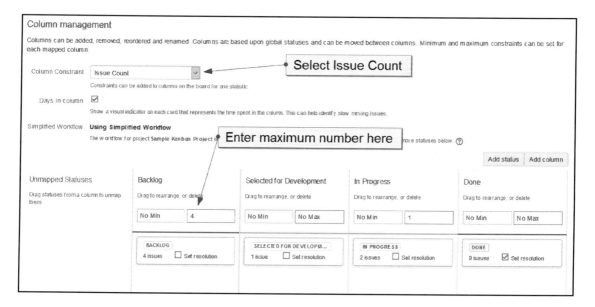

2. In **Column management**, first select **Column Constraint** as **Issue Count**. As shown in the previous screenshot, enter the maximum number of issue counts in the **Backlog** section.

3. Now, create one more issue in your sample project so that your backlog has more than four issues.

4. Go back to your Kanban board and check the **Backlog** column:

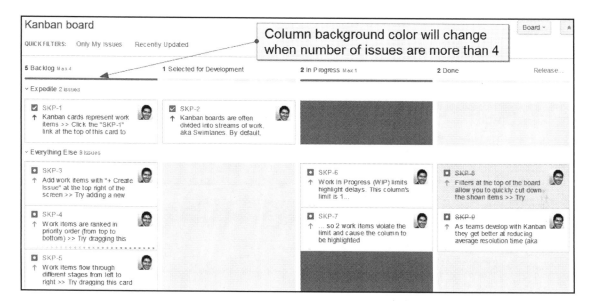

The rest of the configuration is exactly the same as what we have done for Scrum. You can configure swimlanes, add quick filters, and also add a few additional fields in the card layout. The procedure of configuring these was already discussed in the Scrum section earlier, and it's the same for Kanban boards.

Managing multiple teams and projects using boards

The sample projects and boards that we created to understand Scrum and Kanban techniques used only one project, but JIRA Software boards can be configured to use multiple projects too.

If your team members are working on different projects for the same client, then it will make more sense to manage the work from a single board. Scrum and Kanban boards can be configured for issues that either come from one, two, or multiple projects. Perform these steps to manage the work from a single board:

1. In the navigation menu, click on **Boards** | **View All Boards** | **Create board,** and in the **Create an Agile board** pop-up, click on the **Create a Scrum board** button or **Create a Kanban board** button.

2. In the pop-up window, you can either create a new project with a new board or also create a board from a filter, but we can select the second option, that is, **Board from an existing project** and click on the **Next** button:

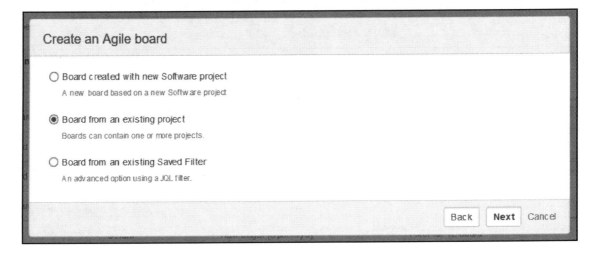

3. On the next screen, enter **Board name** and select multiple **Project(s)**. Click on **Create board** to finish:

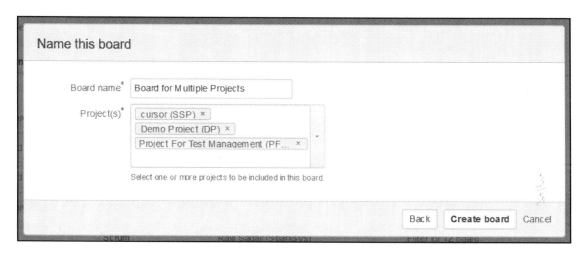

4. Your newly created board will now have issues from all the projects that you have selected.

The issues from multiple projects can now be added for the sprint in the Scrum board or will appear in the Kanban backlog and your team can work on them.

Summary

In this chapter, you learned how to implement Scrum and Kanban Agile methodologies using the Software application. We understood how to use both boards and learned various configurations that can be performed in them. The JIRA Software can either be used as a standalone instance or it can also be installed as an application in an existing JIRA Core application.

In the next chapter, we will discuss Groovy Script Runner, which is an amazing add-on used to perform complex customizations in the workflow, access powerful JQL functions, and run various scripts that can be used by JIRA administrators to maintain the instance efficiently.

12
JIRA Administration with ScriptRunner and the CLI Add-on

When JIRA is used to implement a complex use case with lots of conditions, validations, and workflows, there are certain configurations that are not doable using the existing set of features. For instance, you may want to auto-calculate a custom field value after a workflow transition. Using the **ScriptRunner** plugin, many such advanced configurations can be achieved. It comes with various built-in administration scripts, which give the administrators tremendous power to manage their instance. In this chapter, we will discuss the ScriptRunner add-on, along with the JIRA **Command Line Interface (CLI)** add-on, to perform various JIRA functions from the command line.

We will cover the following topics:

- Installing ScriptRunner
- Installing CLI

Installing ScriptRunner

Just like any other add-on, ScriptRunner can be installed from the JIRA administration interface. Perform these steps to install ScriptRunner on your JIRA instance:

1. Navigate to **Administration** | **Add-ons** | **Find new add-ons** (under **ATLASSIAN MARKETPLACE**).

2. In the search box, enter `ScriptRunner` and press the *Enter* key. The ScriptRunner add-on will appear in the search result list:

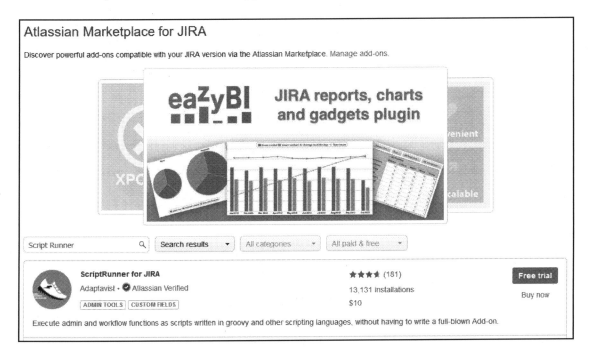

3. Click on the **Free trial** button. Then, press the **Accept** button in the **Accept terms and agreements** pop-up and the ScriptRunner add-on will begin downloading:

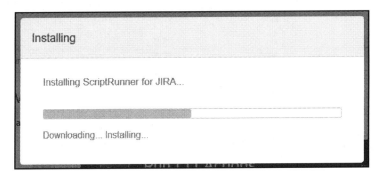

4. ScriptRunner will then be downloaded and installed in your instance. Finally, you will be asked to enter your Atlassian account to generate a trial license for ScriptRunner.

5. In the pop-up window that appears confirming the add-on installation, click on the **Close** link in the bottom right corner:

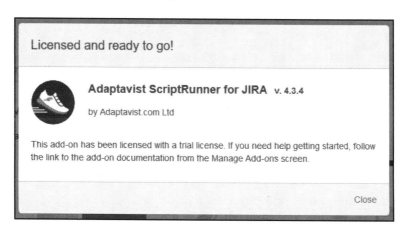

ScriptRunner will now be installed in your JIRA instance.

Built-in scripts for administration

The ScriptRunner add-on allows users to write and run their own scripts. It comes with plenty of nice scripts, which allow JIRA administrators to perform various activities that are otherwise difficult to perform using existing JIRA features, or not possible at all from the UI. Let's take a look at some of these scripts.

Accessing built-in scripts

To access scripts that come with the ScriptRunner add-on, perform these steps:

1. Navigate to **Administration** | **Add-ons** | **Built-in Scripts** (under **SCRIPTRUNNER**).

2. In this section, the list of all the **Built-in Scripts** can be found:

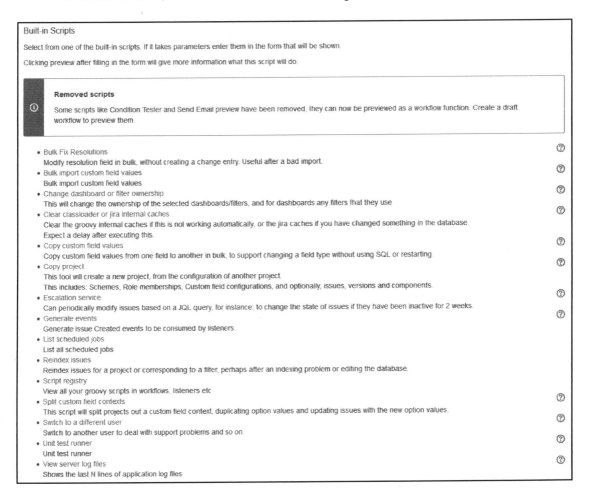

2. Click on any of these links to run that particular built-in script. This will further ask you to enter parameters relevant for that script.

Let's take a look at some of these built-in scripts.

Copy project

Only JIRA administrators have the permission to create a project in JIRA (and change the configurations, too). Whenever there is a need to have an additional project in JIRA, the administrator needs to manually create projects and then change their schemes. It's not a difficult task, and usually takes only 10 minutes, but sometimes there is a need to create ten projects, and creating them manually could take hours.

There is a built-in script in ScriptRunner to copy the project along with its configurations, with or without its issues. Perform these steps:

1. Click on the **Copy project** link:

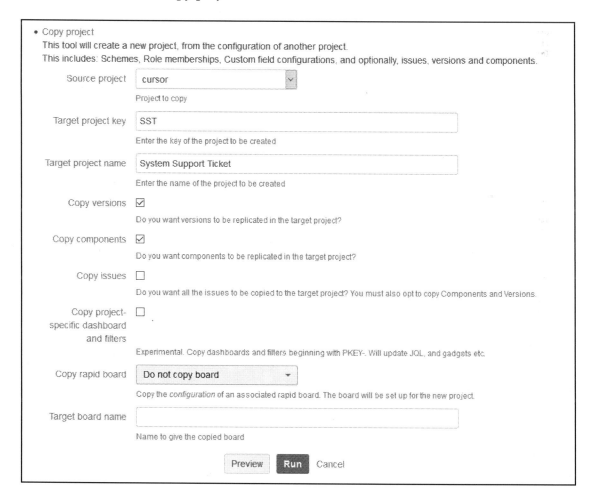

2. On the next screen, select **cursor** as **Source project**, enter **Target project key** and **Target project name**.

3. Check the **Copy versions** and **Copy components** checkbox if you want to copy the project versions and project components as well.

4. Click on the **Run** button to initiate the **Copy project** script:

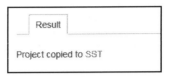

Once done, the message is displayed at the bottom of the screen stating that the project has been copied, with a link to the new project. If you check the new copied project, you will notice that it has all the configurations of the source project. This tool takes less than a minute to run and JIRA administrators can save a lot of time using it.

Escalation service

This is an excellent built-in script that helps JIRA administrators perform periodic actions on a certain set of issues. Let's take the example of a support ticket configuration, in which we have a workflow state called **Waiting for Client** in our project. This is used to signify that further information is required from a client to act further on a ticket. These issues need to be resolved automatically if the ticket has not been updated in the past two weeks:

1. Click on **Escalation service**:

- Escalation service
  Can periodically modify issues based on a JQL query, for instance: to change the state of issues if they have been inactive for 2 weeks.
No escalation services defined - use the link below to create one.
New Service

Cancel

2. Click on **New Service** to create a new service:

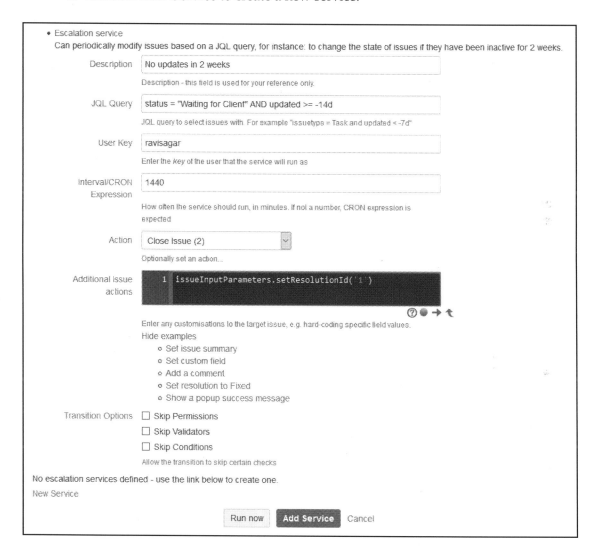

3. Enter `No updates in 2 weeks` as **Description**.

4. In **JQL Query**, enter `status="Waiting for Client" AND updated >= -14d`.

5. Enter your **User Key** and specify **Interval/CRON Expression** as `1440`, which is 24 hours. In the **Action** dropdown, all the workflow states for all the projects in your instances will be displayed. Select the workflow transition that you want to perform as per your project. For instance, you can select **Close Issue (2)**.

 As we want to close the issues that qualify under the criteria in JQL Query, in the **Additional issue actions** field, enter the code `issueInputParameters.setResolutionId('1')`. You can also do this by clicking on **Expand examples** and selecting the **Set resolution to Fixed** link.

6. Click on the **Add Service** button to save this service:

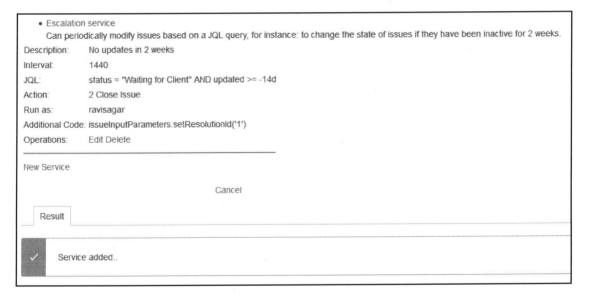

Now, we have a service added that will run after every 24-hour period and will resolve the issues that were not updated in the past 14 days, that is, two weeks.

Switching to a different user

Imagine a situation when a user reports some problem in JIRA. As a JIRA administrator, you need to log in with their ID to understand the problem this user might be facing. You can either ask this user for their password or create a similar user with the same set of permissions. Instead, wouldn't it be better to be able to log in to JIRA using that user's username without asking for the password? There is a built-in script to perform just that:

1. Click on **Switch to a different user**.
2. Enter the **User ID** of the user and click on the **Run** button:

3. Click on the **here** link that appears at the bottom of the screen. You will then be logged in as a different user:

This script is one of my favorites because I can log in with any username I want without asking for the user's password. It also saves a lot of time.

Modifying the JIRA workflow with conditions, validators, and post functions

The best part of the ScriptRunner add-on is the additional features it brings in the JIRA workflow. Out of the box, there are various conditions, validators, and post functions that can be configured in the workflow, but it offers limited functionalities. ScriptRunner simply gives you more options, which you can control in the workflow. Let's take a look at them.

Conditions

ScriptRunner brings a set of additional conditions that you can add in the workflow; it gives you amazing control over a lot of things, which was not previously possible. Perform these steps:

1. Modify the workflow of your choice. For any transition, navigate to the **Conditions** tab and then click on the **Add condition** link.
2. You will find a new condition called **Script Condition**; just select it and click on the **Add** button:

	Name	Description
○	Code Committed Condition	Transition to execute only if code has/has not (depending on configuration) been committed against this issue.
○	Hide transition from user	Condition to hide a transition from the user. The transition can only be triggered from a workflow function.
○	No Open Reviews Condition	Transition to execute only if there are no related open Crucible reviews.
○	Only Assignee Condition	Condition to allow only the assignee to execute a transition.
○	Only Reporter Condition	Condition to allow only the reporter to execute a transition.
○	Permission Condition	Condition to allow only users with a certain permission to execute a transition.
◉	Script Condition	Runs a script to evaluate whether to allow this action, or a built-in script.
○	Sub-Task Blocking Condition	Condition to block parent issue transition depending on sub-task status.
○	Unreviewed Code Condition	Transition to execute only if there are no unreviewed changesets related to this issue.
○	User Is In Any Groups	Allows only users of a given group to execute the transition.
○	User Is In Any Roles	Allows only users of a given role to execute the transition.
○	User Is In Custom field	Allows only users in a given custom field to execute the transition.
○	User Is In Group	Condition to allow only users in a given group to execute a transition.
○	User Is In Group Custom Field	Condition to allow only users in a custom field-specified group to execute a transition.
○	User Is In Project Role	Condition to allow only users in a given project role to execute a transition.
○	Value Field	Allows to execute a transition if the given value of a field is equal to a constant value, or simply set.

Add condition To Transition

Add | Cancel

3. On the next screen, you will get a list of scripts that you can add as a workflow condition:

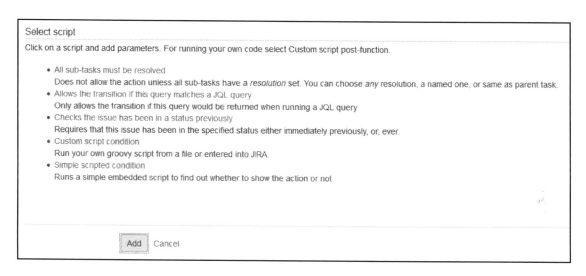

Let's discuss some of these scripts.

All sub-tasks must be resolved

If you want all the sub-tasks of a particular issue to be resolved with a specific resolution, the following condition can be added:

Simply select the **Resolution** that you want your sub-tasks to have after moving them to the **Resolved** state and click on the **Add** button.

Allowing the transition if this query matches a JQL query

While performing a workflow transition, you can use a custom JQL in the workflow condition and allow the transition only when that JQL returns the issue that you will transition:

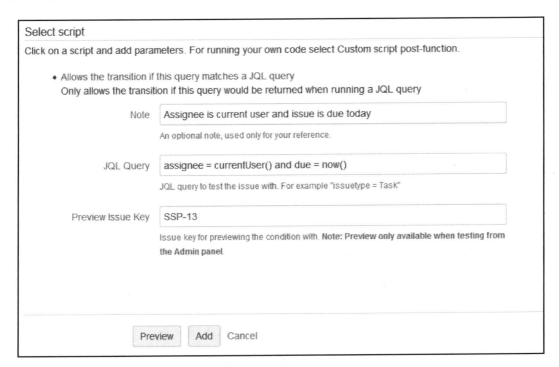

For instance, if you want the transition to happen only when the assignee of the issue is the currently logged-in user and the due date of the issue is today, in the **JQL Query** field add the `assignee = currentUser() and due = now()` query and click on the **Add** button. Optionally, you can also enter the specific issue ID to preview this condition.

Checks the issue has been in a status previously

The workflow can have numerous states and transitions between them. A workflow state can have more than one transition. If for some reason you want the transition to be made from a particular state only, the following condition can be added:

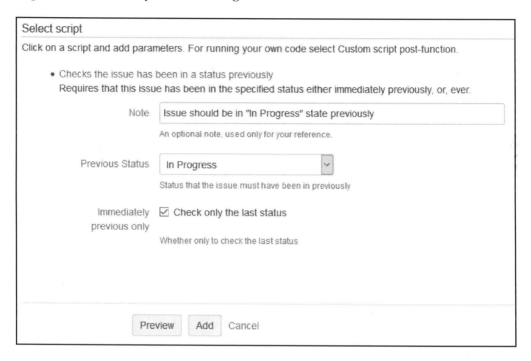

Just select **In Progress** from the drop-down list for **Previous Status** and check whether this status has to be **Immediately previous only**, or uncheck this option if it could be any other previous status, and click on the **Add** button.

Simple scripted condition

ScriptRunner has some ready-made simple scripts that can be added quickly as a condition:

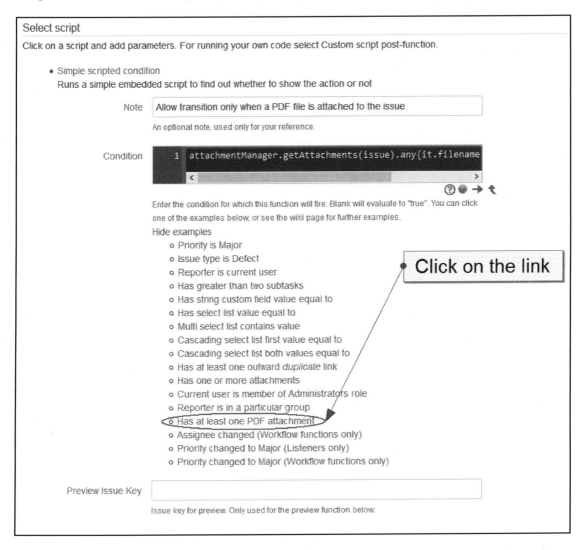

Just click on any of the example links and it can be added as a condition. For instance, I added a condition that will check whether one of the issue attachments is a PDF file or not. Click on the **Add** button to continue.

Validators

Just like additional conditions, ScriptRunner brings a set of additional validators that you can add to the workflow; it gives you amazing control over lots of things that were not previously possible. Perform these following steps:

1. Modify the workflow of your choice and for any transition, navigate to the **Validators** tab and then click on the **Add validator** button.

2. You will find a new validator called **Script Validator**. Just select it and click on the **Add** button:

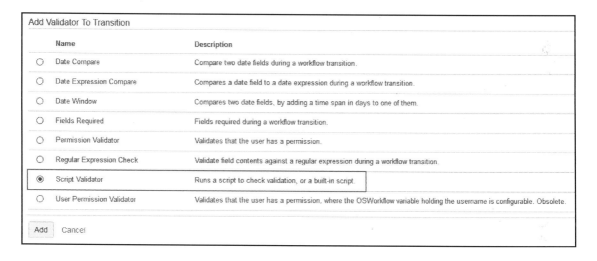

	Name	Description
○	Date Compare	Compare two date fields during a workflow transition.
○	Date Expression Compare	Compares a date field to a date expression during a workflow transition.
○	Date Window	Compares two date fields, by adding a time span in days to one of them.
○	Fields Required	Fields required during a workflow transition.
○	Permission Validator	Validates that the user has a permission.
○	Regular Expression Check	Validate field contents against a regular expression during a workflow transition.
◉	Script Validator	Runs a script to check validation, or a built-in script.
○	User Permission Validator	Validates that the user has a permission, where the OSWorkflow variable holding the username is configurable. Obsolete.

Add Validator To Transition

Add   Cancel

3. On the next screen, you will get a list of scripts that you can add as a workflow validator:

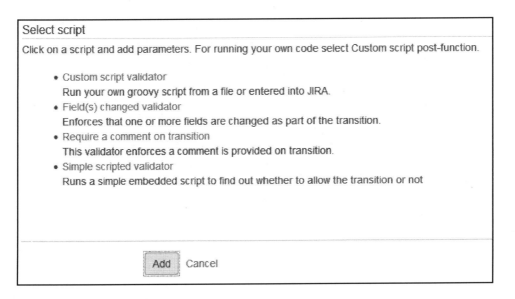

Let's discuss some of these scripts.

Field(s) changed validator

It's possible that you will use a transition view in the workflow transition that pops up a window to the user to capture additional input. These transition views are nothing but a screen containing one or more fields. Use this validator to validate whether those fields present in the transition view have changed:

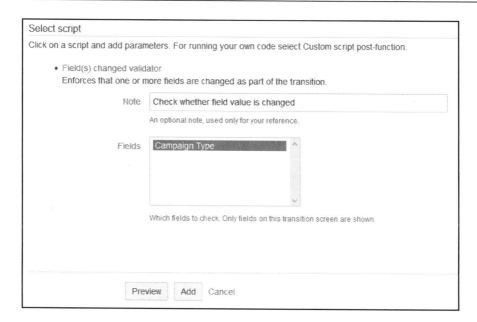

Select all the **Fields** that you want to check for changes and click on the **Add** button. The fields visible here are only the ones that are part of the transition view for the transition you are working on in the workflow.

Require a comment on transition

In the transition view, there is usually a comment field as well. Use this validator to validate whether a comment has been added or not:

This validator doesn't require any parameters to configure. Just click on the **Add** button.

Simple scripted validator

ScriptRunner has some ready-made simple scripts that can be added quickly as validators:

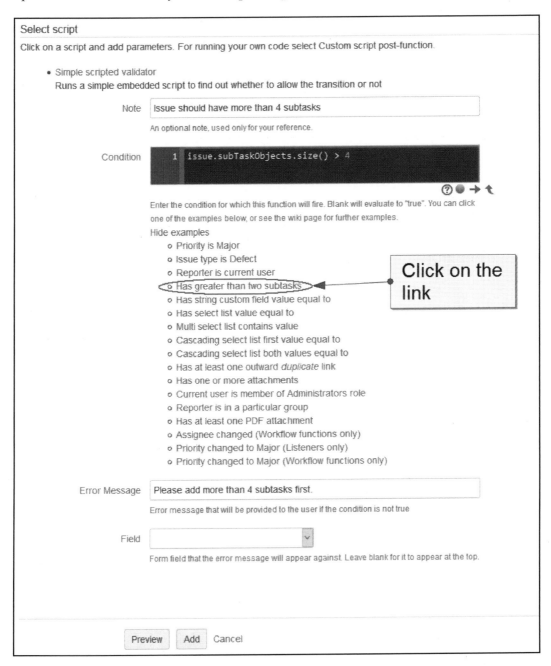

Just click on any of the example links and it can be added as a validator. For instance, if you want to enforce that the issue should have at least four subtasks, then click on **Has greater than two subtasks** and modify **Condition** from 2 to 4 so that it becomes `issue.subTasks.size() > 4`. Click on the **Add** button to continue.

Post functions

Just like additional conditions and validators, ScriptRunner brings a set of additional post functions that you can add in the workflow; this gives you amazing control over a lot of things that were not previously possible. Perform these steps:

1. Modify the workflow of your choice and for any transition, navigate to the **Post Functions** tab and then click on the **Add post function** link.

2. You will find a new post function called **Script Post-Function**; just select it and click on the **Add** button:

	Name	Description
○	Assign to Current User	Assigns the issue to the current user if the current user has the 'Assignable User' permission.
○	Assign to Lead Developer	Assigns the issue to the project/component lead developer
○	Assign to Reporter	Assigns the issue to the reporter
○	Clear Field Value	Clear value of a given field.
○	Copy Value From Other Field	Copies the value of one field to another, either within the same issue or from parent to sub-task.
○	Create Perforce Job Function	Creates a Perforce Job (if required) after completing the workflow transition.
○	Notify HipChat	Send a notification to one or more HipChat rooms.
●	Script Post-Function	Runs a script in a post-function, or a built-in script.
○	Trigger a Webhook	If this post-function is executed, JIRA will post the issue content in JSON format to the URL specified.
○	Update Issue Custom Field	Updates an issue custom field to a given value.
○	Update Issue Field	Updates a simple issue field to a given value.

Add Post Function To Transition

Add   Cancel

3. On the next screen, you will get a list of scripts that you can add as a workflow post function:

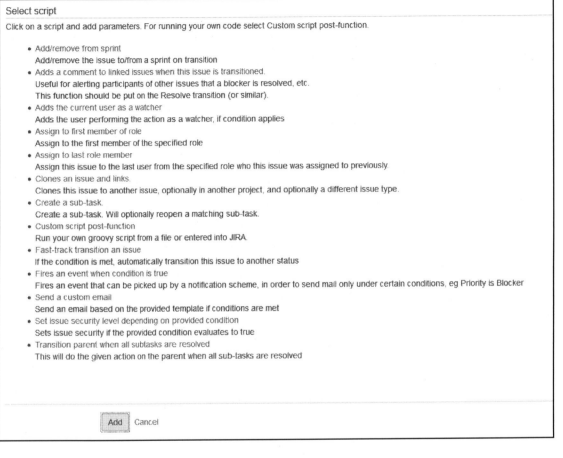

Let's discuss some of these scripts.

Adds the current user as a watcher

Consider a scenario when the priority of the issue is **Major** and the user who is currently logged in and making the workflow transition should be added as a watcher of the issue; in this case, use the following post function:

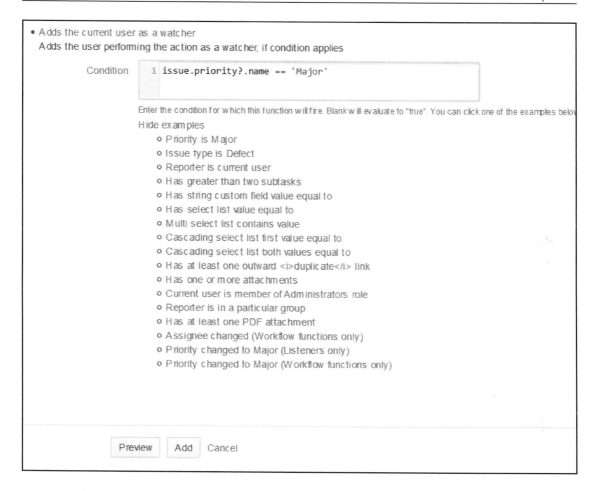

From the list of examples, click on the **Priority is Major** link and a condition will be added. Now, whenever this condition is true during the workflow transition, the post function will be executed. Click on the **Add** button to add the post function.

Transition parent when all subtasks are resolved

If your issue has a lot of subtasks, it's possible to move the parent to a new state in the workflow when all its subtasks are resolved:

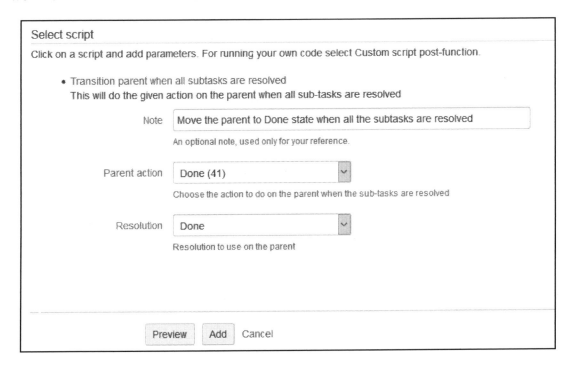

Select **Parent action** as **Done (41)** and **Resolution** as **Done**. Click on the **Add** button to add the post function. This is particularly useful in Scrum boards, when you are to change the state of the story when all of its subtasks are resolved.

There are numerous other post functions that can be used in the workflow. Using the ScriptRunner add-on, a lot of flexibility and control can be added in the workflow to perform actions that were not possible earlier.

Accessing powerful JQL functions

We have already discussed searching issues in JIRA with the **Basic** and **Advanced** search options using JQL. However, JQL has some limitations. JIRA administrators often try to fetch the information directly from the database, which is difficult to do because it requires a good knowledge of the JIRA database schema.

ScriptRunner introduces new JQL functions. You can use these functions in your instance. After installing this add-on, just perform the re-indexing to enable the new JQL functions.

Let's discuss some of these JQL functions.

Returning issues with number of comments

Use the following JQL queries to return issues with the exact number of comments:

```
issueFunction in hasComments(3)
```

The following query will return an issue with more than four comments:

```
issueFunction in hasComments('+5')
```

Returning issues based on comment attributes

Use the following query to return issues commented on by project role administrators:

```
issueFunction in commented("role Administrators")
```

This query returns issues with comments from a specific user in the past seven days:

```
issueFunction in commented("after -7d by ravisagar")
```

Returning issues based on attachments

Use the following query to fetch issues with a PDF as an attachment:

```
issueFunction in hasAttachments ("pdf")
```

This query finds issues in the file that were attached by a specific user in the past seven days:

```
issueFunction in fileAttached("after -7d by ravisagar")
```

Comparing dates

Issues can also be fetched by comparing their date fields, such as **Resolution Date** and **Due Date**.

Use this query to return issues that were resolved later than their due date:

```
issueFunction in dateCompare("", "resolutionDate > dueDate")
```

The following query finds issues that were resolved within one week of their creation:

```
issueFunction in dateCompare("", "created +1w > resolutionDate ")
```

These are just some of the examples of additional JQL functions that you can use. For the full list, I recommend you refer to `https://jamieechlin.atlassian.net/wiki/display/GRV/Scripted+JQL+Functions`.

ScriptRunner is, personally, my favorite add-on, which I use with all of the JIRA instances that I manage. It just gives so much power and control to effectively manage various administrative tasks in JIRA. Apart from various built-in scripts, which give administrators access to ready-to-use features, one can also write one's own script and use it to perform more advanced and complex tasks. This ability to write scripts opens up a lot of possibilities to enhance the workflow and to add more features in JIRA without developing an add-on.

Installing JIRA CLI

Just like any other add-on, Atlassian CLI can be installed from the JIRA **Administration** interface. Perform these steps to install it on your JIRA instance:

1. Navigate to **Administration** | **Add-ons** | **Find new add-ons** (under **ATLASSIAN MARKETPLACE**).
2. In the search box, enter `Atlassian Command Line Interface` and press the *Enter* key. The **JIRA Command Line Interface (CLI)** add-on will appear in the search result list:

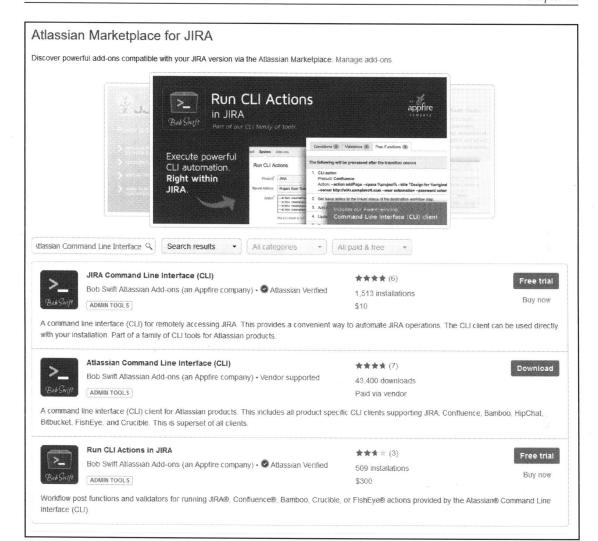

Atlassian Marketplace for JIRA

Discover powerful add-ons compatible with your JIRA version via the Atlassian Marketplace. Manage add-ons.

JIRA Command Line Interface (CLI)
Bob Swift Atlassian Add-ons (an Appfire company) • ✓ Atlassian Verified
ADMIN TOOLS
★★★★ (6)
1,513 installations
$10
Free trial
Buy now

A command line interface (CLI) for remotely accessing JIRA. This provides a convenient way to automate JIRA operations. The CLI client can be used directly with your installation. Part of a family of CLI tools for Atlassian products.

Atlassian Command Line Interface (CLI)
Bob Swift Atlassian Add-ons (an Appfire company) • Vendor supported
ADMIN TOOLS
★★★★ (7)
43,400 downloads
Paid via vendor
Download

A command line interface (CLI) client for Atlassian products. This includes all product specific CLI clients supporting JIRA, Confluence, Bamboo, HipChat, Bitbucket, FishEye, and Crucible. This is superset of all clients.

Run CLI Actions in JIRA
Bob Swift Atlassian Add-ons (an Appfire company) • ✓ Atlassian Verified
ADMIN TOOLS
★★★ (3)
509 installations
$300
Free trial
Buy now

Workflow post functions and validators for running JIRA®, Confluence®, Bamboo, Crucible, or FishEye® actions provided by the Atassian® Command Line Interface (CLI).

3. Click on the **Free trial** button, then press the **Accept** button in the **Accept terms and agreements** pop-up and the CLI add-on will begin downloading:

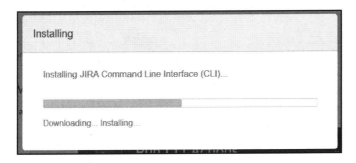

4. JIRA CLI will then be downloaded and installed on your instance. Finally, you will be asked to enter your Atlassian account to generate a trial license for JIRA CLI.

5. In the pop-up window that appears confirming the add-on installation, click on the **Close** link in the bottom right corner:

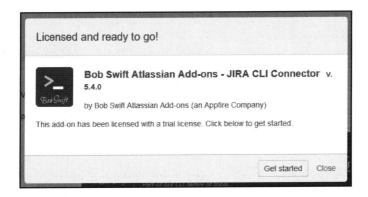

JIRA CLI will now be installed in your JIRA instance. This add-on doesn't really have any UI in a JIRA instance; instead, the add-on is used for remotely accessing JIRA by another utility, called **Atlassian Command Line Interface (CLI)**, which is a collection of scripts and has to be run from your computer. Download it from `https://marketplace.atlassian.com/plugins/org.swift.atlassian.cli/server/overview`.

You will get a file like `atlassian-cli-5.4.0-distribution.zip`. Save it to your favorite location on your computer. Unzip this package, and using the Windows command line, navigate to the uncompressed folder and run the following commands.

Fetch the list of boards

The following command will get the list of all the boards in your JIRA instance:

```
jira --server http://jira.example.com --user "demouser" --password
"demopassword" --action getBoardList
```

The preceding command results in the following output:

```
10 boards in list
"Name","Id","Description","Type","Filter Id"
"Board for Multiple Projects","8","","scrum","0"
"DP board","1","","scrum","0"
"PFTM board","5","","scrum","0"
"SKP board","7","","kanban","0"
"SSP","9","","kanban","0"
"SSP board","4","","scrum","0"
"SSPA board","6","","scrum","0"
"Scrum","10","","scrum","0"
"TZ board","3","","scrum","0"
"TZ board","2","","scrum","0"
```

Fetch the list of comments of a particular issue

The following command will get the list of all the comments of a particular issue:

```
jira --server http://jira.example.com --user "demouser" --password
"demopassword" --action getComments --issue "SSP-16"
```

The preceding command results in the following output:

```
Data for 3 comments associated with issue: SSP-16

ravisagar added a comment on 2016-05-24T03:01:54.000-0500
Created 28 days 5 hours 14 minutes ago
Joined Sample Sprint 1 21 days 10 hours 20 minutes ago
— — — — — — — — — — — — — — — — — — — — — — — — — — — — — — — —
ravisagar added a comment on 2016-05-24T03:01:54.000-0500
Joined Sample Sprint 2 7 days 9 hours 10 minutes ago
— — — — — — — — — — — — — — — — — — — — — — — — — — — — — — — —
ravisagar added a comment on 2016-05-24T03:01:54.000-0500
To Do to In Progress 7 days 4 hours 26 minutes ago
In Progress to Done 6 days 2 hours 38 minutes ago
```

Create an issue from the command line

Use the following command to create an issue from the command line:

```
jira --server http://jira.example.com --user "demouser" --password
"demopassword" --action createIssue --project "SSP" --type "story" --
summary "This is a story"
```

The preceding command results in the following output:

```
Issue SSP-32 created with id 10500.
```

These are some of the examples of JIRA CLI. It is very powerful as these commands can be invoked by any script. It also opens up a wide range of possibilities, not only to JIRA administrators, but also to developers who want to integrate with JIRA. To get a list of all the functionality and examples, visit `https://bobswift.atlassian.net/wiki/display/J CLI/Examples`.

The command-line package can be run from Windows, Linux, and OS X. It just needs Java 7 or higher.

Summary

In this chapter, we discussed ScriptRunner, which is an amazing add-on for performing complex customizations in the workflow, accessing powerful JQL functions, and running various scripts, which can be used by JIRA administrators to maintain the instance efficiently. ScriptRunner is by far the most popular admin tool used by JIRA administrators.

In the following chapter, we will discuss how to access the JIRA database directly to fetch data. JIRA offers lots of good reports, but sometimes they are not good enough and more insight is required. If you know the JIRA database schema and how to access the database, any data can be retrieved for further reporting purposes.

13
Database Access

JIRA offers a lot of project reports to keep track of a project's progress, analyze trends over the past few months, and make decisions based on various statistics regarding time estimates, status, and workload. In most cases, these reports are enough to reach conclusions, but there are times when desirable information cannot be fetched from the existing JIRA reports. However, it's possible to generate complex reports directly from the database. In this chapter, we will discuss common databases that JIRA can use and the schemas these databases use. We will take a look at some reports that can only be generated by querying the database directly.

In this chapter, we will cover the following topics:

- JIRA's database schema
- Accessing **MySQL**
- Accessing **PostgreSQL**
- User table
- The `jiraissue` table
- The `customfield` table
- The `customfieldvalue` table
- Some useful SQL queries

JIRA's database schema

JIRA stores its configuration and data in a database; if you are evaluating JIRA, it's possible to use the embedded **Hyper SQL Database** (**HSQLDB**) written in Java. This is suitable for small applications, and JIRA uses it only in its evaluation version. HSQLDB is not recommended for production usage. For that, JIRA recommends MySQL or PostgreSQL.

No matter what type of database is used, the database schema that is, the tables and the relationship between them, is the same. If you want to take a look at the schema, you can refer to JIRA_INSTALL/atlassian-jira/WEB-INF/classes/entitydefs/entitymodel.xml.

The contents of the file are as displayed in the following screenshot:

```xml
<?xml version="1.0" encoding="UTF-8"?>
<!DOCTYPE entitymodel PUBLIC "-//OFBiz//DTD Entity Model//EN" "http://www.ofbiz.org/dtds/entitymodel.dtd">

<!--

Are you going to add a new column?

Check fieldtype-postgres.xml and others to know exactly what given type means, and you could be surprised!

For example long-varchar is not very long :-}

-->
<entitymodel>
    <title>Entity Model for JIRA</title>
    <description>None</description>
    <copyright>Copyright (c) 2002-2006 Atlassian</copyright>
    <author>The Atlassian Dev Team</author>
    <version>1.0</version>

    <!-- sequence generator table -->
    <entity entity-name="SequenceValueItem" table-name="SEQUENCE_VALUE_ITEM" package-name="">
        <field name="seqName" type="id-long-ne"/>
        <field name="seqId" type="numeric"/>
        <prim-key field="seqName"/>
    </entity>

    <!-- User implementation -->
    <entity entity-name="User" table-name="cwd_user" package-name="">
        <field name="id" type="numeric"/>

        <field name="directoryId" col-name="directory_id" type="numeric"/>
        <field name="userName" col-name="user_name" type="long-varchar"/>
```

This is an XML file that contains the definition of all the tables in JIRA and their relationship with other tables.

Alternatively, you can also check the database schema on the Atlassian website, at `https:/ /developer.atlassian.com/display/JIRADEV/Database+Schema`.

Accessing HSQLDB

As previously mentioned, HSQLDB is used only for evaluation purposes and should not be used for production instances. You may, however, want to run queries to generate reports from the database. Luckily, HSQLDB comes with a built-in console that can be invoked by performing the following steps:

1. Shut down your JIRA service.
2. Use the following command to start the HSQLDB console:

```
java -cp JIRA_INSTALL/lib/hsqldb-1.8.0.5.jar
org.hsqldb.util.DatabaseManager -
user sa -url jdbc:hsqldb:JIRA_HOME/database/jiradb
```

In the preceding command, replace `JIRA_INSTALL` and `JIRA_HOME` with the directory locations, as per your installation. If you have installed JIRA using the Windows installer, the following procedure should work.

First, navigate to the `C:\Program Files\Atlassian\Application Data\JIRA\database` directory.

Then, run the following command:

```
java -cp ../../../JIRA/lib/hsqldb-1.8.0.5.jar
org.hsqldb.util.DatabaseManager -
user sa -url jdbc:hsqldb:jiradb
```

The **HSQL Database Manager** will be displayed on your screen:

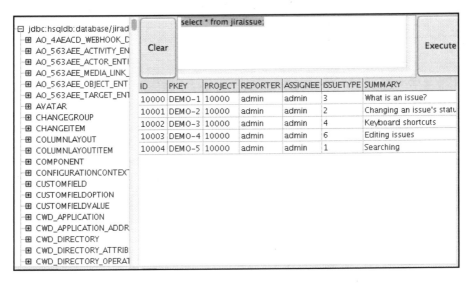

You can now run SQL queries in the **HSQL Database Manager** and check the output in the same window.

Accessing MySQL

The **HSQL Database Manager** should never be used in the production instance because it's prone to data loss. The recommended database is either MySQL or PostgreSQL. Earlier in this book, we discussed how to create a database in MySQL to store JIRA's data and configure it during the setup phase. To access your database in order to run SQL queries, you can either use the MySQL console, which comes with the MySQL server, or you can use **phpMyAdmin**.

phpMyAdmin

The phpMyAdmin application can be downloaded from `http://www.phpmyadmin.net/`.

This is a great web-based tool to manage your MySQL database and it's usually accessed using `http://localhost/phpmyadmin/`. The exact URL can be different, depending on your installation.

Perform these following steps:

1. Open the previous URL in your browser to launch **phpMyAdmin**:

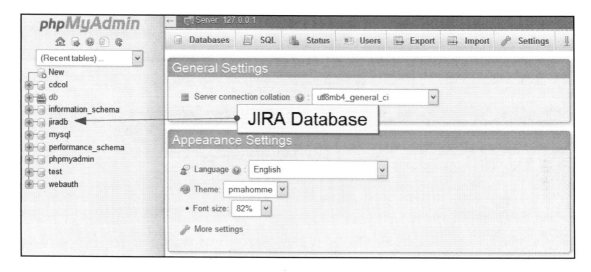

You will notice that the list of databases appears on the left-hand side. Our `jiradb` database also appears in this list. We created this database for our JIRA instance.

3. Click on the plus (+) sign before the database name to expand the table for this database.
4. You can click on any table to browse its content:

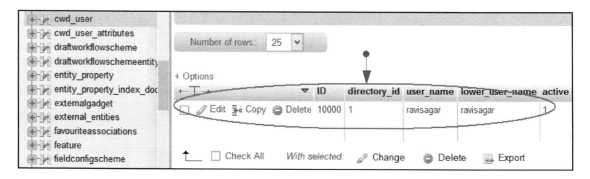

As you can see, we clicked on the cwd_user table and on the right-hand side, we have the list of users in our JIRA instance.

Similarly, you can browse any table you want in your JIRA instance. You should have some knowledge of JIRA's database schema to make sense out of this data. Also, if you want to generate complex reports that involve more than one table, you can write SQL queries as well.

1. Click on the **SQL** tab in the top navigation bar:

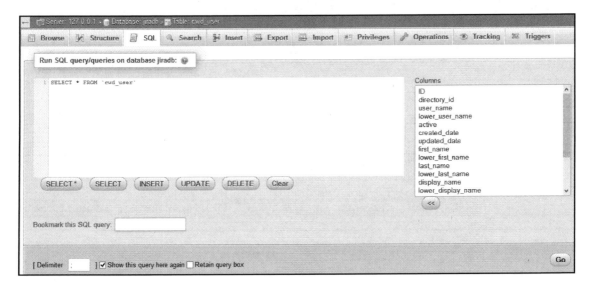

2. To execute your query, perform the following steps:
   1. In the preceding screenshot, you can enter your SQL queries under **Run SQL query/queries on database jiradb:**.
   2. Click on the **Go** button to run the SQL query.

The MySQL console

When you install the MySQL server on your machine, it comes with the MySQL console. This console can also be used to manage your database. It's not very user-friendly compared to phpMyAdmin, but once you remember the basic commands, you will likely prefer the MySQL console for quick access to the database.

Run the following command to enter the MySQL console:

```
mysql -u USERNAME -p
```

In the preceding command, replace USERNAME with your username. In our case, it's root. The command will ask you to enter your password, after which you will enter the MySQL console:

```
C:\WINDOWS\syste

C:\Users\HP1>mysql -u root -p
Enter password:
Welcome to the MySQL monitor.  Commands end with ; or \g.
Your MySQL connection id is 30
Server version: 5.6.16 MySQL Community Server (GPL)

Copyright (c) 2000, 2013, Oracle and/or its affiliates. All rights reserved.

Oracle is a registered trademark of Oracle Corporation and/or its
affiliates. Other names may be trademarks of their respective
owners.

Type 'help;' or '\h' for help. Type '\c' to clear the current input statement.

mysql>
```

In the MySQL console, you can enter your commands and run queries.

Let's take a look at the structure of a few common JIRA tables and generate reports combining these multiple tables. For the following example queries, you may use either phpMyAdmin or the MySQL console, depending on your comfort level.

Accessing PostgreSQL

When you install PostgreSQL using the Windows installer, it comes with **pgAdmin III**, which is another tool for PostgreSQL's administration and management:

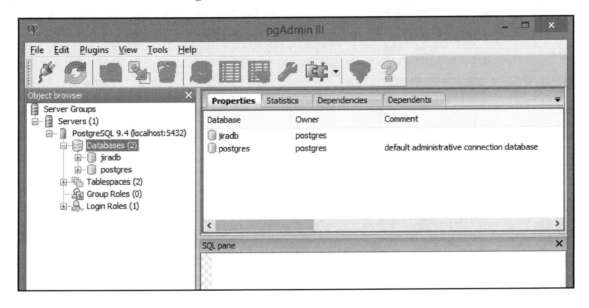

Let's take a look at some JIRA database tables that store useful information.

User table

The cwd_user table is used to store a user in the system. Let's check the structure of this table.

The table structure

Run the following query:

```
desc cwd_user;
```

The output of the query is as follows:

```
mysql> desc cwd_user;
+----------------------+---------------+------+-----+---------+-------+
| Field                | Type          | Null | Key | Default | Extra |
+----------------------+---------------+------+-----+---------+-------+
| ID                   | decimal(18,0) | NO   | PRI | NULL    |       |
| directory_id         | decimal(18,0) | YES  |     | NULL    |       |
| user_name            | varchar(255)  | YES  |     | NULL    |       |
| lower_user_name      | varchar(255)  | YES  | MUL | NULL    |       |
| active               | decimal(9,0)  | YES  |     | NULL    |       |
| created_date         | datetime      | YES  |     | NULL    |       |
| updated_date         | datetime      | YES  |     | NULL    |       |
| first_name           | varchar(255)  | YES  |     | NULL    |       |
| lower_first_name     | varchar(255)  | YES  | MUL | NULL    |       |
| last_name            | varchar(255)  | YES  |     | NULL    |       |
| lower_last_name      | varchar(255)  | YES  | MUL | NULL    |       |
| display_name         | varchar(255)  | YES  |     | NULL    |       |
| lower_display_name   | varchar(255)  | YES  | MUL | NULL    |       |
| email_address        | varchar(255)  | YES  |     | NULL    |       |
| lower_email_address  | varchar(255)  | YES  | MUL | NULL    |       |
| CREDENTIAL           | varchar(255)  | YES  |     | NULL    |       |
| deleted_externally   | decimal(9,0)  | YES  |     | NULL    |       |
| EXTERNAL_ID          | varchar(255)  | YES  | MUL | NULL    |       |
+----------------------+---------------+------+-----+---------+-------+
18 rows in set (0.02 sec)
```

Finding the list of inactive JIRA users

One of the main responsibilities of JIRA administrators is user management. Let's say you want to find the list of inactive users, along with their directory information. In big JIRA instances, it may be possible that there are users in JIRA's internal directory, as well as users from corporate LDAP.

The following query will return the list of inactive users in JIRA:

```
SELECT
u.user_name,u.first_name,u.last_name,u.email_address,d.directory_name
from cwd_user u join cwd_directory d on u.directory_id = d.id where
u.active
= 0;
```

The preceding query relies on another table, called `cwd_directory`. This directory stores the user directory information, whereas whether the user is active or not is stored in the `cwd_user` table under the `active` table field.

The jiraissue table

The `jiraissue` table is used to store JIRA issues. Let's check the structure of this table.

The table structure

Run the following query:

```
desc jiraissue;
```

The output of this query is as follows:

```
Oracle is a registered trademark of Oracle Corporation and/or its
affiliates. Other names may be trademarks of their respective
owners.

Type 'help;' or '\h' for help. Type '\c' to clear the current input statement.

mysql> use jiradb;
Database changed
mysql> desc jiraissue;
+----------------------+----------------+------+-----+---------+-------+
| Field                | Type           | Null | Key | Default | Extra |
+----------------------+----------------+------+-----+---------+-------+
| ID                   | decimal(18,0)  | NO   | PRI | NULL    |       |
| pkey                 | varchar(255)   | YES  |     | NULL    |       |
| issuenum             | decimal(18,0)  | YES  | MUL | NULL    |       |
| PROJECT              | decimal(18,0)  | YES  | MUL | NULL    |       |
| REPORTER             | varchar(255)   | YES  | MUL | NULL    |       |
| ASSIGNEE             | varchar(255)   | YES  | MUL | NULL    |       |
| CREATOR              | varchar(255)   | YES  |     | NULL    |       |
| issuetype            | varchar(255)   | YES  |     | NULL    |       |
| SUMMARY              | varchar(255)   | YES  |     | NULL    |       |
| DESCRIPTION          | longtext       | YES  |     | NULL    |       |
| ENVIRONMENT          | longtext       | YES  |     | NULL    |       |
| PRIORITY             | varchar(255)   | YES  |     | NULL    |       |
| RESOLUTION           | varchar(255)   | YES  |     | NULL    |       |
| issuestatus          | varchar(255)   | YES  |     | NULL    |       |
| CREATED              | datetime       | YES  |     | NULL    |       |
| UPDATED              | datetime       | YES  | MUL | NULL    |       |
| DUEDATE              | datetime       | YES  |     | NULL    |       |
| RESOLUTIONDATE       | datetime       | YES  |     | NULL    |       |
| VOTES                | decimal(18,0)  | YES  |     | NULL    |       |
| WATCHES              | decimal(18,0)  | YES  |     | NULL    |       |
| TIMEORIGINALESTIMATE | decimal(18,0)  | YES  |     | NULL    |       |
| TIMEESTIMATE         | decimal(18,0)  | YES  |     | NULL    |       |
| TIMESPENT            | decimal(18,0)  | YES  |     | NULL    |       |
| WORKFLOW_ID          | decimal(18,0)  | YES  | MUL | NULL    |       |
| SECURITY             | decimal(18,0)  | YES  |     | NULL    |       |
| FIXFOR               | decimal(18,0)  | YES  |     | NULL    |       |
| COMPONENT            | decimal(18,0)  | YES  |     | NULL    |       |
+----------------------+----------------+------+-----+---------+-------+
27 rows in set (0.01 sec)
```

Finding issues of a specific project

It's quite easy to find the list of issues of a specific project using the JIRA **Issue Navigator**, but as we are exploring the database schema and its various tables, let's fetch the issues of a specific project directly from the database:

```
SELECT p.id AS project_id, p.pname AS project_name, CONCAT("SSP-
",ji.issuenum)  AS issue_id, ji.reporter AS issue_reporter FROM project p
LEFT OUTER JOIN jiraissue ji ON ji.project = p.id WHERE p.pkey = 'SSP'
ORDER
BY ji.issuenum;
```

The preceding query will display the list of issues of the project with the SSP key. You can replace the project key with your own and try the previous query. The project name and a few other fields are fetched from the `project` table.

The customfield table

The `customfield` table is used to store all the custom fields. Let's check the structure of this table.

The table structure

Execute the following query:

```
desc customfield;
```

The output of the query is as follows:

```
mysql> desc customfield;
+----------------------+---------------+------+-----+---------+-------+
| Field                | Type          | Null | Key | Default | Extra |
+----------------------+---------------+------+-----+---------+-------+
| ID                   | decimal(18,0) | NO   | PRI | NULL    |       |
| cfkey                | varchar(255)  | YES  |     | NULL    |       |
| CUSTOMFIELDTYPEKEY   | varchar(255)  | YES  |     | NULL    |       |
| CUSTOMFIELDSEARCHERKEY | varchar(255) | YES  |     | NULL    |       |
| cfname               | varchar(255)  | YES  |     | NULL    |       |
| DESCRIPTION          | text          | YES  |     | NULL    |       |
| defaultvalue         | varchar(255)  | YES  |     | NULL    |       |
| FIELDTYPE            | decimal(18,0) | YES  |     | NULL    |       |
| PROJECT              | decimal(18,0) | YES  |     | NULL    |       |
| ISSUETYPE            | varchar(255)  | YES  |     | NULL    |       |
+----------------------+---------------+------+-----+---------+-------+
10 rows in set (0.11 sec)
```

The customfieldvalue table

The customfieldvalue table is used to store custom field values. Let's check the structure of this table.

The table structure

Run the following query:

```
desc customfieldvalue;
```

The output of the query is as follows:

```
mysql> desc customfieldvalue;
+-------------+---------------+------+-----+---------+-------+
| Field       | Type          | Null | Key | Default | Extra |
+-------------+---------------+------+-----+---------+-------+
| ID          | decimal(18,0) | NO   | PRI | NULL    |       |
| ISSUE       | decimal(18,0) | YES  | MUL | NULL    |       |
| CUSTOMFIELD | decimal(18,0) | YES  |     | NULL    |       |
| PARENTKEY   | varchar(255)  | YES  |     | NULL    |       |
| STRINGVALUE | varchar(255)  | YES  |     | NULL    |       |
| NUMBERVALUE | decimal(18,6) | YES  |     | NULL    |       |
| TEXTVALUE   | longtext      | YES  |     | NULL    |       |
| DATEVALUE   | datetime      | YES  |     | NULL    |       |
| VALUETYPE   | varchar(255)  | YES  |     | NULL    |       |
+-------------+---------------+------+-----+---------+-------+
9 rows in set (0.01 sec)
```

Some useful SQL queries

We will list a few useful SQL queries that can help JIRA administrators quickly find the information they are looking for. It's important to mention that new versions of JIRA are released quite regularly, with new features and bug fixes. The database schema may change slightly in new versions. Therefore, verify your SQL queries on the new version of JIRA before using them.

List of shared filters

The following SQL query will list the filters created in the JIRA instance that are shared with others:

```
SELECT sr.filtername, sr.authorname
FROM searchrequest sr
LEFT JOIN sharepermissions sp ON sp.entityid = sr.ID
WHERE sp.entitytype = "SearchRequest" AND sp.sharetype != "global";
```

Fetching users of a specific group

It's quite easy to find users of a specific group from the JIRA interface, but you should know how to fetch this information using SQL. The following query will list the users of the jira-software-users group. You can change it to any group in your instance:

```
SELECT cu.user_name, cu.display_name, cu.email_address
FROM cwd_user AS cu
INNER JOIN cwd_membership AS cm
ON cu.directory_id=cm.directory_id
AND cu.lower_user_name=cm.lower_child_name
AND cm.membership_type='GROUP_USER'
WHERE cm.lower_parent_name='jira-software-users';
```

List of users with count of comments

One of the main responsibilities of JIRA administrators is to find users that are either inactive or not using JIRA a lot in a given month. The next query will fetch the list of users, along with the number of comments they posted in a particular month. This will be useful in cases where it's necessary to find users who are active in system, but not performing much activity:

```
SELECT author, count(author) as comments
FROM jiraaction j
WHERE UPDATED > "2014-12-01 00:00:00"
group by author
ORDER BY author ASC;
```

Fetching the count of issues per component

Let's say you want to find the list of not only all the components in the system, but also the number of issues they are connected to. The following query will give you that information quickly:

```
SELECT count(ji.id), c.cname FROM jiraissue ji
INNER JOIN nodeassociation na ON ji.id = na.source_node_id
INNER JOIN component c ON na.sink_node_id = c.id
GROUP BY c.cname;
```

Listing projects of a specific project category

If you want to retrieve the list of projects in a specific category, use the following query:

```
SELECT p.pname, p.LEAD, p.pkey
FROM project p
JOIN nodeassociation na ON (p.ID = na.SOURCE_NODE_ID AND
na.ASSOCIATION_TYPE
= 'ProjectCategory')
JOIN projectcategory pc ON (na.SINK_NODE_ID = pc.ID)
WHERE pc.cname like 'Category';
```

List of assignees or reporters in a particular project

Sometimes you have to find the list of users who are involved in a particular project as either an assignee or as a reporter. This is particularly useful when you want to migrate a few projects from one instance to another and you also need to migrate the associated users:

```
SELECT DISTINCT reporter AS "User" FROM jiraissue WHERE project IN (
    SELECT id AS "Project ID" FROM project WHERE pkey IN ('SSP','SSPA')
)
UNION
SELECT DISTINCT assignee AS "User" FROM jiraissue WHERE project IN (
    SELECT id AS "Project ID" FROM project WHERE pkey IN ('SSP','SSPA')
)
```

Summary

In this chapter, you learned how to retrieve information directly from the database. This is quite useful when information cannot easily be fetched from the JIRA interface. We discussed some common JIRA tables and looked at some example queries on how to find useful information. The ability to access the database directly empowers JIRA administrators to generate complex reports and seek information faster.

In the next chapter, you will learn how to customize the look and feel of JIRA by inserting custom CSS code. You will also learn to modify the behavior of the HTML elements of the JIRA interface using JavaScript. We will take a look at some examples to show/hide JIRA fields based on the user selection of a specific value of a select list, and to modify the values of text fields to insert text-based templates.

14
Customizing Look, Feel, and Behavior

JIRA offers a simple functionality in its UI to change the colors of various sections and elements, such as the header, footer, and links; you can also upload your custom logo. However, if you want to change the width of a certain section or the whole body element, you can't do it from the UI. It's possible to include your own custom CSS to make changes to the look and feel. It's also possible to load custom JavaScript in a JIRA instance; this enables changes in the behavior of various HTML elements. For example, you can selectively show or hide a field on another field's values and insert text-based templates in JIRA fields. In this chapter, we will take a look at such customizations.

We will cover the following topics:

- Adding your own CSS
- Adding JavaScript to show/hide field
- **Velocity** templates

Adding your own CSS

The JIRA administration interface allows you to change the look and feel of various elements in JIRA and to change the default logo. Perform these steps to customize your JIRA interface:

1. Navigate to **Administration** | **System** | **Look and feel** (under **USER INTERFACE**).

2. The first option on this page is to change **Logo**. Click on the **Browse...** button and then click on the **Upload Logo** button to upload your own custom logo:

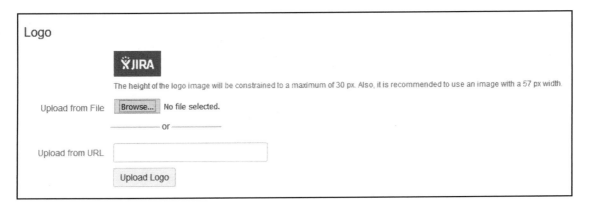

3. The second option is to display **Site Title**, located next to logo. Check the **Show Site Title** checkbox and click on the **Update** button:

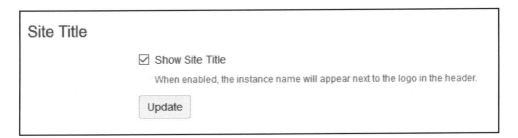

You will notice that the name of your instance, which you entered while installing JIRA, will now appear right next to the JIRA logo. In our example, it's **Sparxsys JIRA Demo**, which now appears next to the JIRA logo:

4. The third option is to update **Favicon**, which appears in the browser tab when JIRA is opened. Click on the **Browse...** button to select the new **Favicon** image and then click on the **Upload Favicon** button:

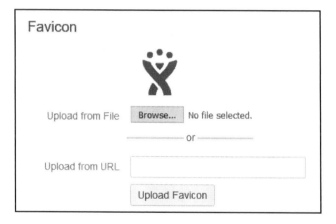

5. The fourth option is to change the color of various sections of JIRA's web interface. For instance, click on any color in the box for **Header Background Color**. In the popup window, select the new color, or enter the color's hexadecimal value directly. Let's change this color to red, with a hexadecimal value of #ff0000. Click on the **Update** button to continue:

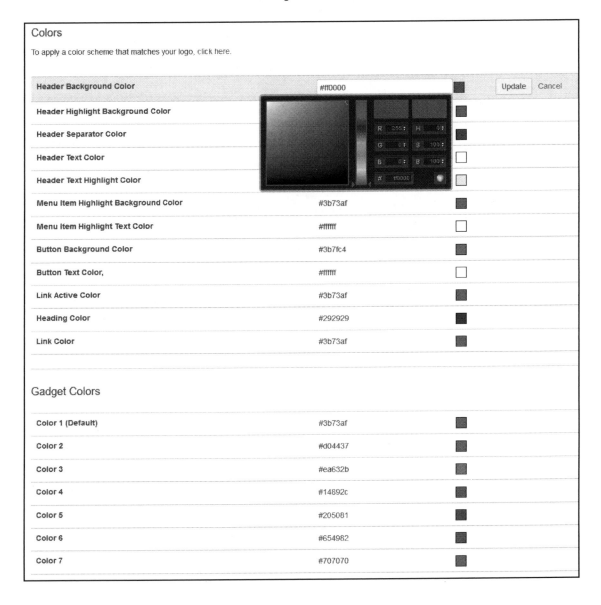

The color of the main navigation bar is now red.

You can change the color of various sections available from this interface and match it with your company's color scheme, but JIRA's interface is limited to changing colors. If you want to change the width of the <body> element or give extra padding and margins to certain sections, it's not possible to do it through this interface.

However, it's possible to insert your own custom CSS in JIRA, which can override the default look and feel. Perform these steps:

1. Go to **Administration** | **System** | **Announcement banner** (under **USER INTERFACE**).

2. In the **Announcement** text area, copy `<LINK href="http://localhost:8080/includes/custom_css/custom_style.css" rel="stylesheet" type="text/css">` and click on the **Set Banner** button:

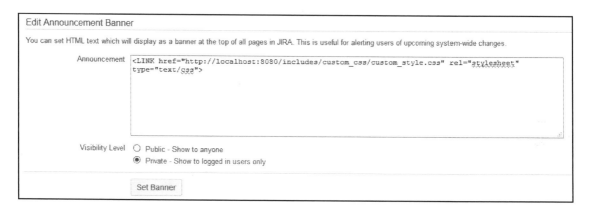

The **Announcement banner** is used to display text common to all the users in JIRA on all the pages in JIRA; the good thing is that it supports HTML tags as well. In our case, we want to load a custom CSS code to all the pages. The `LINK` tag mentioned previously specifies the path where our custom CSS will be found. Perform these steps:

1. Create a `custom_css` folder in the following directory in your JIRA installation directory:

   `JIRA_INSTALL/atlassian-jira/includes/.`

2. Navigate to the `custom_css` folder and create a `custom_style.css` file; the location of the file should be `JIRA_INSTALL/atlassian-jira/includes/custom_css/custom_style.css`.

This file contains the CSS to make changes to the UI of JIRA which are otherwise not possible through configurations. When you save the **Announcement banner,** nothing will be displayed to the user, but this CSS file will be loaded on all the pages. You can also verify this by viewing the source code of any page in JIRA and searching for the filename:

```
269
270  <div id="announcement-banner" class="alertHeader">
271      <LINK href="http://localhost:8080/includes/custom_css/custom_style.css" rel="stylesheet" type="text/css">
272  </div>
273
274
```

In the preceding screenshot, you can see that our custom CSS file is loaded.

Now it's time to add some CSS code to this file and change the look and feel of our JIRA instance. Open the `custom_style.css` code in your favorite editor and enter the following code snippet:

```
body {
   background-color: #e0e0e0;
   padding: 0 70px;
}
#content {
   box-shadow: 0px 0px 5px #232323;
}
#footer {
   background-color: #232323;
   box-shadow: 0px 0px 5px #232323;
}
```

Then, refresh your JIRA instance in your browser. You should now see that the preceding CSS code is applied and the changes have appeared, as shown in the following screenshot:

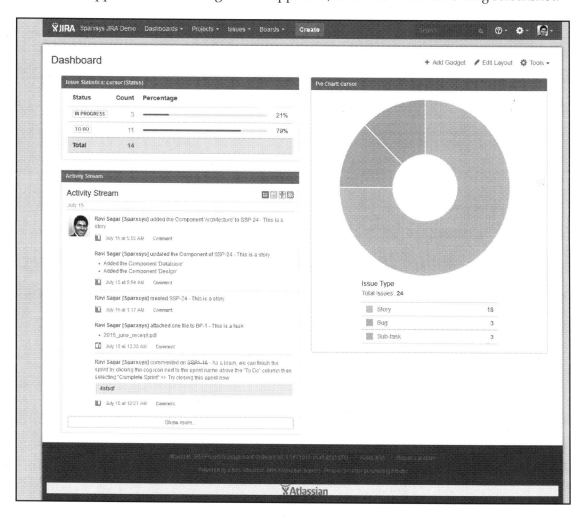

You can further customize the look and feel of the web page by adding your own CSS code. This will be loaded to every page; just make sure that the code in the **Announcement banner** is not removed.

We have added an additional file to the JIRA filesystem. It's very important to keep a note of this file and save it separately too. When you upgrade your JIRA instance to a new version or migrate to a new server, the JIRA administrator should make sure that this file is not removed; otherwise, the customizations to the look and feel of the web page will not appear.

Adding JavaScript to show/hide field

JIRA comes with tons of functionalities and customizations; however, there are times when you want more control over the behavior of HTML fields. For instance, if you want to show or hide a particular custom field on the basis of a value of another custom field, you can use custom JavaScript to do this.

Let's take a scenario where users who create a ticket in JIRA need to enter their analysis in one of the text areas based on the custom field, but they only need to fill it in when the priority of the issue is highest. Now, in order to achieve this, we want to completely hide the **Analysis** field first, and display it only when users set **Priority** as **Highest**.

Unlike the preceding example for inserting custom CSS, the custom JavaScript can be added directly from the JIRA interface. Perform these steps:

1. Go to JIRA **Administration** | **Issues** | **Custom fields** (under **FIELDS**).
2. Click on the **Add custom field** button in the top-right corner and select **Field Type** as **Text Field (multi-line)**.
3. On the next screen, enter `Analysis` as **Name** and enter the JavaScript code (`analysis_js.css`) in the **Description** field of the custom field, as shown in the following screenshot:

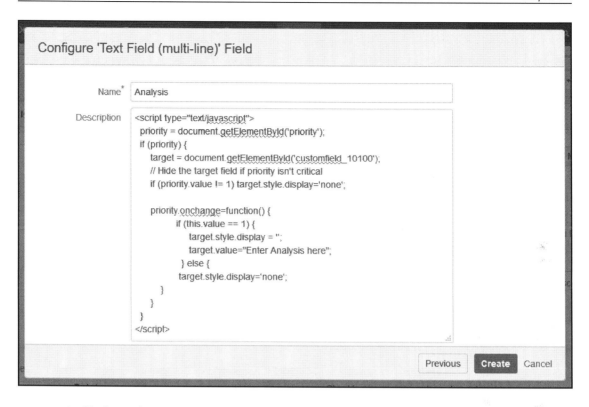

Configure 'Text Field (multi-line)' Field

Name* Analysis

Description
```
<script type="text/javascript">
    priority = document.getElementById('priority');
    if (priority) {
        target = document.getElementById('customfield_10100');
        // Hide the target field if priority isn't critical
        if (priority.value != 1) target.style.display='none';

        priority.onchange=function() {
            if (this.value == 1) {
                target.style.display = '';
                target.value="Enter Analysis here";
            } else {
                target.style.display='none';
            }
        }
    }
</script>
```

Previous **Create** Cancel

4. Click on the **Create** button to continue.
5. Add this field in the screen associated with the **Create Issue** operation just after the **Priority** system field.

Note that the field description of custom fields can also be controlled by **Field Configurations** option. In `Chapter 4`, *Customizing JIRA for Test Management*, we discussed the purpose of field configurations. In the previous example, we added the JavaScript code in the field description while creating the custom field; it will be overwritten if field configurations are used in the project.

Let's understand the important section of this JavaScript code.

The **Analysis** custom field ID is equal to `10100` and we assigned a target variable to this field:

```
target = document.getElementById('customfield_10100');
```

Then, for the **Priority** field, we check whether its value is **Highest**, which is selectable from a list with different numerical values for **Highest**, **High**, **Medium**, **Low**, and **Lowest** (**Highest** having the numerical value 1). For every other value, the **Analysis** field is hidden:

```
if (priority.value != 1)
  target.style.display='none';
priority.onchange=function() {
  if (this.value == 1) {
    target.style.display = '';
    target.value="enter message here";
  } else {
    target.style.display='none';
  }
}
```

When users select the **Priority** as **Highest**, the **Analysis** field is displayed again.

Creating the issue

After creating the**Analysis** field, just add one more issue in JIRA to test it. By default, the **Analysis** field is not displayed to the user:

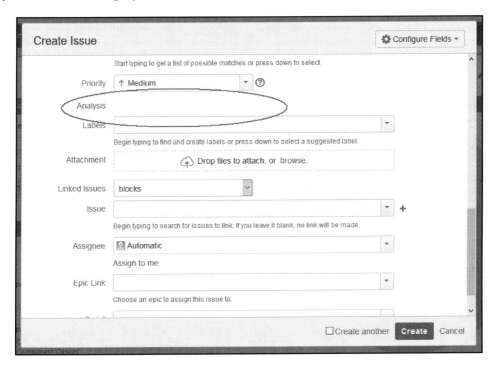

The moment you select **Priority** as **Highest**, the **Analysis** text area will be visible to the user:

This example is just to give you an idea of how to use JavaScript to control the behavior of HTML elements.

Velocity templates

Velocity is a Java-based, server-side template engine used to render page content that allows Java objects to be used alongside HTML elements. As JIRA has been written in Java, it utilizes Velocity templates to display the content. These template files can be modified by the user. However, Atlassian will not provide any support for such changes to the template files; therefore, I recommend taking a backup of the original files before making any changes to them.

In this section, let's discuss a few examples where we will make changes to these templates.

Modifying the description system field with predefined text

JIRA allows you to add a description for every custom field, where some instructions on how to enter the data can be given to the end user. However, it's sometimes useful to present the user with a predefined text, which is like a text-based template. In this example, we will add some default text in the JIRA **Description** system field. Perform the following steps:

1. Edit the following file in your JIRA installation directory:

   ```
   JIRA_INSTALL/atlassian-jira/WEB-INF/
   classes/templates/jira/issue/field/description-edit.vm.
   ```

2. Enter the following code just before the `$rendererDescriptor.getEditVM()` function:

   ```
   #set ($description = "Please enter the details in steps.\
   \
   Step 1:\
   \
   Step 2:\
   \
   Step 3:\
   \
   Issue Occurrence: Once or Always\
   Current Status: Working or Not Working
   \
   ")
   #set ($description = $description.replace('',''))
   ```

3. The code is shown in the following screenshot:

```
17    $rendererDescriptor.getEditVM() function:
18    #set ($description = "Please enter the details in steps.\
19    \
20    Step 1:\
21    \
22    Step 2:\
23    \
24    Step 3:\
25    \
26    Issue Occurrence: Once or Always\
27    Current Status: Working or Not Working
28    \
29    ")
30    #set ($description = $description.replace('\',''))
31
```

4. Restart your JIRA instance.
5. Once the JIRA instance is restarted, click on the **Create** button to create an issue.
6. You will notice that the default text now appears in the **Description** field:

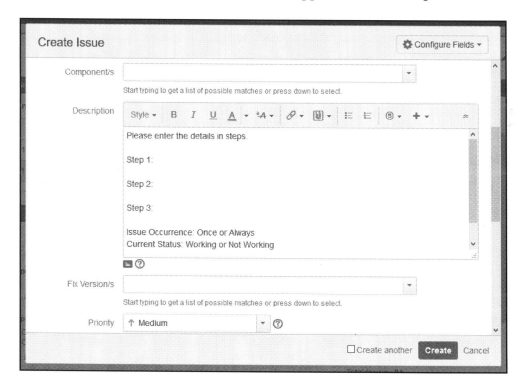

You can use the same method to add custom predefined text to other fields as well.

After modifying the **Description** field template using the previous code, this predefined text will be added to the **Description** field for all the projects and issue types in your JIRA instance, but it's possible to restrict it to a specific project and issue type. Instead, use the following code:

```
#if ($issue.getProject().getString("key") == 'SSP')
  #if(($description == "") && ($issue.getIssueTypeObject().getName() ==
"Story"))
    #set ($description = "Please enter the details in steps.\
      \
    Step 1:\
      \
    Step 2:\
      \
    Step 3:\
      \
    Issue Recurrance: Once or Always\
    Current Status: Working or Not Working
      \
      ")
    #set ($description = $description.replace('',''))
  #end
#end
```

To define the default value of a custom field, the context can also be used, which is discussed in Chapter 17, *JIRA Best Practices*.

In the preceding code, we just added two lines at the top to restrict **Project Key** to SSP and **Issue Type** to Story. Make sure that you restart your JIRA instance before making any changes in the template file. If you don't want to restart your instance, it's also possible to disable the caching of Velocity templates by following these steps in your JIRA installation directory:

1. Uncomment (remove the # sign from `#velocimacro.library.autoreload=true`).
2. Change `class.resource.loader.cache` from `true` to `false`.
3. Open `JIRA_INSTALL/atlassian-jira/WEB-INF/classes/velocity.properties`.
4. Now, any change in Velocity templates will be reflected in your instance without restarting JIRA. Do this only in your development environment.

As mentioned previously, for custom CSS, keep track of any changes you make in the template file and always keep a backup of the original template file. It's important to note that Atlassian will not provide any support for customizations made on the template files.

Modifying the footer

There are various template files you can customize in JIRA, and for various sections of the web page. Let's take a look at another example, where we will add some custom text to the footer section. Perform these steps:

1. Edit the following file in your JIRA installation directory:

   ```
   JIRA_INSTALL/atlassian-jira/WEB-
   INF/classes/templates/plugins/footer/footer.vm.
   ```

2. This file has a lot of content; just navigate to the bottom of the file and add the following lines before #end:

   ```
   <ul>
       <li>This is a Test JIRA Instance and we are adding text in the
   footer.
       </li>
   </ul>
   ```

   The file looks as follows:

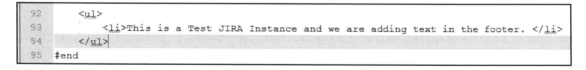

```
92    <ul>
93        <li>This is a Test JIRA Instance and we are adding text in the footer. </li>
94    </ul>
95 #end
```

3. Restart your JIRA instance.
4. Once the JIRA instance is restarted, you will notice some additional text before the Atlassian logo:

Displaying a custom field in e-mails

It's also possible to customize e-mails sent to the users. The e-mail content is also generated using Velocity templates. Let's now customize the template for e-mails that are sent when an issue is created. The custom fields that are created in the system are not included in the e-mail content, but we will modify the Velocity template of the issue creation e-mail and include the **Analysis** field (which we added earlier). Perform these steps:

1. Edit the following file in your JIRA installation directory:

    ```
    JIRA_INSTALL/atlassian-jira/WEB-
    INF/classes/templates/email/html/issuecreated.vm
    ```

2. Add the following code before the final `#parse` at the end of the file:

    ```
    #if ($issue.getCustomFieldValue("customfield_10100"))
    <tr valign="top">
      <td >
        #text("Analysis"):
      </td>
      <td>
        $issue.getCustomFieldValue("customfield_10100")
      </td>
    </tr>
    #end
    ```

3. Save the file and restart JIRA.
4. Once the JIRA instance is restarted, create one issue in JIRA and fill the **Analysis** field.
5. Check the e-mail you receive; it should have the **Analysis** field value now. The e-mail content should look similar to the following screenshot:

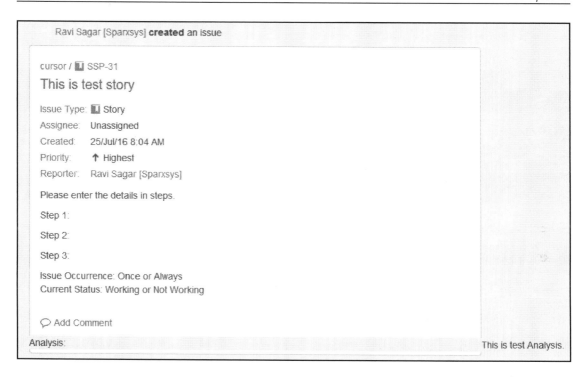

There are templates for similar events and system fields. You can explore them and make changes to them once you get comfortable with Velocity templates.

Summary

In this chapter, you learned how to customize the look and feel of JIRA by inserting custom CSS codes. We also modified the behavior of HTML elements of the JIRA interface using JavaScript to show/hide JIRA fields based on the selection made by the user, of a specific value from a selectable list. Finally, we explored Velocity templates and how to modify the displayed content. We also discussed how to insert custom field values in e-mails.

In the next chapter, we will discuss JIRA Service Desk, which has become the most popular way to cater to your customer support requests. Service Desk is now a separate application, which can either be installed as a standalone application or as an application along with JIRA Core. Service Desk comes with inbuilt configurations that are standard to any support project.

15
Implementing JIRA Service Desk

In this chapter, we will learn how to implement a JIRA Service Desk application for taking care of IT help desks and support requests that is not only easy to use, but comes with the preconfigured features of a ticketing system out of the box. All the support tickets are tracked using a JIRA project, but, it comes with a customer portal that makes it really easy to raise requests. Also, JIRA Service Desk can be integrated with Confluence and users can easily search for related issues while raising new tickets.

In this chapter, we will cover the following:

- Product overview—JIRA Service Desk?
- Installing JIRA Service Desk

Product overview – JIRA Service Desk?

In Chapter 1, *Planning Your JIRA Installation*, we discussed the new JIRA 7, which was split into three separate applications called JIRA Core, JIRA Software, and JIRA Service Desk. In Chapter 6, *Sample Implementation of Use Cases*, we discussed some sample use cases of JIRA and in Chapter 4, *Customizing JIRA for Test Management*, we also looked at how JIRA can be customized for test management. Similarly, JIRA can also be configured for support requests, but in that case, only users who have a JIRA account can log in to raise requests. In cases where there is a need to have unlimited customers who can create tickets, JIRA Service Desk can be used. JIRA Service Desk does not impose any limit on the customers and it also comes with the standard features of a typical support and ticketing system.

Installing JIRA Service Desk

In case you only want to use JIRA for support projects, you can download and install the JIRA Service Desk application. The procedure to install it is similar to that of JIRA Software, which we discussed in Chapter 1, *Planning Your JIRA Installation*. However, if you are already using JIRA Core or JIRA Software in your organization, you can still install the JIRA Service Desk application over your existing instance. Follow the steps mentioned here to install the JIRA Service Desk application on your existing JIRA instance:

1. Download the latest version of JIRA Service Desk available. You will get a jira-servicedesk-application-3.1.7.obr file at https://marketplace.atlassian.com/plugins/com.atlassian.servicedesk.application/versions.

2. Go to **Administration | Applications | Versions & licenses**. On this screen, you will get the list of all the applications such as JIRA Core and JIRA Software that are already installed. Click on the **Upload an application** link in the top-right corner and in the **Upload application** popup that appears, upload the jira-servicedesk-application-3.1.7.obr file that you just downloaded:

3. JIRA Service Desk will be installed. You can also generate an evaluation license for it. Once the license is installed you will be able to create a new Service Desk project:

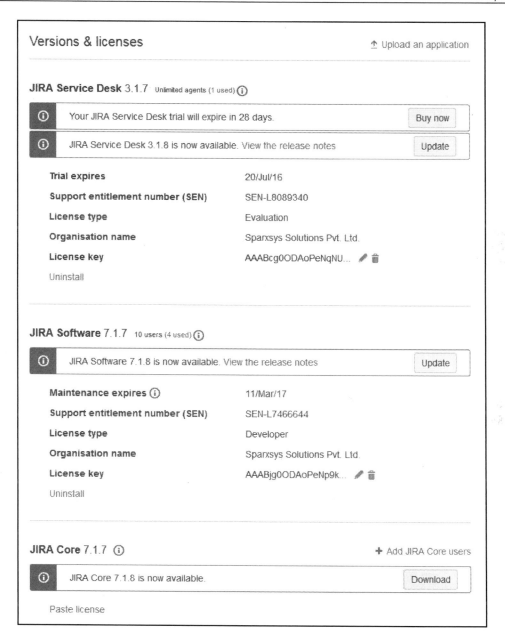

Versions & licenses

⬆ Upload an application

JIRA Service Desk 3.1.7 Unlimited agents (1 used) ⓘ

| ⓘ | Your JIRA Service Desk trial will expire in 28 days. | Buy now |

| ⓘ | JIRA Service Desk 3.1.8 is now available. View the release notes | Update |

Trial expires	20/Jul/16
Support entitlement number (SEN)	SEN-L8089340
License type	Evaluation
Organisation name	Sparxsys Solutions Pvt. Ltd.
License key	AAABcg0ODAoPeNqNU... ✏ 🗑

Uninstall

JIRA Software 7.1.7 10 users (4 used) ⓘ

| ⓘ | JIRA Software 7.1.8 is now available. View the release notes | Update |

Maintenance expires ⓘ	11/Mar/17
Support entitlement number (SEN)	SEN-L7466644
License type	Developer
Organisation name	Sparxsys Solutions Pvt. Ltd.
License key	AAABjg0ODAoPeNp9k... ✏ 🗑

Uninstall

JIRA Core 7.1.7 ⓘ

➕ Add JIRA Core users

| ⓘ | JIRA Core 7.1.8 is now available. | Download |

Paste license

4. Go to the navigation menu at the top of the screen and then click on **Projects** | **Create project**. On the **Create project** popup, select **IT Service Desk** under **SERVICE DESK** and press the **Next** button to continue:

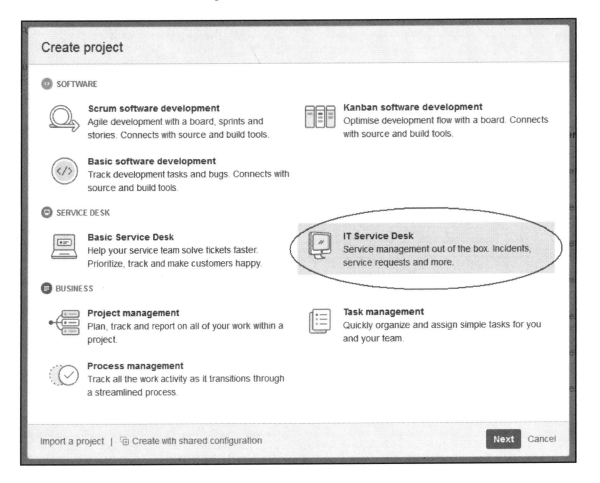

5. On the **IT Service Desk** popup, enter project **Name** and **Key**, and press the **Submit** button to continue:

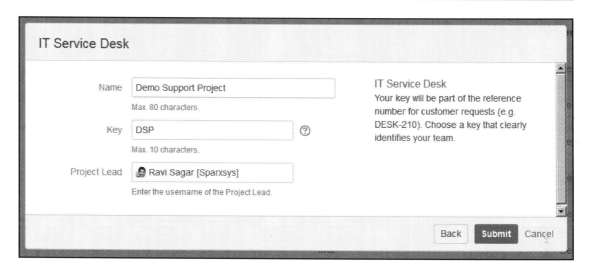

6. A new project with the Service Desk type will be created now. A typical Service Desk project will be quite similar to a standard JIRA project, but it comes with some additional features:

7. Once the project is created, you will be greeted with a **Welcome guide**, which contains several links to Atlassian documentation to get you familiar with Service Desk. In the project sidebar there are three tabs: **Queues**, **Customers**, and **Reports**. Let us understand each of them.

Queues

A queue is simply a filtered list of issues based on predefined conditions. For instance, there are several queues already defined in your project, such as **Unassigned issues**, **Assigned to me**, **Due in 24h**, and more.

Queues are somewhat similar to JIRA filters. You can also create your own queues. Click on the **New queue** link, as shown in the following screenshot:

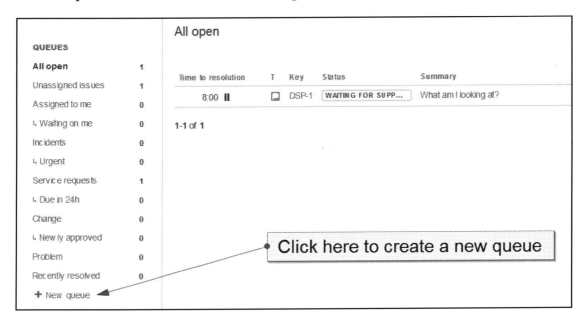

On the **New queue** screen, enter **Name** as `In Progress`, and, under **Issues to show**, select **Status** as **In Progress**. If you are familiar with JQL then click on the **Advanced** link right next to the **Issues to show** section. Press the **Create** button to save the queue:

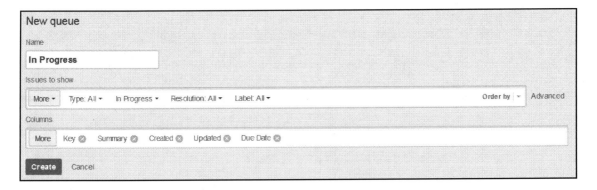

The queue will now be saved and available in the existing list of **QUEUES** in your project.

Customers

Your Service Desk project is, by default, open for **everyone with an account** in your JIRA instance, but we can limit which user or group will be the **Customers**, and can raise requests in this project:

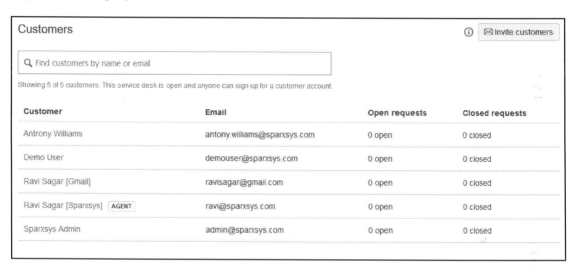

Reports

The Service Desk project comes with some really good inbuilt reports that will help you understand the current progress of your team working on the support project:

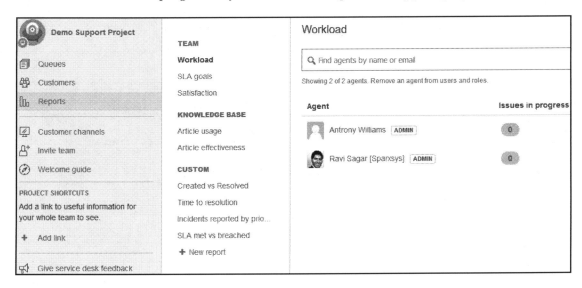

Let us understand the purpose of these reports.

Workload

This is a simple report that shows the number of requests your team is working on right now. It will help you to evenly distribute the workload among your agents. The reports display the number of **Issues in progress** for each agent. This is an important report, which helps the project lead to evenly distribute the work among agents so they are not under- or over-allocated.

SLA goals

Service Desk comes with **Service Level Agreement (SLA)** such as **Time to first response** and **Time to resolution**. This report will tell you if your team is able to achieve these SLA goals or not. The report displays the percentage of successful achievement of the SLA in the last seven days. These reports can quickly tell how the team is performing with regard to resolving the issues, which are measured by time-bound goals.

Satisfaction

This report will display the average customer satisfaction level. This helps you to understand whether your customers are happy with your service or not. It displays an average of the ratings given by users. It is a nice and quick way to get general feedback from users and can help to understand their satisfaction levels.

Article usage

If you have linked a Confluence space with your project, then this report shows the number of times articles were viewed and how many customers found those articles useful. JIRA Service Desk is closely integrated with Confluence spaces; it provides the related articles to the user while they are raising a new request, which might be a known issue or a very common request. In such cases, an article in the linked Confluence space can help the users self-service themselves.

Article effectiveness

This report shows the number of issues created by customers versus the number of issues customers solved themselves by viewing the articles. Understanding how many times users referred to the linked Confluence space articles and helped themselves by reading them can give you an idea of the effectiveness of those articles.

Created vs Resolved

This reports displays the number of issues **Created vs Resolved** for the selected duration, such as **Past 7 days**, **Past 14 days**, or **Past 30 days**. A similar report is usually present in non-JIRA Service Desk projects too.

Time to resolution

This report shows how much time is taken to resolve all the issues, along with how much time is taken to resolve an issue of a particular type, such as **Incidents**.

Incidents reported by priority

A count of issues based on individual priorities is displayed in this report. It is useful to get a quick glance of the issue count broken up by their priorities, such as **Highest**, **High**, **Medium**, **Low**, and **Lowest**.

SLA met vs breached

A simple count of how many issues achieved their SLA goal versus how many issues did not achieve their SLA goals or, in other words, breached. Along with the **SLA goals** reports, this report tells you how many tickets in the project were not able to achieve their SLA goal.

Customer channels

There are two ways customers can raise tickets in the project—**Customer portal**, or **Email**. Let us discuss them in detail:

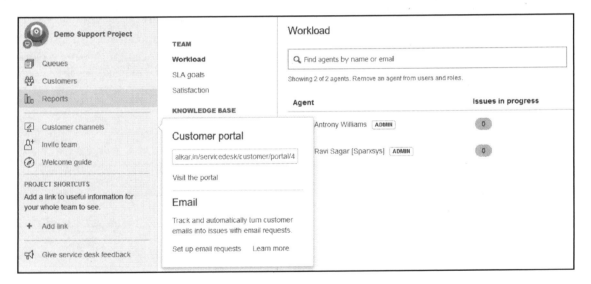

Customer portal

The most important purpose of the Service Desk application is to focus on support requests and ticketing systems to cater to the requests of end users and customers. Using JIRA, a simple project can be created to track the issues and access can be given to the customers provided there are enough licenses, but, in general, the end users may not find it intuitive to log in to an issue tracker to raise their requests. Atlassian understood this concern and created the Service Desk application with a dedicated **Customer portal**, which is a neat and simple interface for raising support requests.

Every Service Desk project will have its own **Customer portal** URL like the one mentioned here `http://localhost/servicedesk/customer/portal/1`.

You will find this URL when you click on the **Customer channels** tab in the project sidebar. The project-specific URL will be displayed in the popup that appears,. You can share this URL with your customers, or publish it on your website. **Customer portal** offers a simple and intuitive interface to raise the request. Let us go through this portal. Open this URL in your web browser:

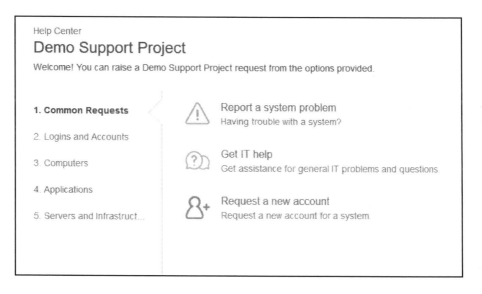

On the left-hand side, five **Groups** are listed and, under each of them, several requests types, such as **Report a system problem**, **Get IT help**, and **Request a new account** are grouped. These request types are actually assigned to a specific issue type in JIRA. We can create a new request type and map it to any existing issue type.

Click on **Report a system problem** and it will open a new page with a form to raise a request:

This form is something similar to the one that opens when you click on the **Create** button in JIRA, but it is much simpler. Customers can fill in this form and click on the **Create** button to raise the request:

Once the request is submitted, a JIRA issue is created with the status **WAITING FOR SUPPORT**. Each Service Desk project has its own workflow, just like any other JIRA project. The issue will start appearing in the **Queues** of the project.

E-mail

You can configure Service Desk in such a way that your customers can raise tickets by simply sending an e-mail to a specific e-mail address. We need to configure our project first to enable this functionality.

Click on the **Set up email requests** link in the popup that appears when you click on the **Customer channels** tab on the project sidebar:

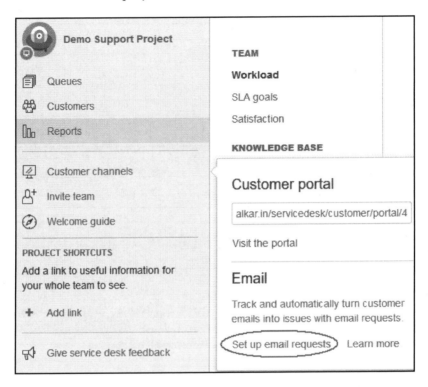

On the next screen, click on the **Add an email address** button:

In the **Set up email channel** popup, enter the details of your e-mail account. If you are using a Google apps account, enter **Email address** and **Password**, but you can also configure POP- and IMAP-based accounts from the **Other** tab. Press the **Next** button to continue:

Now you will need to select which request type will be used to create issues from e-mail. You can select **Report a system problem** and press the **Done** button at the bottom:

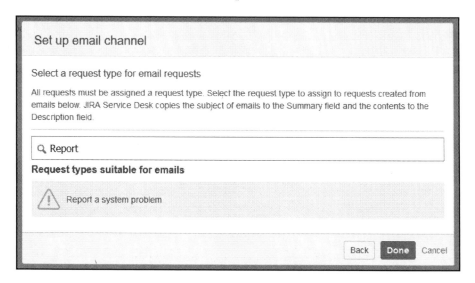

The e-mail will now be configured for this project. JIRA Service Desk will continuously read the specified inbox and whenever there is a new mail, it will copy the e-mail subject in the **Summary** field and e-mail content in the **Description** field.

JIRA Service Desk configurations

Service Desk projects are not much different from a standard JIRA project. Internally, it is also configured using various schemes for **Issue types**, **Workflows**, **Screens**, and **Permissions**. In Chapter 4, *Customizing JIRA for Test Management*, we discussed how to customize the project by modifying these schemes. However, there are certain configurations that are specific to a Service Desk-based project.

Go to **Project Administration** of your project under the project sidebar and just below the **Summary**, you will notice a new set of configurations that are not present in a standard JIRA project:

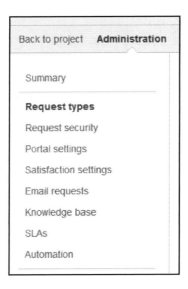

Let us understand them one by one.

Request types

Earlier in this chapter, we discussed how the **Customer portal** is a simple interface for end users. They get to choose the different types of request, which are internally mapped to a specific issue type. Under this section, you can create a new request type and also modify the existing ones:

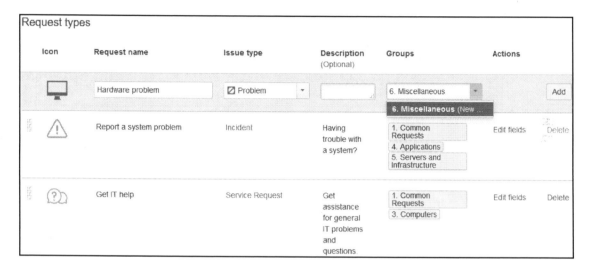

Enter a **Request name**, such as `Hardware problem`, select **Issue type** as **Problem**, and enter text in **Groups** as `6. Miscellaneous`. Then press the **Add** button. Now, if you go back to your **Customer portal**, there will be a new request type added, but it will only contain the **Summary** field. Let us now add a few more fields to this request type:

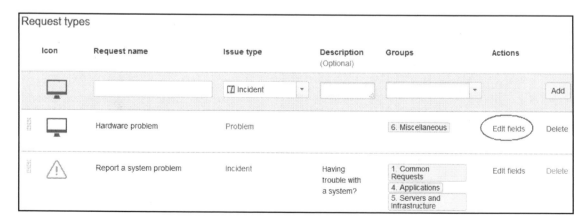

Click on the **Edit fields** link corresponding to the request type you want to modify:

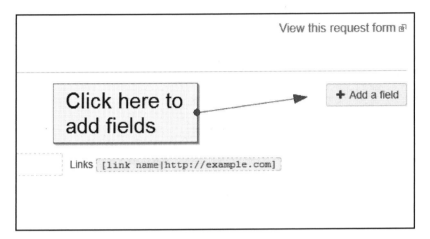

Now click on the **Add a field** button in the top-right corner of the screen:

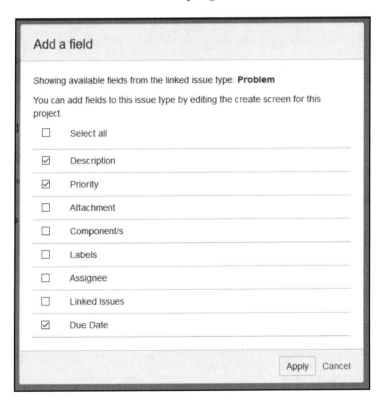

In the **Add a field** popup, select the fields that you want to add and click the **Apply** button:

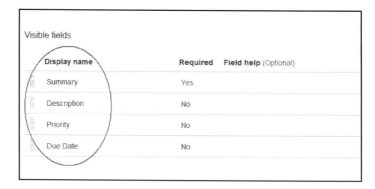

The fields will now be added and will be visible to the end user on the **Customer portal**. You can also add a custom field in your JIRA instance and add it to the screen associated with the project. It will then be available for you to add to the request types.

Request security

You can control who can raise a support request on your Service Desk project:

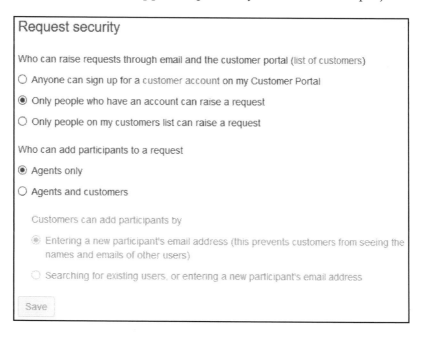

As you can see in the preceding screenshot, you have three options to select from:

- **Anyone can sign up for a customer account on my Customer Portal**
- **Only people who have an account can raise a request**
- **Only people on my customers list can raise a request**

Select the option that is most suitable for your project and click on the **Save** button.

To add the users to your customer list, go to the **Users and roles** of your project and add the user to the **SERVICE DESK CUSTOMERS** project role.

Portal settings

In this section, you can change the **Name** of your **Customer portal**, which is, by default, the same as your project name. You can also upload a custom logo:

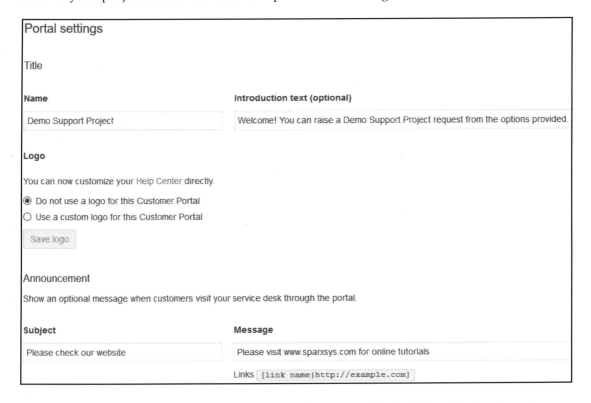

It is also possible to give an **Announcement** to the users, which will be displayed at the top of your **Customer portal**.

Satisfaction settings

In the Service Desk project, your customers can give feedback. This will help you understand their satisfaction levels. Under this section, you can enable or disable this feature.

E-mail requests

Your customers can raise a request by either visiting the **Customer portal**, or by sending an e-mail to the address that you specify. We discussed how to configure it in the previous section on **Customer channels**.

Knowledge base

The Service Desk projects can be integrated with a Confluence space. This is useful because, when a customer raises a request through the **Customer portal**, they can be presented with the related pages on Confluence. Customers can then go through those related pages and can potentially solve their problem without the need to raise a request.

To configure the **Knowledge base**, an application link has first to be added between JIRA and Confluence. Chapter 16, *Integrating JIRA with Common Atlassian Applications and Other Tools*, has detailed information on adding an application link. Let us take a look at how to link a Confluence space with our project:

Knowledge base

Use a linked Confluence space to provide customers with knowledge base articles they can use to help themselves.

Link a Confluence space

○ Don't link to a Confluence space

◉ Link to a Confluence space

Application

Select the Confluence application you would like to use to link a Confluence space.

Confluence (sparxsys-dev.atlas ...   ▼

Space

You can only select spaces you have the permission to view in Confluence.

Customer Knowledge Base   ▼   Create a knowledge base space

Link   Cancel

Under the **Link a Confluence space** section, select the **Link to a Confluence space** radio button. Then, under the **Application** drop-down, select **Confluence** and finally, under the **Space** drop-down, select the name of the Confluence space and click on the **Link** button.

SLAs

Service Desk projects comes with the following SLAs:

- **Time to resolution**: This is the time taken from creation to resolution of the issue
- **Time to first response**: This is the time taken from creation to changing the status of the issue to **Waiting for customer**

We can also create our own SLA, such as `Time to Assign`. Follow the procedure mentioned in the following steps to create a new SLA in your project:

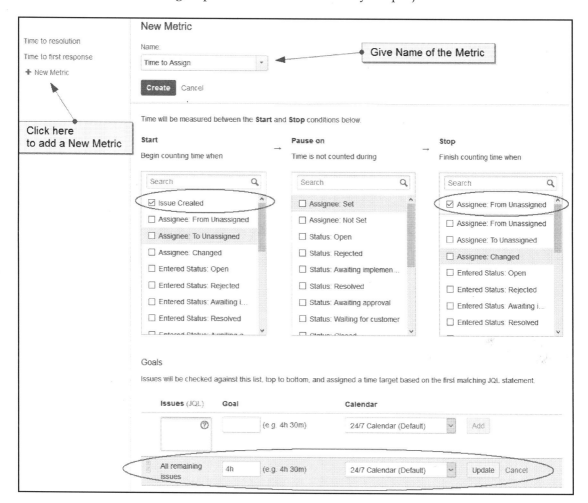

1. Click on the **New Metric** link on the left-hand side.
2. On the **New Metric** screen, enter the **Name** of the metric.
3. Select the **Start** time, when the count will begin.
4. Select the **Stop** time, when the count will finish.
5. Under the **Goals** section, enter the **Goal** as 4h for **All remaining issues** and click the **Update** button.
6. Finally, click the **Create** button at the top of the screen to save the new SLA.
7. The new SLA will be reflected in all existing and new issues in your project.

Automation

Service Desk projects come with a nifty utility to add some automation tasks to the project. This utility is useful to assist the team in performing some recurring tasks, and also to enforce some policies.

For instance, we just added a new SLA: **Time to Assign**, where an issue is assigned to an agent within 4 hours of its creation. We can actually post a comment on the request when only 60 minutes are remaining in this SLA. This comment would be visible only to the existing agents assigned on this project.

Follow the procedure given to add a new rule:

1. Click on the **Add rule** button in the top-right corner:

2. In the **New automation rule** popup, select **Custom rule** and press the **Next** button to continue:

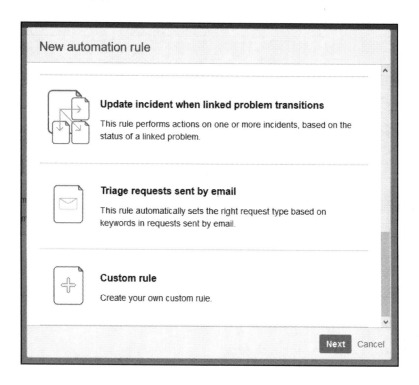

3. On the next screen, enter the name, such as `Alert user`, in the first text box. We now have to **Add a trigger** under the **WHEN** box and we also have to **Add an action** under the **THEN** box.

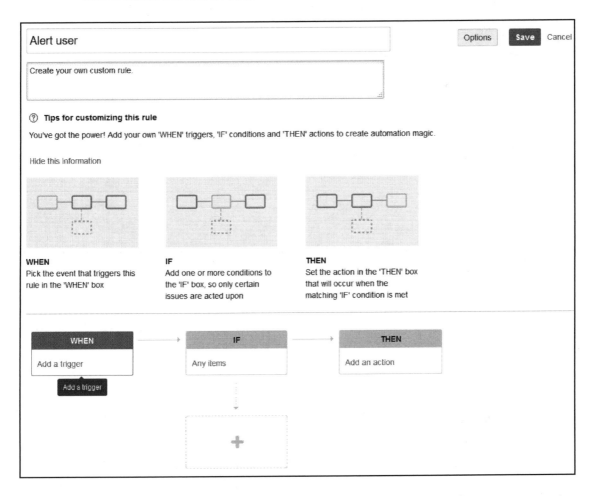

4. Click on the **Add a trigger** link and in the **Edit WHEN** popup that appears, again click on the **Add trigger** link. Then select **SLA time remaining** and click the **Add** button:

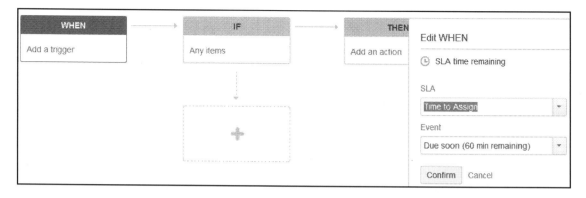

5. In the **SLA** drop-down, select **Time to Assign** and, in **Event**, select **Due soon (60 min remaining)**. Press the **Confirm** button to save the trigger.

6. Now click on the **Add an action** link and, in the **Edit THEN** popup that appears, again click on the **Add action** link. Then select **Add comment** and click the **Add** button:

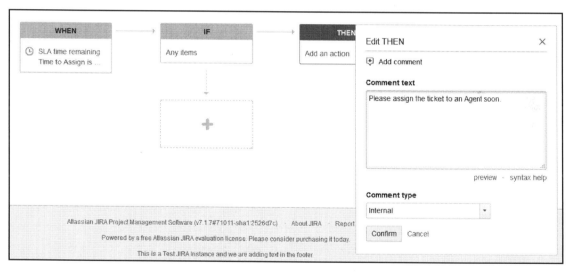

7. Enter a **Comment text**, select **Comment type**, and press the **Confirm** button.

We have now added a new rule that will post an internal comment on the issue when the SLA is due in the next 60 minutes.

Adding users as agents

The Service Desk license doesn't impose any limit on the number of customers but instead limits the number of users that can act as an agent on the project. The requests can only be assigned to an agent, and only they can communicate with the customers.

Follow the steps given here to add users as agents in your project:

1. To make a user an agent, first add them in the **jira-servicedesk-users**, which should be assigned to the **JIRA Service Desk** application under the **Application access** section.
2. Then go to **Project administration | Users and roles**, and add that user in the project role **Service Desk Team**.
3. Finally, check your permission scheme. The **Service Desk Agent** permission should be given to the **Service Desk Team** project role.

Summary

In this chapter, we have learned how to create and use a Service Desk project, which is now one of the most important applications for support projects from Atlassian. This application comes with really nice built-in features that get you started in no time. We also learned various configurations of Service Desk to get the most out of this go-to application for support projects.

In the following chapter, we will take a look at various integrations of JIRA with common Atlassian applications, and other tools that help at various stages of the **software development life cycle** (**SDLC**).

16
Integrating JIRA with Common Atlassian Applications and Other Tools

There are a lot of different tools and applications required at various stages of the **software development life cycle (SDLC)**. JIRA and Confluence act as one of the most important tools, but several other applications, such as Bamboo, Fisheye/Crucible, and other tools, are also used for different purposes to assist development. One of the best features of JIRA is its ability to integrate with a variety of tools from Atlassian and other third-party companies. Let's take a look at some of the common integrations you can perform with JIRA.

In this chapter, we will cover the following:

- JIRA with the **Subversion (SVN)** plugin
- JIRA with **Bitbucket** and **GitHub**
- JIRA with other Git repositories
- JIRA with Confluence

JIRA with the Subversion plugin

SVN is a popular and widely-used version control software. JIRA has an add-on, called **JIRA Subversion plugin**, which can be used to integrate JIRA with SVN. Let's work through the following steps to install the JIRA SVN plugin:

1. Navigate to **Administration | Add-ons | Find new add-ons** (under **ATLASSIAN MARKETPLACE**), enter subversion in the search box, and press the *Enter* key:

2. The **JIRA subversion plugin** will appear in the list. Click on the **Install** button to continue.

3. This add-on will then be downloaded and installed on your JIRA instance. Once installed, you will get a message confirming the installation:

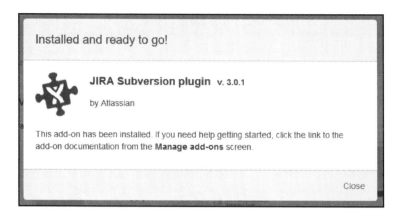

4. Click on the **Close** link to close the popup.

5. Navigate to **Administration** | **Add-ons** | **Subversion Repositories** (under **SOURCE CONTROL**):

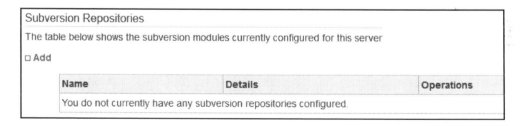

6. Now you will have the option to add SVN repositories to your JIRA instance. Click on the **Add** link. On the next screen, enter **Display Name** and **Repository Root**; if your SVN repository requires authentication, enter the **Username** and **Password**. Select **Web Link** as **WebClient for SVN** if your repository can be browsed through a browser. Finally, click on the **Add** button:

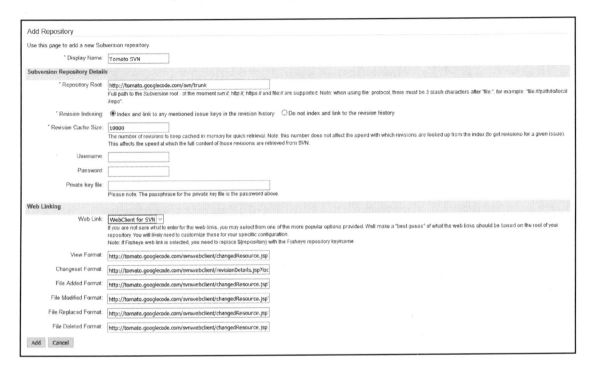

The SVN repository will be added to your instance whenever a user includes the ticket ID such as KEY-1 in the SVN commit message, this specific file will be listed in the JIRA view issue operation, under the **Subversion** tab.

JIRA with Bitbucket and GitHub

JIRA comes with a built-in functionality to connect with the Bitbucket and GitHub repositories. Perform these steps to integrate JIRA into Bitbucket and GitHub:

1. Navigate to **Administration** | **Applications** | **DVCS Accounts** (under **INTEGRATIONS**).

2. On the next screen, click on the **Link Bitbucket Cloud or GitHub account** button:

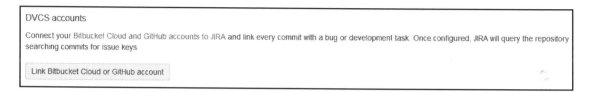

3. In the popup that appears, select either **Bitbucket Cloud** or **GitHub** from the **Host** drop-down list, enter your username in the **Team or User Account** text field, and enter the relevant values in **OAuth Key** and **OAuth Secret**, both of which you can generate from your Bitbucket or GitHub account. Click on the **Add** button to continue:

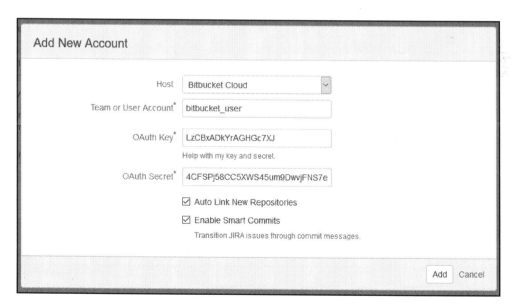

4. On the **Confirm access to your account** screen, click on the **Grant access** button:

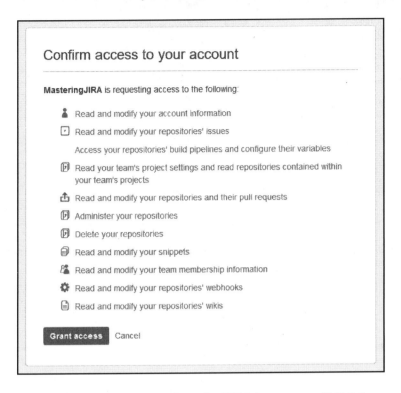

5. After the configuration is complete, the JIRA instance will list the available repositories:

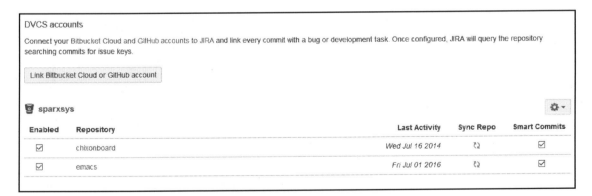

Once the repositories are listed in the instance, the Git commit messages can include the JIRA issues ID, and these files will be displayed under the JIRA view issue **Source** tab.

JIRA with other Git repositories

It's also possible to connect your JIRA instance with any Git repository—not just Bitbucket and GitHub. There is an add-on, the Git Integration plugin for JIRA, which can be installed for such integrations. Perform these steps:

1. Navigate to **Administration** | **Add-ons** | **Find new add-ons** (under **ATLASSIAN MARKETPLACE**), and search for git via the search box.
2. From the search result that appears, select **Git Integration Plugin for JIRA**. Click on the **Free trial** button to install and evaluate this add-on:

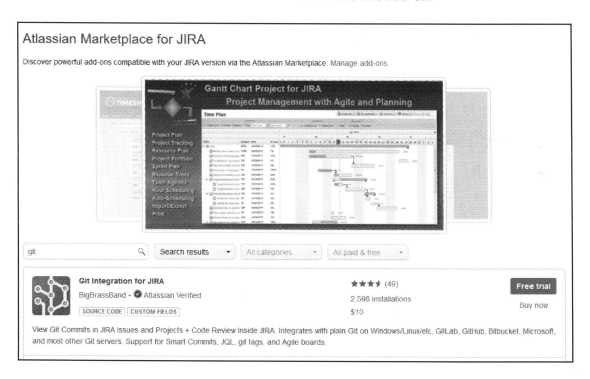

3. Once the add-on is installed, navigate to **Administration** | **Applications** | **Git Repositories** (under **GIT INTEGRATION FOR JIRA**):

4. Click on the **Connect to Git Repository** button:

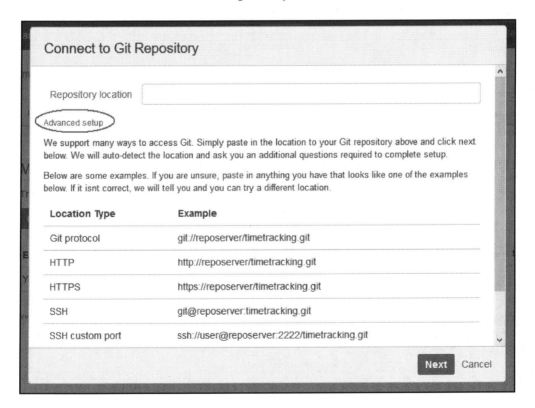

5. In the popup window, click on the **Advanced setup** link to add a Git repository with more configuration options. On the next screen, enter the **Display Name** of the Git repository and provide the **Repository Root** of your Git repository. In our example, we will use a local Git repository, hosted and located at the `c:\git-repo` location. In the **Enable Fetches** radio button, select **Git repository hosted on same server as JIRA**:

Connect to Git Repository

Use this page to add a new git repository.

Repository Settings

Display Name*   Local Git Repo

Repository Root*   c:\git-repo   ⑦

Full path to the Git root on same local machine as JIRA.

Enable Fetches   ○ Git repository hosted on remote server
                  ◉ Git repository hosted on same server as JIRA

Revision Indexing   ◉ Index and link to any mentioned issue keys in the revision history
                     ○ Do not index and link to the revision history

Revision Cache Size*   10000

The number of revisions to keep cached in memory for quick retrieval. Note: this number does not affect the speed with which revisions are looked up from the index (to get revisions for a given issue). This affects the speed at which the full content of those revisions are retrieved from Git.

Main Branch

Specify branch if your repo has no master branch. Leave blank if master branch is present.

Tags   ◉ Show all tags
        ○ Show tags matching the pattern

Optional regular expression to filter which tags to show on issue pages.

Repository Browser

Enabled   ⑦

6. Also, from the **Smart Commits** drop-down list, select **Enabled** and click on the **Add** button to continue:

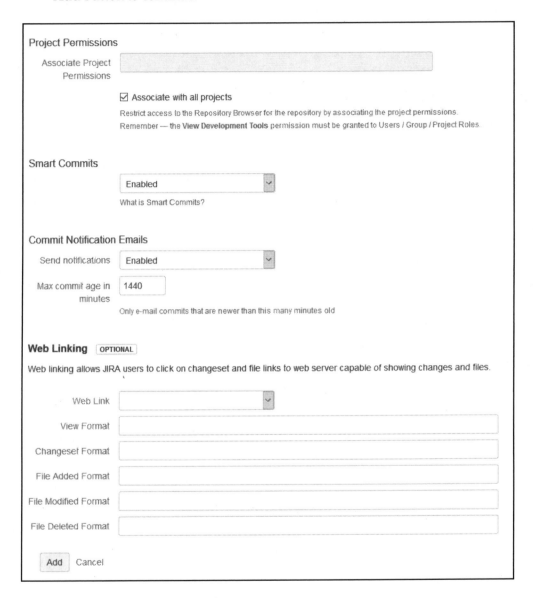

Project Permissions

Associate Project
Permissions

☑ Associate with all projects

Restrict access to the Repository Browser for the repository by associating the project permissions.
Remember — the **View Development Tools** permission must be granted to Users / Group / Project Roles.

Smart Commits

Enabled

What is Smart Commits?

Commit Notification Emails

Send notifications | Enabled

Max commit age in | 1440
minutes

Only e-mail commits that are newer than this many minutes old

Web Linking OPTIONAL

Web linking allows JIRA users to click on changeset and file links to web server capable of showing changes and files.

Web Link

View Format

Changeset Format

File Added Format

File Modified Format

File Deleted Format

Add   Cancel

7. The Git repository will be added and visible in the list:

Also, click on the **Reindex All** button in the top-right corner to index the Git repository. As we have enabled smart commits while configuring the repository, developers can also transition the JIRA issues while they commit the code in Git. To learn more about smart commits, read the documentation at `https://confluence.atlassian.com/display/BITBU CKET/Processing+JIRA+issues+with+commit+messages`.

Although not free, this add-on opens up a lot of possibilities for using any Git repository in your JIRA instance.

JIRA with Confluence

Confluence, another popular tool from Atlassian is used widely for online collaborations. Users can use it to prepare documentation, tutorials, articles, blogs, project reports and various other types of documents. Integrating JIRA with Confluence allows users to create real-time JIRA reports in Confluence. Let's take a look at the steps to set up this integration:

1. Go to **Confluence administration** | **Application Links** (under **ADMINISTRATION**). The link to JIRA can be created here. Enter your JIRA instance URL in the textbox and click on the **Create new link** button:

2. On the next screen, you will be asked to confirm the link for your JIRA instance. Click on the **Continue** button:

3. You will then be directed to your JIRA instance to create a reciprocal link in JIRA to Confluence. Click on the **Continue** button and you will be redirected back to Confluence:

Finally, you will have the application link created both in Confluence and JIRA. After this integration, you will be able to embed JIRA issues on the Confluence page and generate charts as well.

The integration of JIRA with other Atlassian products, such as Bamboo, Fisheye/Crucible, and Bitbucket, is usually performed by creating application links only.

Summary

In this chapter, you learned how JIRA can be integrated with other common tools used in software development processes. Integration with version control software enables developers to associate the code file with the JIRA ticket. Most other tools from Atlassian can also be integrated into JIRA by either installing an add-on or by configuring application links. In the next chapter, we will discuss best practices that need to be employed to use JIRA effectively, especially in enterprise installations with thousands of users and multiple customizations. These best practices and standardized procedures will help administrators to maintain and support JIRA for a long time.

17
JIRA Best Practices

JIRA can become cumbersome to manage when used by many users for different use cases, especially custom schemes that are shared among projects. Imagine a case where a project manager asks you to remove a certain custom field from one of his project's screens, but you accidentally remove it from other projects too. In this chapter, we will discuss the best practices JIRA administrators can employ to maintain their instances.

In this chapter, we will cover the following:

- A word of caution before modifying default schemes and configurations
- The JIRA customization process
- Using project context to assign different options in multiple projects
- Creating too many custom fields—a factor in slow performance
- Choosing a custom field type wisely
- Defining permissions
- JIRA's **Audit Log**
- Adding the announcement banner
- Adding an introduction
- Performing regular indexing
- Final tips

A word of caution before modifying default schemes and configurations

A newly-installed, fresh JIRA instance comes with a lot of default schemes for issue types, workflows, field configurations, and permissions. These default configurations are suitable for simple bug tracking and have a process that is applicable to any generic project. Don't be tempted to start customizing the configurations too soon. If JIRA is being used for the first time in the company, then it's a good idea to pilot it with default configurations. This will give users a good idea of what JIRA has to offer and collect feedback from the users.

When you are ready to customize configurations, either start with the blank configuration, or create a copy of the default configuration and then make your changes in that.

The JIRA customization process

Customizing JIRA should be considered a project in itself. It's quite easy to start making changes while configuring JIRA, but you should always plan your customization first and document them.

You can perform these steps to begin the customization process:

1. Pilot JIRA with default configurations.
2. Gather feedback.
3. Document the proposed configurations.
4. Test the configurations on **sandbox**.
5. Implement it on production.
6. Standardize the configurations.
7. Set up a **Change Control Board** (**CCB**).

Piloting JIRA with default configurations

The move to a new tool always faces resistance from users. JIRA is no exception; however, JIRA has the advantage of being intuitive and it allows you to have a clear distinction between usage and administrative sections. When deploying JIRA for the first time, always use the default configurations and ask users to test it for a few days. This will make sure that users first get comfortable with the features that come with JIRA out of the box. This pilot should ideally be done for at least one candidate from each team, consisting of a project manager, project lead, developer, and tester.

Gathering feedback

At the end of the pilot phase, ask the users to give their feedback. The following questions can be asked on the feedback form:

- Were the default issue types sufficient for your project?
- What changes would you like to perform in the workflow?
- Were the default fields enough to capture the information?
- Do you want e-mail notifications?
- How many types of users will be using JIRA?
- Do you want some users to have restricted access?
- What kinds of reports would you like to have?

The answers to these important questions will give you a very good understanding of desired customizations from various stakeholders in the project.

Documenting and finalizing the proposed configurations

Merely collecting the feedback is not enough to start the customizations. It's very important to first document these customizations in a document to describe the requirements.

We discussed in detail how to gather the requirements in Chapter 6, *Sample Implementation of Use Cases*. Ideally, a separate document for each use case should be prepared. This document should be updated before making any changes in the system. This will ensure that if a new JIRA administrator joins the company, they will not have any problems understanding JIRA's customizations.

Once this document is prepared, share it with the stakeholders and ask them to give their input. Organize a meeting with them to fine-tune the requirements and make necessary changes to this document. Eventually, this document should have the details of all the actual customizations that will be performed in JIRA. What new issue types need to be created, workflows should be visualized in the documents along with the new states that need to be created, and permission schemes and notification schemes should also be mentioned.

Testing configurations on sandbox

Once the requirements are finalized, you should test them in a test environment first. For this, set up a sandbox JIRA instance (which is an exact copy of your production). All the new and old changes in the existing configuration should first be tested in the sandbox. It's really important to have the sandbox for cases when JIRA needs to be upgraded to a new version and when you want to evaluate a new plugin.

The sandbox, which is an exact copy of production, will give the stakeholder a chance to test their requested customizations without worrying about any damage being done in production.

During this testing phase, the stakeholders will surely give you a lot of feedback and ask you to improvise certain customizations that they couldn't perceive earlier. Note down all these changes and make any necessary amendments to the document.

Implementing on the production stage

Once the implementation is successful on the test environment, you can then perform the customizations manually, on production. At this time, the JIRA administrator will have all the information in front of them in the JIRA configuration document. Making actual implementations on production will not take much time.

However, if you are making any changes in the JIRA instance, which is already being used by several users, then it's a good idea to first notify them of the change. You can write a short release note and mention the changes that are being made. This will avoid surprising the users with unexpected changes. Applying changes in the configurations usually doesn't require any downtime, but if you make changes in the workflow, it's always a good idea to do it when no one is using the instance. For this reason, notify users of any downtime well in advance.

Standardizing configurations

JIRA has a wide range of applications. It's an issue tracking and project management tool. This tool can be used not only for bug tracking, but also for test management, helpdesk, requirement management, and agile tracking.

Now initially, when JIRA is implemented, it will be customized for a specific use case for one or more projects, but eventually, as more teams start using JIRA, they will request more customizations. JIRA allows you to use the same configurations in multiple projects, but when the number of projects grows, the same schemes cannot be used for all of them. So, it becomes very important to standardize your configurations in JIRA and ask the new teams to follow them.

Let's take a look at the following scenario in JIRA with three different use cases:

Use case	Number of projects
Test management	10
Helpdesk	5
Requirements management	2

As you can see in the preceding table, there are multiple projects using the same configuration. Now, one of the project managers using the test management scheme may request that you add a new custom field in their project or make one of the existing fields mandatory. These minor customizations will affect all the other projects using the same configurations. We can limit these customizations to a single project by creating a new set of schemes, but this will lead to more maintenance for the JIRA administrator.

Avoid creating multiple schemes for the same use case and, before accepting any change in the existing configurations, talk to the stakeholders of all the projects using that configuration. If one project manager requests an additional custom field, discuss this with other project managers and make the changes after confirmation from all the stakeholders.

So, it's very important to standardize your configurations as much as possible, and reuse these configurations in other projects.

In Chapter 4, *Customizing JIRA for Test Management*, and Chapter 6, *Sample Implementation of Use Cases*, we discussed how to customize JIRA in detail, with various examples.

Setting up a CCB

JIRA administrators have the responsibility of implementing customization requests. As discussed in the previous section, configurations should be standardized as much as possible, but sometimes changes need to be done in JIRA to support JIRA's requirements. Any change, be it large or small, needs to be analyzed first, because it may lead to further issues. I recommend a CCB, whose job is to study the customizations before implementing them.

I recommend the following process:

1. Create a project in JIRA for support requests with various issue types such as bug, improvements, and new feature.
2. Ask your users to raise a ticket in this project for any JIRA support.
3. Once the ticket is created, analyze the requested customizations and perform an impact analysis.
4. If there is no impact, implement the changes directly in JIRA.
5. If there is any impact on other projects, discuss the changes with the stakeholders of the other projects.
6. On the basis of your discussion with stakeholders, make a decision on whether or not to implement the change in JIRA.

Various scenarios for impact analysis

Let's take a look at some of the customization requests from users and their possible impact on the instance:

Request	Used by other projects?	Impact	Conclusion
Addition of a new custom field	Yes	Minor	Confirm this with other stakeholders first
Addition of new values in a select list custom field	Yes	Minor	Either confirm this with other stakeholders or use context to create a different set of values for that project
Change the workflow condition	Yes	Major	This is a major change and should be discussed with all stakeholders
Addition of a new workflow state	Yes	Major	This is a major change and should be discussed with all stakeholders

Create a mandatory custom field	Yes	Major	This is a major change and should be discussed with all stakeholders
Installing a new plugin	Yes, applicable globally	Major	Install this plugin on sandbox first and ask the stakeholders to evaluate
Creation of new issue type	Yes	Major	Discuss the needs of this new issue type with all stakeholders

These are some examples of the requests that JIRA administrators will receive. For each request, analyze the impact first before implementing it in the system.

Using project context to assign different options in multiple projects

Let's say we have a custom field called **Customer**. This is a select list with different values, which users can select while creating an issue. If JIRA is used by multiple teams, each working on a different project, it's quite possible that the customer list will be different. One project may cater to a different set of customers than others. One approach to deal with this situation is to enter all the customers in a single list, but this will lead to confusion among the team members who raise the tickets and it will also lead to errors, because users might select the wrong customers.

A different custom field can be created for each project to deal with this problem (each having its own list of customers), but this leads to redundancy, as we would store the same type of information in each list.

JIRA's custom fields offer a solution to this problem using context. Perform these steps to create a new context:

1. Go to **Administration** | **Issues** | **Custom Fields** (under **FIELDS**) and you will see the list of all the custom fields in your system.
2. Click on the gear icon for your custom fields and select **Configure**:

3. On the next screen for **Configure Custom Field: Customer**, click on the **Add new context** link.

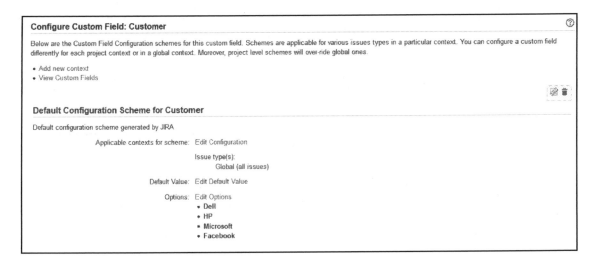

4. On the next screen for **Add configuration scheme context**, enter the **Configuration scheme label** and **Description**. Under **Choose applicable context**, select the name of the project for which this context will be available:

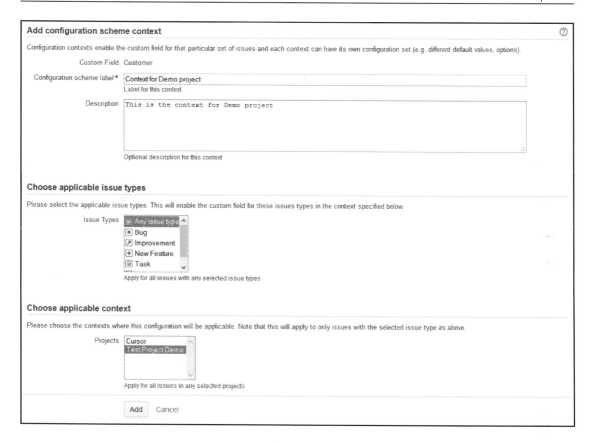

5. You will now have a new **Context for Demo project**, but there are no options yet. Click on the **Edit Options** link:

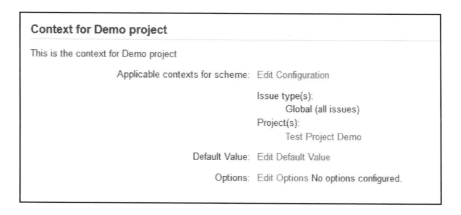

6. On the next screen, enter the customer names that are relevant only to a particular project:

7. Finally, you will have two sets of options for this custom field. One is default and the other is for a specific project:

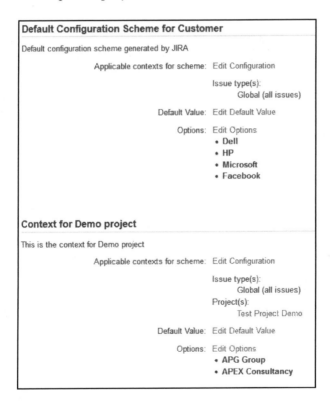

Creating too many custom fields – A factor in slow performance

We just discussed how companies should devise a process to manage their customizations in their JIRA instance. As the JIRA instance grows in terms of number of issues, projects, and users, the performance of the instance will start degrading over a period of time. One of the major factors that leads to slow performance is a lot of custom fields.

JIRA administrators create custom fields to store data that can be filtered out in the reports. This is fine, but an attempt should be made to reuse the existing custom fields. For this reason, create fields with generic names so that they can be reused easily in different projects.

Let's take a look at some generic custom fields that can be created in JIRA instances:

Custom field	Type	Description
Client/Customer	Select List	This uses project context to create different options for multiple projects
Category	Select List	These labels and components should be used in most cases, but this generic field can be used in many projects with different options using project context
External ID	Text Field	This field will be used to store the ID of issues, which is stored in some external tool
Type of testing	Select List	This field can be used when JIRA is used for test management
Start date	Date Picker	JIRA does come with a due date, but the start date of a task is not available

Think twice before adding new custom fields in the system. Your users will request that you create many fields, but remember, having too many custom fields can cause performance issues. Always try to optimize the use of custom fields. For instance, before creating custom fields for **Text Field (multiline)**, try to reuse the **Description** field; if you want users to fill in the details using a template with a predefined text template, then use the method described in `Chapter 14`, *Customizing Look, Feel, and Behavior*.

Choosing a custom field type wisely

When you are gathering the requirements from various stakeholders, they will ask you to create new custom fields to capture a specific piece of information. In the previous section, we discussed how you should always try to optimize the usage of these fields. However, once you have decided on the custom fields that need to be created, before creating them in the instance, spend some time working with the types of custom fields. Once created, the type of fields cannot be changed easily.

For instance, if you want to store a single value, use **Select List (single choice)**, whereas to select multiple values, use **Select List (multiple choices)**. To capture dates, there is a date picker, and to store lengthy text, **Text Field (multiline)** can be used.

Defining permissions

It's very important to secure your data stored in JIRA. There could be several client projects in JIRA whose information cannot be shared with other teams. JIRA can also be accessed by your clients and it becomes more important to hide other projects from your clients and only give them access to the projects relevant to them. In Chapter 4, *Customizing JIRA for Test Management*, we discussed how a project can be accessed only by users of a specific group.

JIRA comes with an amazing permission system, which allows configuration at a granular level. JIRA has three types of permissions. These are:

- **Global permissions**: These permissions apply to the whole JIRA instance. Permissions such as who can log in and who will be the JIRA administrator can be configured here.
- **Project permissions**: These permissions apply to a specific project. Permissions such as who can access the project, create issues, and close issues can be configured here.
- **Issue security levels**: These permissions apply to the issues of a specific project to control who can view the issues.

The permissions need to be defined at all these levels, so make sure that people with right access can view the data in JIRA.

JIRA's Audit Log

There is an **Audit Log** in JIRA that keeps track of all the configuration changes that happen in JIRA. This log is quite useful for tracking any changes in the schemes; the best part is that this log is available through the JIRA administrative interface.

Let's access JIRA's **Audit Log**:

Navigate to **JIRA Administration** | **System** | **Audit Log** (under **TROUBLESHOOTING AND SUPPORT**):

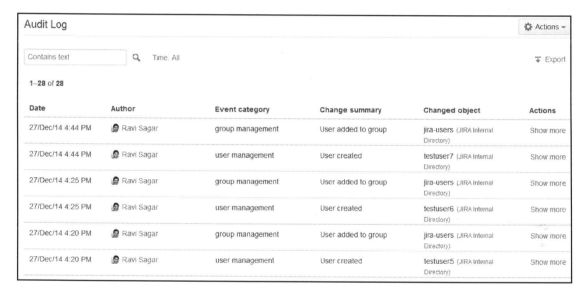

As you can see in the preceding screenshot, events such as new user creation and modifications in the user group are recorded. The changes tracked by **Audit Log** are as follows:

- User management
- Group management
- Project changes
- Permission changes
- Workflow changes
- Notification scheme changes

- Custom field changes
- Component changes
- Version changes

The JIRA administrator can refer to this **Audit Log** for troubleshooting purposes.

Adding the announcement banner

JIRA is a critical part of the software development life cycle and is used to store many kind of issues. Users rely on JIRA to check whether their daily tasks and managers use JIRA to keep track of their projects. JIRA administrators sometimes need to perform maintenance activities that require downtime for users. As a good practice, all the users, or at least the stakeholders, should be notified, but to avoid any surprises for the user, it's a good idea to give them an indication of any planned downtime.

JIRA has an option to add an announcement banner, which is visible all across the JIRA instance just after the main navigation. Perform these steps to add the announcement banner:

1. Navigate to **Administration** | **System** | **Announcement Banner** (under **USER INTERFACE**).
2. In the **Announcement** text area, enter your message and click on the **Set Banner** button. You can also include HTML tags. Select **Visibility Level** as **Public – Show to anyone** to show this announcement to users who are not even logged in:

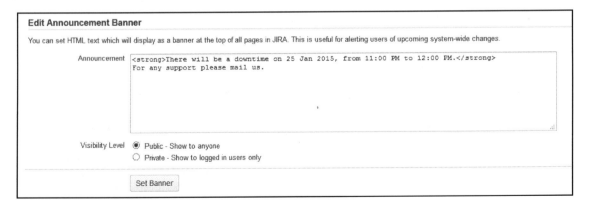

3. The following screenshot displays the announcement:

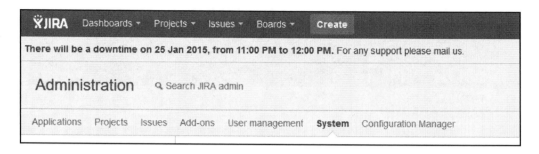

Adding an introduction

When you deploy new JIRA instances, users need to be trained; however, JIRA doesn't require in-depth training to start with basic usage and it's a good practice to give useful introductory information to users. This introduction will be visible not only to the users who are logged in, but also to the users who are logged out.

Perform these steps to add the introductory text:

1. Navigate to **Administration** | **System** | **General Configuration** and click on the **Edit Settings** button in the top-right corner:

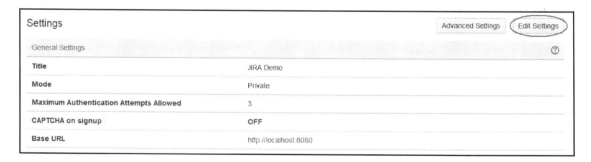

2. On the new screen that opens up, scroll down until you see the text area for **Introduction**. Just type in the instructions for the users and click on the **Update** button.

2. Now, visit your dashboard and note the **Introduction** box, which is updated with your message:

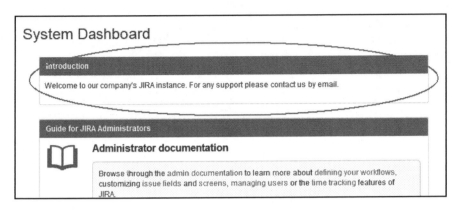

Performing regular indexing

In Chapter 2, *Searching in JIRA*, we discussed in detail the search capability of JIRA and how to find the information you are looking for. JIRA maintains and builds an internal search index, which is important for the quick retrieval of data. However, after making configuration changes, such as the creation of new field configuration schemes, adding new custom fields, and installing new plugins, the search index becomes out of sync. It's important to rebuild this search index from time to time so that users experience fast search times and can find the information they are looking for easily.

Whenever you make configuration-level changes that involve the search index (such as the creation of a new custom field), JIRA will prompt administrators to perform the search and you will get a message similar to the following in the administration section:

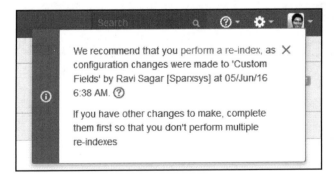

You can either click on the **Indexing** link that appears along with this message or navigate to JIRA **Administration** | **System** | **Indexing** (under **ADVANCED**) to perform the indexing process.

You will get two options to perform **Re-Indexing**. The first option is **Background re-index**, which doesn't lock the JIRA instance and allows users to continue working on the JIRA instance, but takes more time. The second option is **Lock JIRA and rebuild index**, which locks the instance and blocks users from accessing JIRA, but is quite quick:

Click on the **Re-Index** button to start the re-indexing process. Depending on the size of your instance, this process may take anywhere from a few seconds to a few hours, for large instances.

So, plan your indexing for every 15 days, during a period when there are fewer users accessing the instance.

Final tips

Apart from the information shared in this chapter, there are some important maintenance activities, which any JIRA administrator should take care of to ensure the longevity and smooth functioning of your application:

- Perform backups from time to time
- Clean up old, big log files
- Plan your re-index only when it is prompted
- Scan your log file regularly
- Run **Integrity Checker**

These additional points should be part of your maintenance checklist.

Summary

In this chapter, we covered some of the best practices JIRA administrators should follow to maintain their instances. We discussed the customization process they should employ in their company to ensure that their JIRA instance doesn't get messed up with tons of configurations. We also covered some important aspects of housekeeping and regular maintenance activities good JIRA administrators follow.

What should you do when JIRA is running slow or not working at all? As JIRA administrators, it's important to make sure that the JIRA service is not impacted. JIRA is a critical tool as it's a part of the development process. Developers rely on it to check their day-to-day tasks. In the next and final chapter, we will cover some common problems that may arise in your instance and, most importantly, how to troubleshoot these issues.

18
Troubleshooting JIRA

One of the most important responsibilities of JIRA administrators is to provide support to users who rely on JIRA for their daily work. As JIRA administrators, it's important to make sure that service is not impacted. In this chapter, we will cover common problems that may arise in your instance. Most importantly, we will cover how to troubleshoot these issues.

In this chapter, we will cover the following:

- Atlassian support
- Common configuration issues
- Increasing memory
- **Integrity Checker**

Atlassian support

When you purchase JIRA, you are entitled to get official support from Atlassian, and they are quite responsive when you raise a support request. You can raise a support ticket with Atlassian when you are not able to find the solution yourself.

Atlassian Answers

We all learn from our experiences and it takes time to become an expert in a specific tool or technology. Atlassian has a great online community of fellow JIRA administrators and users. Here, they share knowledge with each other and also seek help. I recommend that, before raising a support ticket with Atlassian, you should always try to find the possible solution on the *Atlassian Answers* online portal, at `https://answers.atlassian.com/`:

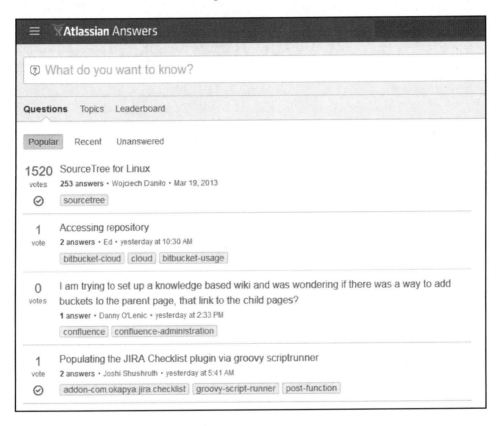

In this portal, you can see the questions that other users have posted. You can go through these questions and also respond to them, if you want to contribute and help others. Each question is usually marked with tags (such as **jira**, **jira-administration**, and **confluence**). You can click on any of these tags and find all the questions related to a specific tag. *Atlassian Answers* is a wonderful online portal to seek help from.

Reporting a problem

Raising a support request with Atlassian is quite easy. Atlassian has a support portal where you can raise your tickets. Depending on the urgency of your problem, you will get your response from Atlassian. In my experience, the support provided by Atlassian is quite good and they respond in a timely manner. If you have further queries on your ticket, you can post a follow-up comment and close the ticket only when you are satisfied with the solution provided.

Perform these steps to raise a support request ticket:

1. Enter `https://support.atlassian.com/customer/servicedesk-portal` in your browser and click on **JIRA** from the list of tools. Then click on **JIRA Core**, **JIRA Software**, or **JIRA Service Desk**:

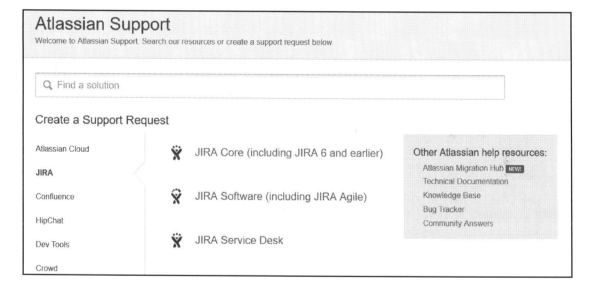

2. On the next screen, click on **Submit a problem report to us**:

3. On the next screen, you will be presented with a form. This form contains various fields, where you can explain the issue. Fill in the **Affects Version/s** field to help Atlassian support to understand on which version of the application you are facing the issue, and press the **Create** button to create the issue:

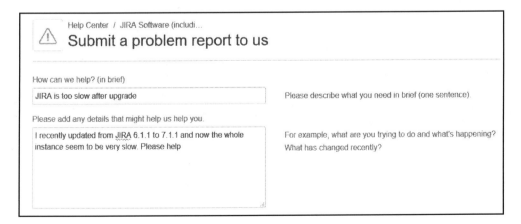

4. After the issue is created, you can also upload screenshots, if any, or attach log files:

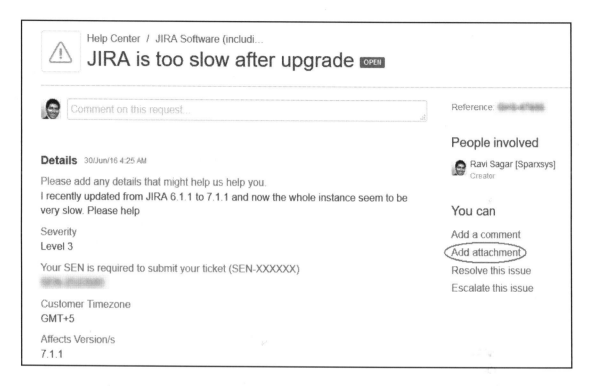

Log scanner

If you ever run into an issue of any kind, you should first check the log file located at `home/log/atlassian-jira.log`, in your `JIRA HOME` directory.

All internal error messages are logged in this file and it provides very useful information about the possible source of the problem. You will get good clues about where to start your troubleshooting. You can search for the respective error message from your log file on *Atlassian Answers*.

If you find looking into the log files daunting in the beginning, you can also use the log scanner option that comes with JIRA. Perform these steps to run log scanner:

1. Go to **Administration** | **System** | **Support Tools** (under **TROUBLESHOOTING AND SUPPORT**):

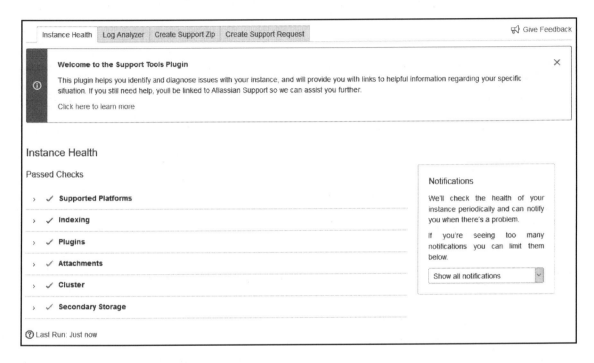

2. Click on the **Log Analyzer** tab link to run the scanner. You will get the option to either run the scanner on the standard log file or any other log file whose location you can enter. We will select the standard log file. Click on the **Scan** button to continue:

3. The scanner will run and look into the log file for error and warning messages; the good thing about the log scanner is that it will also provide various links to *Atlassian Answers* and JIRA issues based on similar error messages other users might have faced. As a JIRA administrator, you should run this scanner regularly, read these recommendations, and take appropriate action:

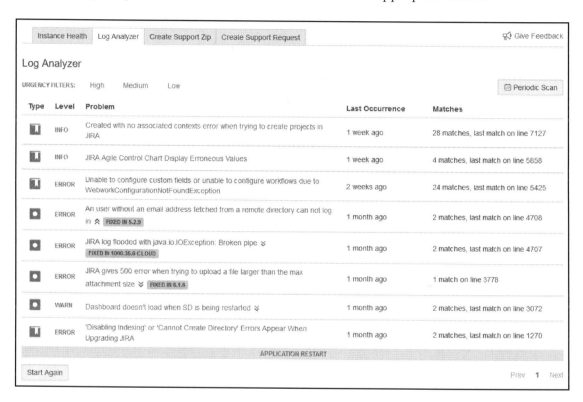

4. Apart from manually running **Log Analyzer**, you can also schedule this scan to happen periodically and mail you the output. Click on the **Periodic Scan** button in the top-right corner to schedule this scan:

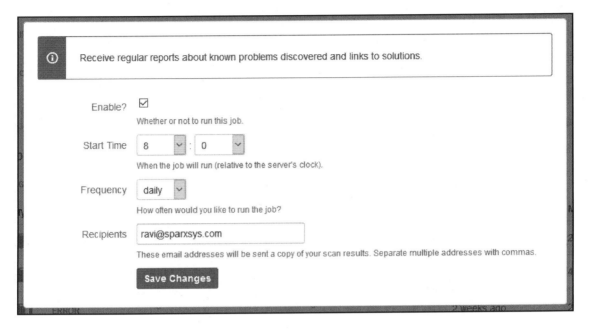

5. Select the **Enable** checkbox, set **Start Time** and **Frequency**, enter your e-mail in the **Recipients** text field, and click on the **Save Changes** button.

Support ZIP

When you raise the support request ticket with Atlassian support, it's always a good idea to attach the log files. You can manually copy the whole `log` folder in your JIRA's home directory and send Atlassian the compressed version of this folder; however, JIRA makes the job easier for you. You can generate the support ZIP file. This not only contains the log files of your instance, but also contains **Application Properties**, **JIRA Configuration Files**, and a few other important files that give Atlassian a very good idea about your instance, which will enable them to give you better answers for your issues.

Under **Support Tools**, click on the third tab, called **CreateSupport Zip**. Here, you will have the option to select the files to include in the support ZIP file. Then, click on the **Create** button to generate the support ZIP file:

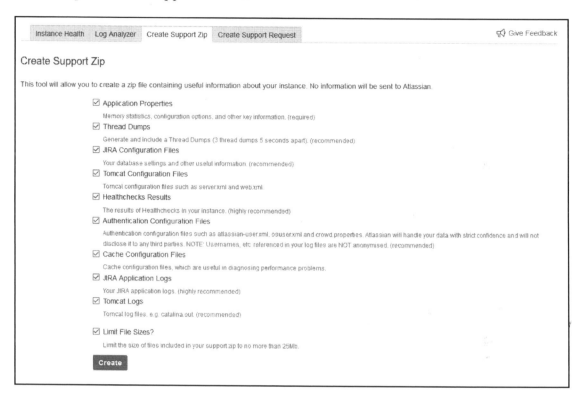

The support ZIP will be suffixed with a timestamp and its zipped version will be placed in your `export` folder, under JIRA's home directory. You can copy this file and attach it to your support ticket.

Common configuration issues

In `Chapter 17`, *JIRA Best Practices*, we discussed various best practices you can employ in your organization to implement customizations in JIRA. We also described the process (from gathering the requirements to testing new configurations) used to perform customizations. If testing is not done properly, then it's quite possible to have issues later on and users will complain. Let's go through some common configuration-related issues and their possible causes.

User is not able to log in

Let's say that you receive a request to create a new user account in JIRA. You create the account manually and assign appropriate groups to the user to provide access to the relevant projects, but you receive the complaint that the user is not able to log in to JIRA at all.

Solution

First, check in your JIRA instance's global permissions, whose groups are part of the JIRA user's permission. In the default JIRA configuration, the **jira-users** group is part of this permission. Just check whether this user is part of the **jira-users** group or not.

Users don't see the project

If you are using different permission schemes in your projects to hide specific projects from everyone, it's possible that users will not be able to see the projects they want to work on.

Solution

In Chapter 4, *Customizing JIRA for Test Management*, we discussed how to limit the visibility of a project to a certain group. The **Browse Projects** permission in the project's permission scheme decides who will see the project and who will not. Just check which group or project role is assigned this permission and add the user to this group or project role.

Permission helper

JIRA comes with a handy tool, called **Permission helper**, which can quickly tell whether a user has a specific permission or not:

1. Go to **Administration** I **System** I **Permission helper** (under **ADMIN HELPER**).

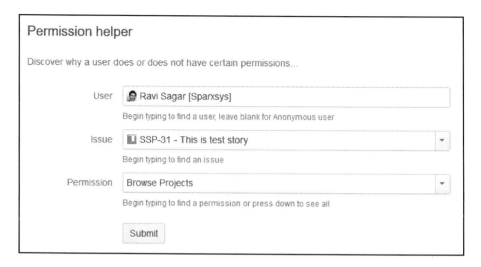

2. Enter the **User**, select the **Issue** and the **Permission** you want to check for, and click the **Submit** button:

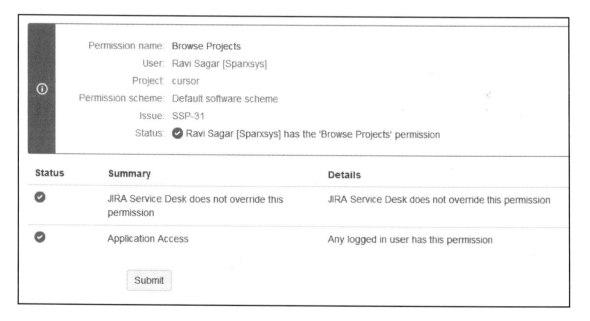

3. As shown in the preceding screenshot, you will then get the details of permissions that user has on a specific Issue.

This is a great tool to quickly check the permissions of any user.

User complaints about e-mails not being received

JIRA has the capability to send e-mail notifications to relevant users on various events, such as issue creation, resolutions, and workflow transitions.

If the user is not able to receive e-mails, seek more clarification based on the following questions:

E-mail not received	Solution
E-mail not working for some events or not working at all	If e-mails are not working at all, then check the outgoing mail configuration. It can be an issue with the **Simple Mail Transfer Protocol** (**SMTP**) mail server.
E-mails are not received for changes in a particular issue	Check whether the user is the reporter, assignee, watcher, component lead, or project lead. Then, check whether the project notification scheme is configured to send e-mails on issue events.
E-mails are not received on state transition	If a custom workflow is used, then check whether the post function on any custom event is triggered or not. Then, in the project notification scheme, check whether any user, group, or role is configured to receive e-mails on this custom event.

Workflow buttons are missing

Customized workflows have the ability to add conditions on various transitions and a common usage is to limit who can perform these transitions. For instance, in the default workflow, once the issue is created, only the assignee of the issue can move it to the **In Progress** state. In a customized workflow, you have to be very careful about these conditions, because users might not be able to move the issues in the workflow if these conditions are not met.

Solution

If users complain about not being able to perform workflow transitions, check the condition for that transition. Either modify or remove the condition, if it's not required, or add the user to the relevant group or permission to be able to make the transition.

The options in the select list suddenly changed

In Chapter 17, *JIRA Best Practices*, we discussed using the same custom field of the type select list in multiple projects by using context to create different sets of options that appear in the field. The request to add different sets of options for an individual project is quite common, and can easily be done using the context. However, if two or more projects are using the same context, then it's equally easy to make a mistake by not selecting the project name.

While configuring, choose applicable context; the project names are available in the list, and to select multiple projects, you need to press the *Ctrl* key.

The custom field disappears from the project

Working with context can be tricky in the beginning. Another common problem JIRA administrators face is that users complain about a custom field, which suddenly went missing from the project, even though this custom field is present on the screen.

While creating the context, as discussed in Chapter 17, *JIRA Best Practices*, there is an option, **Choose applicable issue types**. By default, **Any issue type** is selected, but if you mistakenly select a specific issue type (such as **Bug**), then this issue type will be present in the project and the content will be limited to this issue type only. Unless there is a specific request to limit the custom field for a particular issue type, it's better to select **Any issue type**.

Increasing memory

As your JIRA instance grows, both in terms of the number of users and data, you will need to keep track of how much memory is consumed by your instance. In Chapter 1, *Planning Your JIRA Installation*, we discussed hardware recommendations, where we mentioned the minimum amount of RAM and CPU required based on the usage; there are times when JIRA will consume more memory than usual (such as taking XML backup, which consumes a lot of memory), so make sure that not many people are using the instance before performing these activities. However, when your instance grows, it will consume a lot of memory and you might get degraded performance. It's quite possible that, due to a lack of sufficient memory, your JIRA instance might stop working.

Perform these steps to check the consumption of memory:

1. Go to **Administration** | **System** | **System info** (under **TROUBLESHOOTING AND SUPPORT**).
2. Scroll down until you see **Java VM Memory Statistics**:

Java VM Memory Statistics	
Total Memory	742 MB
Free Memory	86 MB
Used Memory	656 MB
Memory Graph	**12% Free** (Total: 742 MB) (Force garbage collection)
Non-Heap Memory (includes Metaspace)	**Used: 720 MB**
	Get more detailed memory information.

In this section, you can see how much memory your instance has and how much is currently free. To free up some memory, you can also click on the **Force garbage collection** link.

If you notice degraded performance or `Java Heap Out of Memory` errors in your log file, then you can increase the available memory for JIRA. Follow these instructions to modify it:

1. Open `setenv.bat` in your `bin` directory, under JIRA's installation directory.
2. Increase the **Java virtual machine (JVM)** maximum memory from 768 MB to 1024 MB or more, depending on the number of issues in your instance:

```
set JVM_MAXIMUM_MEMORY=1024m
```

Atlassian that the JVM maximum memory of 1 GB is enough to handle 5000 issues. You can increase it appropriately for your case, making sure that you have enough physical RAM on your server.

Integrity Checker

Whenever there is an issue with the instance, any experienced JIRA administrator will always have an idea of where to look first to fix these problems; however, there is a built-in tool called Integrity Checker that can be used to identify any possible problems. Perform these steps to use Integrity Checker tool:

1. Go to **Administration** | **System** | **Integrity Checker** (under **TROUBLESHOOTING AND SUPPORT**).

2. Check the **Select All** checkbox:

Integrity checker

Select one or more integrity checks from the list below to check for out of date information in the database.

- ☑ **Select All**

- ☑ Check Issue Relations
    - ☑ Check Issue for Relation 'ParentProject'
    - ☑ Check Issue for Relation 'RelatedOSWorkflowEntry'
    - ☑ Check that all Issue Links are associated with valid issues

- ☑ Check Search Request
    - ☑ Check search request references a valid project

- ☑ Check for Duplicate Permissions
    - ☑ Check the permissions are not duplicated

- ☑ Check Workflow Integrity
    - ☑ Check workflow entry states are correct
    - ☑ Check workflow current step entries
    - ☑ Check JIRA issues with null status

- ☑ Check Field Layout Scheme Integrity
    - ☑ Check field layout schemes for references to deleted custom fields

- ☑ Check for invalid filter subscriptions
    - ☑ Check FilterSubscriptions for references to non-existent scheduled job
    - ☑ Check FilterSubscriptions for references to non-existent SearchRequests

[Check]

---

3. Click on the **Check** button to continue:

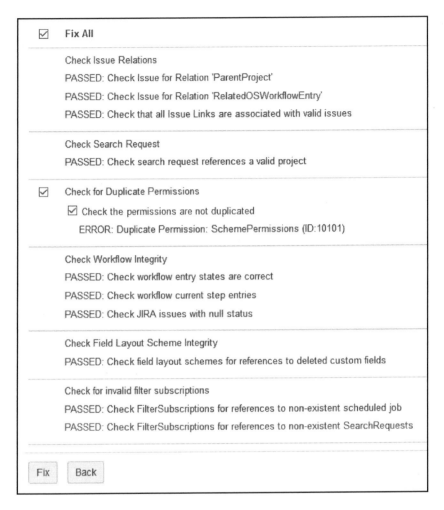

On the next screen, the system will display the list of problems with the configurations found in the instance. You can check the **Fix All** checkbox and click on the **Fix** button to resolve these issues. Alternatively, if you know the actual reason behind these problems, you can resolve them manually and run **Integrity Checker** again.

Summary

In this chapter, we discussed the various problems that may arise in your JIRA instance. Most importantly, we discussed how to handle these issues. If the configurations are not tested properly, users will complain about usage-related issues, which can be fixed by making appropriate changes to the configurations. In this chapter, we discussed such configuration-related issues and their solutions.

This is the last chapter of this book. I hope you enjoyed reading these chapters and I am sure you must have learned about a lot of interesting things that JIRA has to offer. In recent years, JIRA, along with other Atlassian tools, has become a popular choice in organizations. These days, JIRA is treated not just as a tool to manage issues, but is considered a competency. If you are a project manager, scrum master, or are managing any project, learning JIRA will certainly help you get the best out of this amazing tool.

Index

Made in the USA
Middletown, DE
20 April 2018